THE FAl

SAXON
ENGLAND

Mike Kelley

The Fall of Saxon England

ISBN: 978-1-291-96733-3

Typeset in 11 Garamond

Mike Kelley (Publisher)

Second Edition

mgkelley@hotmail.com

Ordering Information:
Special discounts are available on quantity purchases by corporations, associations, educators, and others. For details, contact the publisher at the above listed address.

MAIN CHARACTERS

SAXON

Alric – General of the Housecarls; the full-time professional warriors of Saxon England

Copsig – Tostig's Lieutenant; a traitorous Saxon fighting for the Vikings

Ealdred – Archbishop of York

Edgar Atheling - The grandson of former King Edmund Ironside, closest bloodline to King Edward, but he is only 13 years-old.

Edith – Queen of England and Earl Harold's sister

Edith Swan-Neck – Common law wife of Earl Harold, not legally married in the eyes of the church (Their union produced around six children)

Edward-the-Confessor – King of England

Edwin – Earl of Mercia, central England - brother of Morcar

Gyrth – Earl of East Anglia; Earl Harold's brother

Harold Godwinson – Earl of Wessex and later King of England. Son of the deceased Earl Godwin.

Leofwin – Earl of Kent; Earl Harold's brother

Morcar – Brother of Earl Edwin. Replaced Tostig as the new Earl of Northumbria

Ordgar – General of the Fyrd, the part-time territorial Saxon army

Ricbert – Archer with the Fyrd, the part-time territorial Saxon army

Stigand – Archbishop of Canterbury. He replaced the Norman Robert of Jumieges (but without the Pope's approval)

Tostig – Earl Harold's brother; former Earl of Northumbria and now outlawed. Married to Judith sister of Duke William's wife, Matilda. he was a full blooded traitor not only to England, but also his family.

NORMAN

Odo, Bishop of Bayeux - Half brother of Duke William

Richard Fitz-Gilbert – Guardian to the Duke of Normandy during William's infancy, and a close friend as adults

Robert Count of Mortain - Half brother of Duke William

Robert of Jumieges – Former Archbishop of Canterbury; deposed by the Saxons and replaced by Stigand

William Duke of Normandy - Illegitimate son of deceased Robert of Normandy

VIKING

Harald Sigurdsson (Hardrada) – King of Norway, Iceland, Greenland, Isles of Scotland, Northern Scotland, Isle-of-Man and parts of Ireland

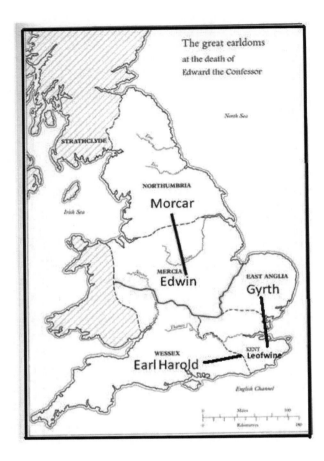

When Harold became king, his brothers ruled all of southern and eastern England, Kent, Wessex and East Anglia: whilst in the north the grandson's of Lady Godiva, two brothers Morcar and Edwin ruled the midlands and the north, Mercia and Northumbria

Mike Kelley

PRELUDE

The nine-year-old boy awoke suddenly, his heart pounding with fear. Men were running up the narrow stone spiral stairs of the round corner turret of the castle, toward the small door leading into his bedroom. They were shouting as they came, it was not a friendly sound. Only a single candle lit the dark walls of his room. The candle was almost burnt out, but still managed to send weird shadows dancing along the aged stone walls. The boy gripped the bed covers and looked across to the larger bed in this same room, placed next to his. Osbern, the boy's guardian, was already awake and feverishly trying to dress, stumbling around, and reaching for his sword, all at the same time. Instinctively the boy knew they were coming for him. It had to be him they wanted. He shuddered, whimpered, and slid beneath the bedclothes, the sweat of fear drenching him. Would they hear him breathing? He kept still, frozen in his sweat.

His former guardian, Alain of Brittany, had already been poisoned; most of his councillors had also been killed, one by one, as had his tutor, Thurold. Was it now his turn to be killed as well? He prayed silently, 'Please God help me. I fear they are coming to kill me.' Tears welled up and streamed down his face, but he dare not make a sound. Surely, they must hear his heart, he thought, as it pounded in his chest. Osbern was only half dressed when the door burst open and three armed men rushed in.

'Where is he? Where is he?' Yelled a wild eyed, chain mailed man, with his sword already draw. 'Where is that bastard boy?'

Osbern did not look round toward the small bed, he dare not give the boy away. Instead he swung with his own sword at the intruders, turning them away from the small bed. Two men dived on him and pushed him backwards onto his own bed. A long dagger was drawn and plunged several times into Osbern's chest and neck. Osbern's scream turned into a gurgle. Blood spouted everywhere, drenching the bedclothes, where he had been sleeping so peacefully just moments before. Again the dagger was struck, and again.

The boy did not move, even though Osbern's warm blood was now running from the larger bed onto his own smaller one, which had been pushed up close by the side of the larger one, where it had always been. Blood was now soaking the boy's nightshirt.

'He must be here somewhere,' snarled one of the intruders. 'Get some light so we can see where the bastard is.'

A mailed hand reached out toward the spent flickering, candle, just as shouts came from below, telling the killers it was time to leave. They couldn't wait and risk capture, so rushed to make their escape into the night.

The boy cried; mouth open, sobbing, eyes staring into the dark, but he still stifled any sound. Involuntary shaking took hold of the child, terrorised in this living nightmare. The boy was the bastard son of Robert the Magnificent, Duke of Normandy, abandoned by him while he went off to fight in some pointless distant war. After his father's death in a far off land, it was not long before the Norman barons forgot the oath they had sworn to their absent Duke to uphold his bastard son and the dukedom. They wanted the power and wealth such a position carried, for themselves.

When help finally arrived, the boy was traumatised, inconsolable. Whom could he trust? So many ruthless men wanted what his father had promised to him, those men wanted to kill him to take what was rightfully his. Now he was just a child, and a bastard child at that, abandoned by his father. Even so, his father had named him as his heir and successor. Yet so many had not approved of this and wanted this frightened child killed, so with his father now dead, power could be theirs. They had murdered his guardians, his tutor, and now Osbern. His mother, Herleva, was merely the daughter of Fulbert, a lowly tanner of Falaise. In the Tannery she had worked well outside the town, tending to the 'piss-pots' of the Tanner; a noxious foul smelling trade which required constant amounts of human urine and dog faeces. The stink from the work her father did was so bad it had to be performed well outside the town. She was just a simple piss-pot carrier, with no power to protect her son.

Now he had no one to turn to, no one to protect him, no one he could trust, and no one to love him. One day he would be a man, one day he would get even with all the wrongs done to him. One day, one day, one day it would come, but not now. 'My time will come,' he said to himself gritting his teeth so hard they hurt. Sitting on the edge of his bed, tears streaming down his face, his nightshirt wet through with his sweat, his own urine mingling with Osbern's blood.

He would never learn to read and write, never have an education, save that of how to survive. The boy had been his father's only son, and although a bastard, he had inherited his father's title and lands. Now though, as a boy, William Duke of Normandy was stressed, abandoned, scorned, and unloved; an experience that would help to mould him, into the hard and unforgiving man he would later become.

WINTER 1065/66

'Ride Welland, ride my beauty!' The warrior shouted his words, yet the howling gale took away the sound of his voice; only his fine horse could hear him. The landscape was cold and desolate, no leaves were left on the trees, as the wind and rain swept relentlessly down the long valley, blasting hard into the man's face.

'Ride Welland, speed me on! Fly my beauty!'

Rain cut into Alric's weather-beaten face, his long beard sodden. A sea of angry dark clouds rolled over the hills as the rider drove his horse onward.

'Come on Welland, come on, we must get there.'

Alric spurred on his magnificent, yet exhausted horse, headlong into the unremitting harsh weather. 'I must get to Winchester in time', he kept shouting to himself. 'I must get there.' The rain came heavier, yet still he urged Welland on. The old Roman road he followed was not in good repair; potholes were frequent and all were full of water; but still this road was better than the rutted muddy cart tracks, which meandered across most of the country. Alric's face was taught with tension, he gripped his teeth together so hard, his jaw was hurting. For long years, he had led the Anglo-Saxon armies in the service of his noble master, the Earl of Wessex. Alric's whole life had been in the service of this Earl, Harold Godwinson. Alric felt there was no finer man on earth and now he had to warn him as quickly as he could.

With sodden clothes making his weight and his discomfort all the greater, Alric swept into the yard of a wayside inn. The building was a larger version of the others in the village; mud and wattle walls, with plaster falling away in places and a high thatched roof reaching down to the first floor window.

Alric quickly dismounted and turned his troubled face to look at his faithful horse Welland. His horse was in a bad state, with the steam of the beast's perspiration forming a cloud around the exhausted animal. It disturbed Alric, but he knew his mission was too important to be jeopardised by a tired animal. Alric's eyes flashed with anger, furious there was no one about to attend him outside the inn; he stood alone in the wet muddy yard. Striding up to the entrance threw open the door, yet remained standing outside. 'I need a new mount,' he yelled above the storm, his eyes squinting against the rain. 'Innkeeper,' Alric's voice rose to an even higher pitch. 'Innkeeper, I need a new horse quickly.' He yelled again staring at the startled faces huddled around a large table laden with food in front of them. The warm light issuing from inside the inn looked very homely and tempting; it was in stark contrast to the winter's darkness outside. Alric could see a fire burning in a circular grate in the middle of the floor, with smoke rising up to escape through the round chimney above, in the roof; also, because it was Christmas Day they had candles, which were usually too expensive for most families to use. On a normal day, they would have used rush-lights, simple rushes dipped in animal fat.

The innkeeper, a small man, with a balding head and wearing a grubby leather apron, left the group and came to the door, the cold wind removing the warmth they had built up inside. The innkeeper looked dazed and bewildered by this unexpected visitor, yet his keen eyes were soon taking in his rich apparel and his expensive horse, which was of the highest quality thoroughbred.

'Good sir, 'tis Christmas Day! There are no mounts ready today. No one travels on the feast of Christ's Mass!'

'Damn you. I know it's Christmas Day you fool, but I must get to Winchester, before night sets in. This is the King's business. I have an important message for our lord, the Earl of Wessex, Harold Godwinson. For God's sake, get me a horse: get me one now. Do you hear me?' Alric's throat was becoming hoarse with his shouting.

Stunned, the innkeeper gulped his breath, seeing clearly Alric's need for help and the importance of this traveller. 'Right away sir, I'll get the stable boys to help.' So saying he turned and disappeared into the inn, glad to be out of the rain. A sudden flurry of activity saw men and boys running all around the stables adjacent to the inn. Soon the innkeeper reappeared, with a jug of warm mulled ale. 'Take some refreshment sir, the hot irons have warmed this for you,' he offered the warm ale, as a flummoxed gesture to gain some time, while a new horse was readied.

'No time, no time,' was Alric's response. 'I still have ten more miles to go and daylight has all but gone. These winter days are too bloody short.' Then looking up at the dense clouds above, he added, whimsically. 'What daylight there is on a day like this; I have seen more daylight in a cave, than there is out here this day.'

A short time later Alric was climbing onto this new, but very much inferior mount, he turned to the innkeeper, 'Look you well after my horse for me, stable, groom and feed him; I shall be back shortly for him.'

'Certainly sir, I shall look after him well.' Then he added, 'May God bless your journey sir.'

Alric was soon on his way again, but the night was already gathering and the darkness slowed him down to a canter. The road was far too poor to push the horse any harder. It seemed to take forever. After what felt like an eternity, eventually Alric could just discern Winchester's dim shape in the gloom and several oil lights flickering amidst the murkiness. It was a welcome sight indeed.

He rode straight up to the castle. Anxious to fulfil his mission, Alric immediately made his presence known to the guards. Taking large strides his escort found it difficult to keep up with this tall man as he headed for the great hall. Alric's chainmail armour was well worn; his helmet marked from where it had saved his life, more than once. His appearance was as hard and unforgiving, as the winter earth. He had mastered his trade serving in the Welsh wars under the military leadership of Earl Harold who had appointed him as General of the Housecarls. His escort of guards were shocked at this unexpected visit of the general to Winchester, and on Christmas Day at that. They quickly ushered Alric into the warmth of the Earl's great hall.

From the hall came the sound of revelry, the music of harps and loud drunken voices, which greeted Alric as he entered the room within. There were two hundred or more people, all enjoying the festival of Christmas. In the presence of their lord and master, Earl Harold Godwinson, Earl of Wessex, who sat with Edith-Swan-Neck. The Earl's friends and relatives lounged on resplendently carved chairs placed on a raised dais of stone at the upper end of the hall, opposite to the entrance, away from cold winter drafts and intrusions. This was a special feast, in which the earl had invited not just the nobles of the land, but also the tenant farmers, tradesmen and many of the local military. These Anglo-Saxons were fond of meat and fish, but for most of the common people, meat was a luxury, which only the rich could eat frequently. So on the feast of Christ's Mass the ordinary people were invited to feast with their lord. It was in stark contrast to their usual diet of bread, cheese, eggs and vegetables. They were all in a happy mood for today there was meat, and plenty of it, swan, goose, lamb and venison, but most of all was the succulent mouth watering smell of roasting pig, being turned on a spit, over a roaring fire; all washed down with ale and cider.

Earl Harold occupied a heavy wooden chair, on the raised dais, with a red and gold canopy over it, by way of emphasizing his status. Everyone else in the hall sat on wooden benches. Most were dining and drinking at temporary trestles made into tableis for the joyous feast of Christmas. The huge fireplace radiated heat from the stonesat the back, and from the hearth, the warmth felt so welcoming to Alric. A great red banner emblazoned with the large golden dragon of Wessex, hung over where the earl and his privileged guests sat. It was the two-legged Dragon of Wessex, originally the symbol Wessex and now that of all England as well. The sight of this banner made Alric's heart swell with pride, for he well knew this same emblem had been on the battle flags under which King Alfred-the-Great had halted the Viking advance into England at the Battle of Edington. It was the flag under which the mighty King Athelstan defeated the combined Scottish, Welsh, Irish and Danish armies, at the battle of Brananburgh: the flag under which Earl Harold now proudly sat.

A sudden and startled silence greeted Alric's entrance, when all there saw this sodden, giant of a man stride boldly forward. Removing his conical helmet, Alric's long dark blond hair, all matted and filthy from the exertions of his ride, fell about his shoulders. He had a ruddy face normally, but even more so now, after riding headlong into the wind and rain for so long. The minstrel stopped singing, as all in the hall looked up from their food, some still holding tankards of cider, mead or beer to their lips; as if frozen in the act of drinking. All were now wondering what this could mean. Dropping his heavy wet cloak behind him on the floor, for others to pick up, Alric revealed the sword by his side, as he walked the length of the long banqueting hall. His large hands held the hilt of his sword in one and his helmet in the other. Alric was known to all. He was an important man, the General of the Housecarls, which were acknowledge by all Europe as the most elite troops in England.

At this sudden silence Earl Harold looked up, his heart jumped, knowing only trouble would bring his general to him like this on Christmas Day. Harold reached out and washed his hands in the finger bowl, held out by a servant.

Stooping on one knee, head bowed Alric spoke loud and clear for all to hear, 'My lord I bring dire news.' Water from Alric's wet leggings and tunic made a pool on the floor.

'Stand good Alric, stand,' invited Harold. 'It would seem you have important news for me.' Alric rose to his feet, 'Yes my lord, Edward our King is dying. He is not expected to live much longer. I have ridden hard from London to inform you.'

Earl Harold stood, contemplating this news; his face was expressionless, not willing anyone to interpret his feelings. Harold, Earl of Wessex had a presence about him, a man of compelling personal authority, and the essence of a great leader. Others were instinctively drawn toward him, a very handsome man, with remarkable physical strength for someone of normal stature. His courage, eloquence, his ready jests and acts of valour in battle, were all truly proven. His people loved him and were ready to follow wherever he commanded.

Earl Harold raised his hand to silence even the serving women who were still busy carrying in fresh trays of food, jugs of mead and ale. Harold looked resplendent in his fine linen shirt. His thick mat of dark blond hair, although shorter than most other men in the room, was still long enough to be tied about, with a band of embroidered cloth, woven with small finely crafted beads, around his forehead.

Earl Harold of Wessex was an impressive figure, and so well liked by all. Unlike most of his countrymen, Harold was clean-shaven, but grew a thick moustache. Muscular, from countless battles as leader of the army, educated and a good orator, with a noble presence about him which few men could equal. He was the very epitome of a warrior and statesman. Everyone knew whenever Harold walked into a room, so powerful was his charisma, every inch a leader of men, a man others were proud to serve.

'This is dire news indeed good Alric. What is the nature of the king's sickness?' He beckoned to Alric to sit with him, others quickly standing to offer him space at the table.

Alric sat down on the vacated chair, much relieved to do so, and addressed the Earl, 'His mind has been wayward for some weeks now. He has taken to his bed and your sister, Queen Edith, fears he will not rise again from it.' Alric was handed a tankard of warm mulled ale, which he downed quickly, without taking it from his lips in one long grateful swallow.

'How long do we have?' Harold asked as he put down his goblet of wine, the blood visibly draining from his face. He well knew, as all there also knew, the implications of this news for his country. King Edward was childless with no direct bloodline heir; this lack of a natural successor had been worrying nobles for some time and had been a common theme of gossip amongst most of the people.

'Difficult to say my lord, maybe three days, maybe seven at the most I fear.'

'Take refreshment Alric, and get some dry clothes.' Then turning to the assembly, raising his voice, Harold thundered out an order, 'Call my council; call the Thanes of the Witan who are here this night in Winchester. Call them together, immediately. We have work to do this night.' So saying Earl Harold left the great hall and strode quickly out to the chambers above. When Harold issued an order like this everyone immediately responded without hestitation.

A short while later, the befuddled heads of the Witan members found it difficult to concentrate on climbing the stairs to the meeting chamber.

'One moment it's Christmas and the next this,' whispered one Thane, to no one in particular, as they began to gather in the upper chamber.

By tradition the Witan was always called by the king, and only the king; but all knew that King Edward had been no more than a puppet king for several years now. Earl Harold had become the man who was now looked upon, as the one responsible for maintaining the kingdom's defences against the Welsh.

The local aldermen, together with a few royal Thanes, who were landowners of regional importance, and Aelfwig, the Abbot of Winchester gathered in the council chamber as they had been instructed.

Harold, tense and worried turned to them, sat down at a large table, with Alric by his side. 'Men,' he waited as he prepared in his mind what to say, 'Men, King Edward is childless.'

Harold's mind was troubled. 'I believe those who tell me that King Edward never consummated his marriage to my sister Queen Edith, for this was a way to get back at my father, Earl Godwin, who saw fit to have this marriage arranged.' Harold reflected on the marriage of the king to his sister. His dead father relished the power and influence this alliance would bring to all his family, and indeed it had; but it had not been a happy marriage. 'Edward did not want this marriage, yet my father forced it on him.' Harold paused, and then smiled, 'I now believe King Edward would rather pray than take a lady to his bed.' Muffled smirks were quickly stifled by the seriousness of the situation.

Harold's mind was in turmoil. How should he react to this news? What would be the right thing to do? He did not let his feelings show. 'We must go hastily to London, call the full Witan to assemble there to elect our next King. The issue of succession is a matter for the Witan, and only the Witan, to decide. We will not let the king's preference for Norman ways influence our law. The Normans would never elect their king, no by God; he would be imposed upon them, regardless.'

Harold looked pensive. Then through teeth gritted, he added slowly for all to clearly understand, 'The Norman way is not the Anglo-Saxon way. No King of England has greater authority than the Witan, and this is a matter for the Witan: and only the Witan will decide.' Harold's voice rose to a higher pitch as he repeated these last words so that they would sink deep into their hearts.

'My Lord, God will bless you and we will pray for guidance for the kingdom and the Witan,' so spoke Aelfwig, Harold's uncle, the Abbot of Winchester. Aelfwig was well aware that he was one who had benefited richly from Harold's sister marrying King Edward.

Alric had watched theses proceedings and Harold's actions carefully, but said nothing. He had pondered what would be Harold's response to the news he carried. He also knew of the rumours that the Normans had their eye on this kingdom of England, but no one in England could conceive of a Norman on the English throne.

Alric now stood up, 'My Lord, the Housecarls here in Winchester will join me to escort you to London.' Then as he lifted his helmet from the table, he place it under his arm and added, 'We can be ready at first light.'

'Good,' smiled Harold. He was surprised to feel a buzz of excitement coursing through him. 'Send messengers Alric, for all the Housecarls to muster at Westminster in London. We will leave early in the morning.'

Edith, the Queen of England, was sitting on the floor warming the feet of King Edward in her lap. She looked older than her forty-six years, her face drawn, with a tired aura about her. She was slim, some would even say thin. She had never come to terms with her childless marriage to the king, who all but shunned her. Even so, in spite of this, she had come to love her husband, especially in these later years as he began to rely on her support more. Due to his illness Edward was unable stand, so he lay on cushions by the fire, trying to keep warm; away from the bitter cold winds, which blew through this, the king's Palace at Westminster. Edward was drained of energy, having little strength left in him, he felt so tired and weak. His long swan-white beard was not as trimmed and neat as normal, but was now wild and ragged. In better days, his form had been of admirable proportion, his countenance florid; but now as an old man, he was deathly pale, with a burning temperature. He could hardly speak.

The most serious result of the constant squabbles and rebellions within his kingdom was the breakdown of the king's health. Throughout his reign, not only did he have the powerful Earl Godwin to reckon with, and the ambition and squabbles of that earl's children; now he found after Godwin's death, he had that earl's son Harold Godwinson, acting as though he were the king. The final blow to Edward's stability was the violent division between two of Godwin's sons, Harold and Tostig. This stress had become all too much for him; sorrowing at all this, he had fallen ill in the autumn of this year.

King Edward had loved Harold and his younger brother Tostig, when they were children, but Tostig had become so very difficult to deal with, as he grew into a man. Queen Edith was the eldest of the of the late Earl Godwin's children, she had six brothers, who all had lived and played together as children in the court of King Edward; Sweyn, Harold, Gyrth, Tostig, Leofwin, and Wulfnoth. These siblings of Earl Harold became the most powerful family in England; yet in truth, they were so very different to each other.

Sweyn and Tostig had brought infamous disgrace to their noble family. Both of these men were violent, arrogant and aggressive; and both had been exiled from England due to their criminal behaviour.

Sweyn had raped the Abbess of Leominster, which was not only a violation of the woman; it was also a sacrilege against the church. For this act he was exiled abroad for three years, then, although allowed to return, he had to forfeit his estates, as Earl of Herefordshire. When King Edward had heard of the rape and was told of Sweyn's many other crimes the king rightly refused his reinstatement. The king pointed out that a lesser man would have been put to death.

Then just a few months before King Edward took to his sick bed, Tostig, as the Earl of Northumbria, had been overthrown by his own Thanes, after holding the title for ten years. Several members of the Witan had charged that glorious earl with being too cruel; they had accused him of punishing men more for a desire to obtain their property, which would be confiscated to the earl's estates, than for a love of justice. Tostig was subsequently removed by force from his office, and replaced by Morcar, the brother of Edwin the Earl of Mercia. Tostig did not take kindly to being extricated from his earldom and now sought his bitter revenge.

Then there was Wulfnoth, the youngest of the siblings at twenty-six years of age and the sixth son of the late Earl Godwin. Wulfnoth had been forced to stay as hostage in Normandy, when the Godwin family living in exile there, keenly wanted to return to England. Wulfnoth, along with Harold's nephew Hakon, had been seized by the hated Robert of Jumieges, who was at that time, the Archbishop of Canterbury. This was just one of the reasons why the Normans were so detested by the common English.

Now though, Edward had within him a sickness of the mind. He protested to God ten times a day, with deep sorrow, complaining constantly, that he had been deprived of the due obedience from the men of his kingdom.

He could not see that the English had never forgiven him for bringing in so many of his Norman friends and appointing them to positions of great power, over the heads of the native population. It was evident to the English that if Edward pursued this course, he would turn England into a province of Normandy, which no Englishman would readily contemplate. Frequently ranting and raving at no one in particular, Edward called down God's vengeance upon the English for not respecting his authority.

When he was just a child, Edward's Norman mother took him to Normandy to live in exile where he had spent many happy years as a youth, after the Danish invasion of England. In Normandy, Edward saw for himself, that no one ever ventured to question Duke William, or his Barons; and yet in England it was different, so very different. Here the king was not the only voice to be heard; here they questioned all decisions they either did not like, or could not understand. At times, in Anglo-Saxon England, they even *voted* who was to be their next king: it was so unlike the Norman way.

'They should obey me without question', had been the attitude of Edward's mind. 'Why is it the English not only show no fear of my authority, they even show no respect for those I have appointed?' These questions had infuriated Edward.

Some years before his present sickness, the high-ranking Count Eustace of Boulogne, who was married to Duke William's sister arrived in Dover, to visit Robert of Jumieges, the Norman Archbishop of Canterbury. The people of Dover deliberately turned their backs on Eustace as a calculated insult. Eustace was an arrogant man, full of his own importance. He liked nothing better than to display to others his magnitude, so this insult riled him considerably. Expecting no reprisal, he cut one man down with his sword, to show these lowly people his power and authority.

Angered by such unwarranted aggression, the people of Dover attacked Eustace and his entourage with stones and other missiles, so that he had to make a hasty retreat out of the town. 'How dare they do this to a nobleman of Normandy?' complained King Edward bitterly. He refused to acknowledge that the problem was of his own making. Indeed, Robert of Jumieges was just one of the many Normans Edward had put into a position of power, above the local English. The people of England would spit on the ground at the mere mention of the names, Robert of Jumieges and Count Eustace.

Edward demanded justice from Earl Godwin to punish the people of Dover, but Godwin refused, saying that the towns' people had been provoked beyond all reason. Edward simply could just not understand how any man would refuse the command of a king. The mental pressure and strain on Edward all built up over the years from several events like this. Edward knew such actions would never be allowed to happen in Normandy. He even drove Earl Godwin into exile because of this Dover incident, but it had not worked, for later, he had been forced to accept the earl's return.

Count Eustace was now an embittered enemy of England, he would never forget how the English insulted his dignity, and he vehemently vowed to someday wreak vengeance upon them.

Such pressures and stresses had taken their toll on Edward.

Walking purposefully, with heads bowed against the chill wind, a small, but important group of men, headed to the room where Edward, their king now lay dying. Alric felt the tension of the occasion, in the pit of his stomach. Alric was accompanying Earl Harold, along with Rodbert, the Steward of the Royal Palace, who was a relative of the king, and Stigand the English Archbishop of Canterbury, who had replaced Robert of Jumieges. Harold's face was grim as the door to King Edward's sick room was open for them. All four men looked tired and strained, as they quietly entered the room. It was hot inside due to the large fires lit to keep the king warm, but there was a smell of sickness within there, which all chose to ignore. They walked over to where King Edward lay and the reclining figure of Queen Edith.

'Harold!' cried Edith as she saw her brother. She rose and ran toward him in a loving embrace. 'Harold, it is so good to see you,' she almost gleefully said. 'Yet under such a sad time,' she quickly added. 'I fear yesterday, the fourth day of Christmas, was a bad day for Edward our king. He insisted on trying to go to the wonderful new Abbey at Westminster for its consecration.' She grimaced, shaking her head slowly. 'It was such a cold day. He tried so hard to get there, now, look at him,' she pointed to the curled heap of bedclothes, 'he can hardly move.'

Both Edward and Edith were truly proud of the new abbey and its outstanding beauty. Edward had earnestly wanted this to be an ecclesiastical and royal complex. A palace with a large monastery, and the new Abbey church suitable for royal functions and burials. Edith breathed shallowly, with the mixed emotions, of pride in her husband's achievements and sadness at his current state.

'Now that this wonderful abbey is finally finished, I have heard that the French intend to copy this wonderful edifice and build one of their own in the city of Paris.' She almost had girlish joy at the prospect of the French copying the English to such an extent.

Her mixed emotions though felt strange to her, for she had been forced to marry a man who did not love her, and who would not take her as a true wife. Yet in these later years, they had grown to be very fond of each other, especially as the king grew older and weaker. She well knew Edward had been driven by guilt to complete this major building project, for when Edward had been forced to flee into a long exile in Normandy, he made a solemn vow that if he ever regained his throne, he would make a pilgrimage to Rome in gratitude. He did indeed manage to regain his throne, but the politically uncertain climate made it unwise for him to leave England and go to Rome. Pope Leo, excused Edward from his vow to go to Rome, on the condition that he was to spend the money put aside for his pilgrimage, on the building of Westminster Abbey instead.

Harold knowing the turmoil his sister must be in gently put his hand on Edith's shoulder. 'Tell me about the consecration of the abbey later sister, I will love to hear more of this, but now I must speak with the king.' So saying Harold, and his group, walked over to the curled up heap surrounded by cushions on the floor, that was, for now, the King of England.

Opening his eyes dimly Edward smiled on seeing the tall stately figure of Earl Harold standing before him. 'Harold, it is good to see you have come.' Harold squatted on the floor beside the ailing king and the warm fire. 'We need to talk, while I still can,' Edward's voice crackled, barely above that of a whisper. He was happy to see the man before him; the man he had so loved when he was a child.

Edward was burning with fever and he struggled to raise himself up from his fireside bed. Edith rushed over to his side and put more pillows under his back so that he could be better supported.

'I know what pains you Harold,' Edward had deliberately kept the matter of his succession dangling, so as to keep better control of things; or at least that is what he once thought, but not now. He went straight to the heart of the subject, beckoning Harold now to his side, 'Once, I spoke about the succession of this kingdom to Duke William, when he visited me here in England.' Edward gasped for breath and struggled to gather his thoughts. 'That was more than fifteen years ago. We spoke together for some time about the succession of this kingdom. He tried to get me to promise England to him.' Edward was panting, clearly struggling to get his breath. He waited some time before gaining control of his breathing enough to carry on, 'He was determined I should leave this kingdom to him, but I would not.' Edward summoned all of the little strength he had left, his mind now purposefully set. 'We both know I could not do this.' Then for emphasis he repeated, 'I could not do this. I tried so hard to explain to him the workings of the Witan and the Anglo-Saxon way; which he:' Edward waited and a thin smile spread on his weak lips, 'which he was determined *not* to understand.'

Edward started to cough incessantly. Recovering just enough to continue, he went on. 'I had been too long away from England and William had been kind to me. Even so he persisted to try to get me to admit the Norman way of kingship and dukedom to be a better way to that of the English. I could not agree.' He looked at Harold straight in the eye, 'How could I?'

Edith bathed a wet towel on the King's forehead to wipe away his sweat.

Alric's clenched his fists. He could not believe what he was hearing. How could this foreign duke even think he could barter for the throne of England based on a friendship, or even as a distant relative?

Edward was now composed again, so continued, 'William said that with my authority as king, I could appoint a successor myself. Yet I know full well such authority in England rests only with the Witan.'

Edith wiped the spittle from the corner of Edward's mouth with a dry cloth. 'I remember William got very angry at the time. His temper is truly one to be feared. I saw that for myself, and since I have heard of the harshness of Duke William and his cruelty; I should not want this to be imposed upon our English people.' Edward's words tailed off as he slipped into a temporary sleep whilst speaking, his mouth wide open.

All were quiet, no one whispered, they just looked at each other and waited for Edward, who slowly struggled to force out his words in order to continue, 'During William's recent conquest of Maine my nephew Count Walter of the Vexin was imprisoned by William. It was there that Count Walter died in very suspicious circumstances while in William's custody. They say it was by poison. Such things do not endear me to Duke William.'

All this time a messenger had been standing silently by the door; aware now was not the time to interrupt. Alric had walked over to him, then returned to Harold and whispered in his ear, 'The Witan will be assembled here in three more days. The word has gone throughout all the land. All is made ready.'

Harold just nodded an acknowledgement, but said nothing.

Edith wiped tears from her eyes. 'He was so proud yesterday at the consecration of the abbey, but he could hardly stand and had to be carried much of the time,' tears ran freely down her cheeks. 'He tried so hard, but in the end he could not get there, although he would have liked to have seen it so much.'

Edward reached for some water, which Edith had readied for him by his bedside.

Harold was now irritated, looking straight at Rodbert, Stigand and Alric, he expressed his irritation, 'William also tried to force a similar promise out of me,' Harold admitted as they sat huddled around the prone king. 'It was when I went to Normandy to try to negotiate the release of my youngest brother, Wulfnoth and my nephew Hakon; for as you know, both men were being held as hostages by Duke William.' Harold stepped away from the bed and continued in a whisper, 'It was the only way I could get their release from this monster.' Harold was referring to the demand Duke William had put on Harold. 'He demanded what he laughingly called, "my good behaviour and support," or he would not let Wulfnoth and Hakon return to England.'

Alric had heard whispers of such happenings, but he had always rejected them as just idle gossip.

Harold took a deep breath before continuing, 'I took William a vast amount of wealth to buy my brother's freedom, which he confiscated and then refused to let me leave. I was trapped. It was then I was forced into making a promise to him; a pseudo promise,' he added, 'that he the bastard Duke William, should succeed Edward as our king. He simply did not understand, or would not understand, that I did not have the authority to make such a promise to him.' Harold showed his obvious irritation with the matter. 'Neither I, nor my kin, would have been allowed to leave that land, had I not have quenched this outrageous request, and pacified him. I saw the blood red fury, which raged in his eyes.'

Harold hesitated, unsure how to say what came next, 'The man is a monster, a trickster. It is true, I made a vow to him, I had to, but it was of little worth. He just did not seem to understand that neither did I have the authority to give such a vow, nor would the Witan have honoured it anyway. As it was, I did return home safely with Hakon, but I had to leave my poor young brother Wulfnoth behind, where he remains as hostage to this day.'

Harold looked decidedly embarrassed at these admissions of perceived weakness, 'I fear that that devil, Robert of Jumieges will have stirred up more trouble for us, for I hear tell that when we removed him from being the Archbishop of Canterbury, he deliberately and with malice, went straight to his brother-in-law, Duke William with lies upon his lips. He lied to William that Edward had promised the kingdom to him. We know he made this up, and yet if William believes that devil's lies he will expect the kingship.'

The blood had drained from Alric's face, and he now looked quite pale.

'Harold,' King Edward weakly lifted up his head as he came round from his semiconscious state. 'Harold,' Edward reached up a hand and held tightly onto Harold's tunic, as a child would grasp hold of his mother's skirts, 'Harold, tell the Witan, I commend my wife to your care and with her my whole kingdom.' Then turning to Edith, he looked up and said, 'May God be gracious to this lady, my wife. She has served me devotedly and has always been by my side like a beloved daughter.' With that, Edward slipped into a deep sleep.

The group looked silently at each other as they departed, leaving the king with Edith, knowing they had heard what they had come to this place to hear. Alric now knew what all had whispered, that Edith had been as a daughter to Edward and not a wife. More importantly, what they had just heard from Edward was a ringing endorsement for Earl Harold Godwinson. He pushed to the back of his mind any thought that Duke William may even still think he had any claim to the throne of England.

Four days later, on the second day of January, Gyrth, the Earl of East Anglia and younger brother of Earl Harold, was ready to address the Witan assembled at Westminster Palace. At thirty-four years of age, he was ten years younger than Harold. His eyes were bright and searching; with something of menace and of authority in their quick glitter, his mouth was firm set and hard, as befitted one who was wont to set his face against danger.

Gyrth had always looked up to his older brother with full admiration for him and his achievements. He would do anything for Harold, and now was set to support him during this crucial moment. Gyrth looked resplendent, wearing a dark brown tunic gathered at the waist, with the hem and collar richly embodied in gold thread. A fine red cloak was held in place with a beautiful ornate clasp of gold over his left breast. He wore a solid gold torque amulet around his left bicep. As it was with Harold, so it was with his brother Gyrth, he had the muscles of a warrior, his blond hair neatly dressed and cropped.

All around the assembled Witan looked on, tense under the gaze of the high vaulted ceiling of the Palace of Westminster. The richest and most powerful noblemen of the kingdom were now hushed.

'My Lords, Royal Thanes, Bishops and noble Captains of the Housecarls,' began Gyrth's address to them all. 'Good King Edward is sick unto death, and as we all know, he is childless. Therefore we, as members of the Witan according to our English custom must agree and elect a suitable successor.' A sea of heads nodded in approval. 'His closest living relative is Prince Edgar Atheling, the grandson of our former King, Edmund Ironside, and great-nephew of King Edward, called the Confessor. He is the last surviving male relative of King Alfred-the-Great. Prince Edgar is the closest living relative to King Edward,' then he added with a lower tone of voice, 'but he is only twelve-years-old.' There was a long silence and some uncomfortable fidgeting.

Young Hakon the son of Harold's disgraced brother Sweyn, and the man Harold had negotiated the release of, when he had been held as a hostage by Duke William, rose to his feet. Hakon had seen well the calibre of the Norman threat, while being held in that country as hostage for twelve years. The torment of his captivity told in his face, with bags under his eyes and a permanent wrinkled furrow on his brow.

'Nobles of England, we are threatened on all sides, by Vikings from the east, by Normans from the south, by Welsh from the west and by Scots in the north. I ask you, could Prince Edgar, who is just a young boy, lead an army against these our foes?' The challenged was stark and all well knew the truth in what Hakon said. No voice raised in answer. 'Your silence says it all. I submit therefore to this assembly that Prince Edgar is too young and too far removed from the king to ascend to the throne.' At the buzz and nods of agreement, he sat down.

Alric had been impatient to speak and now quickly stood up. In keeping with the tradition of the Witan, only the man standing was allowed to speak, so Hakon nodded his head toward Alric.

'In the Housecarls we have the finest warriors in all of Europe. Together with the Fyrd, no one can stand against us. We are strong, but only if we have a strong leader.' He looked around the assembly before continuing, 'I put it to you we need a strong leader; we cannot be led by a boy. We need a man of strength, we need a warrior.' Alric pointed his finger to Earl Harold, 'We need Earl Harold of Wessex.' A cheer went up and a stamping of feet in approval.

Gyrth again stood to speak, asking, 'Raise your hand above your head, if you would have Prince Edgar as our next king; the king of all England?' No one moved, so Gyrth cynically questioned, 'Is there any support for Edgar in this room, who should be heard?' Then, lifting his voice to a shout, he declared, 'Then I submit Prince Edgar is not chosen.'

Individual conversations now broke out among the nobles, distracting from the seriousness of the occasion. Irritated Gyrth stood up, 'This is not the time for private conversations,' he rebuked them. Silence now fell over them. Gyrth then stated, 'The second distant relative of King Edward is so far distant we will not even discuss the matter.' He raised his voice, shook his fist and continued. 'We well remember the hated Danish yoke we fought so hard to be free from during the days of King Canute. King Harald Sigurdsson of Norway is a *very* distant relative of King Edward. If we bring in a Norwegian King we will be appointing another Viking king to rule over us.' Slapping his hand hard on the table in front of him, 'He would even bring the Danes back with him. Do we want that?'

'No! No!' Was the combined word of the assembly.

Gyrth knew where this was heading as he slowly shook his head from side to side. 'The name of this man says it all. This man King Harald Sigurdsson of Norway, everyone calls 'Hardrada' meaning "The Ruthless." We in England have driven out the Vikings from this *our* land,' Gyrth again thumped his fist on the table in front of him. 'We will not let them return.' The assembled Witan all rose to their feet in wild applause. Gyrth had to shout above the noise, 'Hardrada can stay in Norway.'

It took some time before Gyrth could restore order to the assembly. 'We must now consider another distant relative of King Edward, namely the bastard Duke William of Normandy.' Moans, hoots and boos came from the assembly. 'Bastard Duke William is still a relative of the king,' rebuked Gyrth, 'Albeit a bastard line!' The laughter from the assembly was more cynical than jolly.

Gyrth now went through the heritage of Duke William, with a strong hint of sarcasm in his voice. 'King Edward's mother was Queen Emma, daughter of the Norman Richard-the-Fearless. Her brother was Richard-the-Good, whose son was Robert-the-Magnificent, whose illegitimate son is now Duke William-the-Bastard.' Pointing a wagging finger to the air Gyrth added, 'So this family link to our king is not strong, just second cousins; and a bastard one at that. Let me put it more simply, his grandfather's sister, Emma, was the mother of King Edward.' Laughter came from the Witan, because of this detailed explanation of the weak and illegitimate family link.

'Also we know he tried illegally,' Gyrth hit the table again with his fist and repeated the word, 'Yes, I say, illegally, to get King Edward to appoint him as his successor. This was an illegal act and one we would not, and could not recognise.'

Esegar, Sheriff of Middlesex was a thin-faced older man, yet still comely and well shaped, with clear pensive grey eyes. He rose to his feet, so Gyrth sat down.

'The bastard duke has no legitimate claim to the throne of England. If our king, spoke of succession to him he had no legal jurisdiction to do so, and certainly no authority to offer the crown to William. There is no precedent for this to happen under Anglo-Saxon law. A unilateral decision by the monarch has never occurred in this country before, even to bequeathing his throne to another Anglo-Saxon. The normal English way, is either by birth or by election from the Witan. We neither know of, nor do we accept any other way.' Nods of approval were evident all around.

Esegar went on, 'Not only this', he paused and repeated, 'not only this, we would never elect a king who has been shown to be so capable of such unbridled cruelty. For example, when he took the rebellious town of Alencon in Normandy by assault, the defenders had taunted him about being illegitimate and the son of a stinking tanner's daughter, the son of a piss-pot carrier. Once the town had fallen, thirty-two of the defenders had their hands and feet cut off and cast over the castle walls. No such man should ever rule England.' Esegar sat down to sound of genuine applause.

Leofric, the Abbot of Peterborough, stood up, resplendent in the robes of his office. 'Noble lords, we should not even be discussing this man's right to the throne of England. Duke William has no claim whatsoever to this kingdom. His name say's it all,' he paused for dramatic effect, 'William-the-Bastard. For it is written in our own law that this man may not inherit the kingdom. King Offa of Mercia presided over the Council of Chelsea, in the year of our Lord 787. That year the synod laid down that only legitimate kings were to be chosen by the Witan and Bishops. Papal legates also attended this synod and so thereby gave this decision the Pope's blessing. We have no need to discuss the candidature of this person any further.'

Gyrth returned to stand before them all, and continued, 'Well said good bishop. Still I must ask the question, Is there any support for bastard Duke William of Normandy in this room, is there anyone who should be heard?' No one moved. Gyrth smiled for he now knew that all were of the same mind, 'Then Duke William-the-Bastard is not chosen to be our king.' A more relaxed atmosphere pervaded the hall of Westminster.

We must now consider the next claimant to the throne, Harold Godwinson, Earl of Wessex.'

Stigand the Archbishop of Canterbury rose to his feet, so Gyrth sat down again. Stigand was an old man, with his hair cropped in the traditional way of the clergy, in a tonsure. He had served King Canute as a chaplain and as his advisor in 1020. He had continued in this role to the king during the reign of Canute's son, Harthacanute. All now looked intently toward Stigand, 'I have evidence to put now before this council,' all leaned forward in their seats intent to hear what he had to say. 'We have all seen how Earl Harold, during the king's sickness, and before, has run the affairs of state of this country and has protected this kingdom well from the Welsh attacks on us.'

'True. True. Agreed,' were the words uttered from the assembly.

Stigand went on, 'Good King Edward himself has let it be known Earl Harold should take hold of this kingdom. I ask those who were there on this occasion to now stand.'

Queen Edith, Earl Harold, Rodbert the Steward of the Royal Palace and Alric General of the Housecarls all stood up. The whole Witan turned to look intently at those now standing.

Stigand knew the importance of what he had to say next. 'I call you all to witness in God's name that King Edward in the presence of those now standing and myself said for all to hear, "Tell the Witan, I commend my wife to Earl Harold's care and with her my whole Kingdom."' The ripple of applause was spontaneous; thumping on the tables and then cheering burst forth from the whole council. The Archbishop sat down, smiling.

Gyrth again stood up, 'Earl Harold and I have royal blood from the Danish branch of our family, but I value talent over blood any day. It is talent which our country needs now, and proven talent at that. We do not need some boy who happens to have closer family of royal blood in his veins, or some foreign tyrant who will not treat us kindly. In Earl Harold we have a proven warrior, a great and respected leader, who also happens to have royal blood, for he is the great, great grandson of Harold Bluetooth, King of Denmark.' Gyrth's heart was pumping hard now, as his excitement rose. 'Earl Harold is a man who will protect this kingdom, in its time of need. I ask you all for a show of hands, that Earl Harold Godwinson of Wessex be designated as our next king.' All hands shot up and loud cheering ensued, which went on for some time. Feet stamped on the wooden floor and fists banged on the tables. It was pandemonium. Finally, when Gyrth could eventually be heard above the noise, he smiled, then asserted, 'Earl Harold is hereby elected and designated as the next King of England.'

The tumultuous response brought laughter and joy to all the assembly, as they spilled out of the hall to tell everyone the good news.

Alric was overjoyed with this decision of the Witan. He grasped the hands of anyone who was within reach, his face beaming with joy. His relief at this decision was plain for all to see. 'What a great decision,' he told everyone. 'What a great decision, God is smiling on us today.' Alric, along with the rest of the Witan, flung their arms around each other, at the sheer exuberance of electing their new king. Alric had never felt so happy for a long time. It felt good to be alive on such a joyful occasion.

The Twelfth Night of Christmas was normally a celebration almost as important as Christmas Day itself, but not this year. On the fifth day of January, the eve of the Twelfth Day of Yule, King Edward-the-Confessor died. Most thought the date of his death significant. The following Day of Epiphany the last day of Christmas, was considered to be when the three wise men had visited the baby Jesus, and as such this was a special holy day. At his death King Edward-the-Confessor was aged sixty-four years and had ruled England for the last twenty-two of those years. His body now lay, wrapped in linen in the painted chamber of the palace at Westminster. A great sadness hung like deep shadows all over the kingdom. Town criers went around London and the shires declaring, 'The king is dead, long live the king.'

Harold and his advisors had to work quickly. On the same day that Edward died, Stigand, the Archbishop of Canterbury and Ealdred, the Archbishop of York were summoned to the presence of Harold. Both were dressed in their full traditional ropes as bishops, even though both were political churchmen. In the year 1058 Ealdred had made a pilgrimage to Jerusalem, proud in the knowledge he was the first English bishop ever to make such a difficult journey. Ealdred was a man of extraordinary influence and energy, and had been in great favour with King Edward. Now both he and Stigand were standing expectantly before Harold, the chosen new king. Stigand's thin face looked drawn and tense. It was a sombre and difficult task, which Harold now had to deal with.

'By our law', Harold began, 'the Archbishop of Canterbury should be the one to crown the King of England, but I fear we have a problem with that.'

Stigand knew exactly what that problem was.

Harold related the story to both archbishops, without needing to, but felt he must, to justify his next action. 'When bringing in his Norman friends to positions of great power within England, King Edward appointed that arrogant Norman upstart, Robert of Jumieges, as Archbishop of Canterbury. This greatly incensed all true Anglo-Saxons. Then, as you well know, in the year 1052, Robert was forcefully removed from his office at the insistence of my father Earl Godwin.' The bishops nodded with submissive respect for Harold. 'You Stigand were then appointed in his stead. My father well knew you to be an honest and just man who was also vehemently opposed to Normans taking positions of power in our land.' Harold cast his eyes down and fumbled with his loose long sleeves. 'Unfortunately for you Stigand, this appointment has been condemned by the Pope, as it had not gone via his office, so he subsequently excommunicated you. The Pope asserting only he could replace an archbishop, so he would not recognise your appointment.' Harold looked intently at Stigand, while pressing his hands together.

Stigand interjected, by way of his justification, 'We all know the Pope is beholden to the Normans for his protection and for their success in fighting the heathen Mohammedans in Italy and Sicily. That is what lies behind this.'

Harold nodded, 'True Stigand, but what this means for us now, is that if you were to officiate at my coronation, there are many who will say the ceremony is null and void, due to your excommunication; even though your appointment is the will of all England.'

'Your majesty I fully understand. I would not wish to bring any such problems to you.' So saying Stigand pointed toward Ealdred, the Archbishop of York. 'There is your answer sire.'

Stigand looked to Ealdred for confirmation, but Harold did not wait.

'Yes indeed Stigand and that is what I wish to do.' This was not an easy decision Harold had to make. Looking both men in the eyes, he reached out putting his hands on the shoulders of each churchman in turn. 'Stigand, you will prepare for the funeral of King Edward tomorrow morning, and conduct a most solemn ceremony, and you good Ealdred, will prepare for my coronation that same afternoon.' This was something that had never been done before, but it would stop the coronation of Harold from being under-valued by his enemies. Harold sat back down, 'Neither of you must be seen in the presence of the other tomorrow, so that none may construe wrongly who is officiating at these two most solemn events. Do I make myself clear?'

Both Archbishops showed their agreements to the king's command. 'Sire,' said Ealdred, 'It is indeed a wise move to use this opportunity, when all the noble Lords and Thanes of the land are gathered in London for the Twelfth Night celebrations and the Festival of Epiphany. All will be gathered here anyway for the funeral of the King and to celebrate Twelfth Night, we will not have to wait now for the nobles to assemble. If they are here for festival, then they can also be here for the funeral and the coronation, they can now partake in the two. Not only will Edward be laid to rest with great ceremony, in the new Abbey of Westminster, this same edifice will now also see its first coronation of our new king.' Both archbishops could see the wisdom of their new king already and the deep thought Harold had put into this.

Stigand was amazed at Harold's display of forethought and intellect, 'This is well thought out sire. It shall be as you say.' Respect for Harold radiated from these noble archbishops.

The sixth day of January dawned the next morning, the Feast of Epiphany. It was a bitterly cold day, with frost covering the ground, there was not a breath of wind and a dull mist hung as a fog, greatly limiting visibility. Frost glistened all around, on the bare branches of the trees, on the grass and on the thatched roofs of the buildings. The town's people were coming together, wrapping themselves in fur and woollen blankets against the biting cold. The breath of the people could be physically seen, like that of smoke from a chimney, whilst stamping their feet in a vain attempt to keep warm. It was so cold, and yet the people had all ventured outside. None remained in their houses, this was an event all wanted to see and to be a part of.

The people lined the streets as they waited patiently for the day's important events to transpire. Slowly a solemn procession made its way toward the new Abbey at Westminster. All felt that this magnificent building was the most impressive building in all of England. From its tower a mournful bell rang, tolling a single strike, and had been doing so for hours.

The grim procession approached the abbey and the great wooded doors, thirty or more feet high, slowly opened. The procession entered beneath the richly carved stonework of the entrance. For many it was like entering a magnificent simulation of heaven itself, with the high vaulted roof, majestic pillars and a perfusion of candle light, giving the onlooker a feeling of being that much closer to heaven.

First in the procession came the wardens holding large silver candle sticks each one with a white unlit candle, then followed a number crosses which were held aloft by the clergy, next were the choristers singing a solemn anthem, their breath rising as little clouds above the heads of boy singers. These were followed by those who led the horses pulling a carriage bearing the body of the dead king. His body was completely wrapped in a shroud on an open bier, covered by a richly embroidered pall, with an attendant either side ringing a bell. The king's widow, Queen Edith, followed immediately behind the bier, her head and face completely covered by a dark veil. Harold, the newly proclaimed king, followed a pace or two behind the queen. After Harold came his brothers Gyrth and Leofwin. Behind the brothers, Alric led one-hundred Housecarls, each one marching in full armour and carrying a long spear, tipped with steel and held upright, each with a small pennant flying from it. The Housecarls had their leaf-shaped shield slung across their backs, looking magnificently intimidating.

The vast banner of the golden dragon of Wessex and England was held horizontally by six page-boys of the king, four taking a corner each and two holding the centre length. This long procession stretched for one-hundred yards, as it entered the vast empty space of the church's nave, quickly filling it up. Once the procession had entered the abbey, the throngs of people, who had been waiting patiently outside in the cold, also entered in their turn. As Stigand conducted the service, the dead king was laid to rest in a stone sarcophagus sunk into the main altar, amid a great deal of weeping and sighing. Stigand, the Archbishop of Canterbury ordered a month of prayers to be said in all churches for the soul of the dead king, and money to be distributed to the poor.

After the funeral, the people spilled out into the fair outside, which had been set up around the abbey. In spite of the cold, merchants and traders had used the occasion to set up stalls of hot chestnuts, hot mulled wine and warm mulled beer. Trade was brisk. The spices in the mulled drinks gave off pleasant aromas, which tempted the pallets of the customers to partake in this mid-winter beverage. Others used this opportunity to sell their wares, of wooden bowls, linen cloth, earthenware jugs, fleeces of wool and much more. Soon the crowds were in a less sombre mood, when just after midday, a war-horn sounded the call for all to return to the abbey, and its bells began to ring a more joyous sound.

Having bid farewell to the old king in the morning, the mourners now prepared to acknowledge their new king in the afternoon. Ealdred, the Archbishop of York, stood before the high-alter, as Harold made his way to the throne. The banner displaying the Golden Dragon of Wessex and England, which had been so solemnly carried in earlier, now hung over the throne.

Harold looked resplendent as he slowly walked up the centre of the nave to take his seat on the throne. He was followed by his Pages, then his brothers Gyrth and Leofwin, after which came the Thanes, nobles of the land, and Alric, representing the Housecarls.

A gasp of unrepressed admiration came from the congregation as Harold stood and slowly turned to face them, before gracefully taking his seat on the throne. He was dressed in a red calf length tunic, trimmed in gold cloth around its short sleeves, its neck and waist. Under the red tunic, he wore a royal blue, long sleeved silk shirt, all royally set off by a ten-foot long robed cape made of the finest cloth of gold. He looked every inch the true King of England.

This was the first coronation of a king in the new Abbey of Westminster. The standing congregation hushed as the Archbishop of York anointed Harold's head and chest with holy oil; he then lowered the gold crown onto his head, placing in his left hand the golden orb and in his right the sceptre. Turning to the congregation Ealdred declared, 'I give you King Harold the Second, King of all England.' Loud cheers echoed throughout Westminster Abbey, as all in unison chanted, 'God save the king, God save the king, God save the king.' All the lords, nobles along with the people submitted to him and paid homage. England had a new king.

Just a few days later Alric led one-hundred Housecarls, all in full armour, to escort King Harold north, along with his brother Gyrth and Wulfstan, the Bishop of Worcester. Wulfstan had reason to feel close to King Harold. His family had lost their lands when the Danish King Canute came to rule

England. Then, in the year 1062, Harold had helped him to secure his bishopric. Wulfstan was noted for his preaching, his personal asceticism, his simplicity, earnestness and incessant labour for his pastoral life. He had been consecrated as bishop, by Ealdred. Harold had a deep respect for Wulfstan and vice-versa. Now, Harold would need Wulfstan on the task that was before him.

As they moved north, it was a royal procession, on state business. Harold wanted to use this opportunity to be seen by his people, and thousands were turning out to greet and wave as he passed through towns, villages, hamlets and cities on his journey. There was suddenly a general feeling of well being among the population who willingly came out to greet their new king. Harold had wanted this to be a royal display, for as many as possible to see.

Alric was full of pride when he saw how well the horses of the Housecarls had been groomed. His men had made sure their horses were all turned out at their very best. His mounted Housecarls, wore chainmail armour, which glinted in the winter's sun, making an impressive sight, with their long knee-length chainmail coats, with short sleeves to enable freedom of movement in battle. They wore pointed conical helmets to help deflect blows from sword attacks, with a nosepiece to guard the front of their face. A long double-edged sword hung at their waist and they carried the Norman style leaf shaped shield, which was long, with tapering point to the bottom. These shields were strung across their backs as they rode along. Pennants flew from every lance with banners of the golden dragon of England and Wessex proudly flying at the front. Alric reflected on his Housecarls; they were, justifiably he felt, the highest status of warrior in England, a paid professional army, and renowned as the best fighters in Europe. His fulltime soldiers were dedicated to the service of the king, all very proud of their position. Any problems of internal discipline were dealt with by a meeting of his senior officers. The worst sentence issued as a punishment to a Housecarl, was to be declared a coward and cast out from their membership.

This royal progress journeyed first to Repton, capital city of the Earldom of Mercia, the large and powerful central district, forming the midlands of England. After a brief stay there, they quickly moved onward, to the furthest northern earldom of England, Northumbria.

This was urgent business, because the first problem of Harold's reign was to win over the men from Northumbria, who at first refused to acknowledge him, complaining they had not been consulted over Harold's crowning, but Harold knew he had to deal with a far deeper fear that was troubling them.

As this royal procession approached Northumbria, the fierce Northumbrian weather set in. At first the cold rain came, which soon turned to snow, making progress difficult. Each day they planned to reach a town, where all men could be billeted for the night, each householder expected to feed and shelter several men for the night. After the snow came the frost, freezing the snow hard, with a bitter cold wind blowing in from the North Sea. It was not the time of year to be travelling, most would not dream of it, yet still they went on, until the city of York eventually came in sight.

'Sire, messengers are already in York to announce our coming,' Alric informed Harold. 'Tonight we will dine with Edwin, Earl of Mercia and his brother Morcar, Earl of Northumbria.' Alric knew why they had come and he felt a little apprehensive at the prospect of what lay ahead.

That evening King Harold and his retinue were given a truly wonderful feast, but it was the warm fires the travellers really enjoyed the most.

In spite of the cordial friendship offered by the brother earls, there was an obvious tension between them and Harold. After the feast, Harold, Gyrth and Alric were invited into an anti-chamber together with Earls Edwin and Morcar. It was plain both earls were troubled; as indeed was King Harold, for he greatly needed their support and their armed men. These earls were in control of the second largest part of England. In the past, both Mercia and Northumbria had rebelled against former Anglo-Saxon kings and Harold knew they had the power to do this again, if they so wished.

Alric was also curious to meet up with these brother earls, whose famous paternal grandparents were Leofric III of Mercia, one of the all-powerful lords who ruled England under the Danish King Canute, and Lady Godiva Countess of Mercia. This same lady who had once ridden naked through the streets of Coventry in protest to heavy taxation. Their maternal grandparents were Ethelred-the-Unready, King of England and Aelflaed Queen of England. Therefore, these brother earls were clearly from a family just as powerful as that of King Harold's family. Harold knew he had to tread very carefully in what he planned to do next.

Earl Edwin was an honest and good man, a true noble Anglo-Saxon Thane, loved and respected by his people of Mercia. His short beard had more white in it, than his natural blond colour. His hair was curly and going a little thin on top. His clear blue eyes were almost covered by his bushy eyebrows, his straight nose standing out clear from his hairy face. What he wanted more than anything was peace and stability for his country, as well as for his family. Edwin's younger brother Morcar had only recently been granted the Earldom of Northumbria, which were formerly the lands and estates of Tostig, Harold's outlawed brother.

The northern lands of Northumbria had long been almost lawless, which Tostig had used to his full advantage. Men could scarcely travel in those parts without either being killed or robbed by the multitude of robbers and outlaws who frequented those parts. Tostig met violence with violence and used such lawlessness to his own ends, when gangs of his thugs forcefully extracted money, goods and cattle from the population, on Tostig's orders, to line his and their own pockets.

Tostig's oppression of Northumbria had become so bad that, just a few months before this visit, on the third day of October

1065, over two-hundred of Tostig's senior Thanes had met in York. Then, after plundering Tostig's treasury, they killed more than two hundred of his armed gangs and bandits, who Tostig had used to plunder the people of Northumbria. They had chosen to make their attack while Tostig was away hunting with King Edward in Wiltshire. These same Thanes then summoned Morcar of Mercia, and proclaimed him as their new Earl. Marching south they pleaded their case with King Edward, ravaging Tostig's lands on the way. Earl Edwin of Mercia joined them at Northampton, where Earl Harold joined them as the emissary of King Edward. Edward reluctantly agreed to replace Tostig with Morcar. Tostig's lands were forfeited and he was made an outlaw. This had been the final stressful act for Edward, for after this his health collapsed, leading to his death a few months later. He had liked Tostig as a young man and trusted him with the Earldom of Northumbria, but like so many times in his life, Edward's trust had again been misplaced.

With Morcar now installed as the new Earl of Northumbria, the influence and lands of these brother earls stretched from the south Midlands, north to the Scottish borders, almost half the kingdom of England was therefore in their hands. Clearly, they were second only to the Godwinson family. But these brothers were stressed. Worried by the fear of Tostig's possible return, now that his brother Harold was king

and the evil revenge Tostig would disseminate on Morcar. This very real threat clouded the gaining of Morcar's newly acquired lands.

Anglo-Saxon influence had never been as strong in the north as it was in the south. During the long wars with the Viking invaders, many Danes had settled in the north and made it their home. Now after several generations, the Vikings had slowly become part of England itself and treated it as their own country rather than their country of origin, Denmark. Some could still remember when the whole of England was ruled by Canute the Danish king, who had encouraged his Danish people to settle in the sparsely populated north. Now though, the races were blending, but still they were not always sure the Anglo-Saxons fully trusted them, even though they had lived as one kingdom for the last fifty years.

'You well know what pains us,' said a grimfaced Edwin as they settled down to talk in the anti-chamber room. 'What if Tostig your brother should return? Now that you are king, he will expect to regain his lands.' Edwin, brought his hand to his forehead in a worrying act, he was clearly very distressed. 'My brother Morcar and I have much to lose if this villainous brother of yours should try and return to claim his forfeited estates,' Edwin wagged his finger at Harold. 'Tostig will not give way easily. He will beseech you, as his brother and king to restore his fortune.'

'Yes, what then?' agreed Morcar. 'With you as king, Tostig will think he can just walk in and claim back Northumbria.' Morcar was clearly Edwin's brother, for although much younger, and with no white hair, he was the image of Edwin.

Harold knew this was coming; it had been the reason for his journey. He needed these earls of the north and their army, he could not risk them turning against him.

'That will not happen,' stated Harold categorically.

'How do you know he will not try? It is easy for you just to dismiss this,' snapped Morcar without thinking. 'I have more to lose than you.'

'I give you my word,' retorted Harold

'Ha! Words, what are words?' The excess beer at the earlier banquet was now speaking, instead of the head of Morcar. 'Words are easy. You could tell us what we want to hear and then go away and still give our lands back to your brother.

'What!' exclaimed Harold, his temper rising and failing to repress his irritation, 'You question my word? How dare you? How dare you?'

Gyrth reached out and held Harold's forearm firmly in a tight grip. He did not have say anything, he just glared at his brother.

For a moment, there was a stunned silence, as both men stood back from the brink of alienating each other beyond repair.

'Sire, forgive my young brother,' interjected Edwin. 'He is not thinking clearly. This whole situation has given us many sleepless nights. We both fear you will restore your brother to his former estates to pacify him. This would cause us, our family and our people a great deal of suffering.'

Alric was truly relieved to see Harold's temper quieten quickly. He could see the distress of these two nobles and, more importantly, England needed them. They needed their support, more than any of them realised at the time.

'I am newly crowned as the true and elected king of all England. I come here, not just to greet you, but to seek your help.'

'How so, sire?' both brothers said in unison.

Turning to Alric, Harold gestured to him, 'Alric: explain.'

Alric had been rehearsing this in his mind for some time, 'My lords, as our king rightly said, this country needs you now more than ever before. We are surrounded on all sides by hostile nations who would attack and take our rich and blessed land if they could. We have Welsh in the west, Scots in the north, Vikings to the east and the Normans to the south. We do not know from where, or when, any of these may strike.' Alric clearly now had all of them concentrating on his words. 'King Harold has ordered us to strengthen and man all our defences.' He waited for this to sink in. 'And you great lords are our strong defence in the north. The Housecarls are ready, but it may well be that soon the Fyrd will be called out, so all men should be ready to serve their country.'

The brothers looked pleased, but said nothing. Harold broke the silence, 'Good noblemen what Alric said is true, we need each other.' Harold sought for a moment to find the right words to continue, 'I understand your concerns, and I want to reassure you. This kingdom has urgent need of you both. You are both honourable men, so I will make a pledge to you now.' Harold stood up and raised his hand. 'I swear by God's holy grace that Tostig will never be reinstated to his former estates in Northumbria.'

Edwin lifted his head up suddenly, scarcely able to believe his ears. 'Thank you sire, this is wonderful to hear.' Edwin smiled in satisfaction and looked at his brother. The relief of both men was clear to see.

'There is more,' continued Harold. 'Your family is the second most powerful family in the land. Therefore, I seek to unite our two families into one. I have no legal wife, so I will cement an alliance between our two great households and take your widowed sister Ealdgyth in Christian marriage. Then if God grants us a son he will inherit the whole kingdom of England.'

The two brothers beamed with delight; this was indeed a great gesture, it would give their family the power and influence, not only in the North, but also throughout the whole kingdom.

'Sire,' hesitated Edwin, unsure if he had heard right. 'Sire you do us a great honour, and one I am truly proud of. All Northumbria and Mercia will stand as brothers with you, truly as one.' Then standing with Harold, he clasped his hand. 'Let those who threaten us dare to take on this kingdom.'

All there beamed with delight, except Morcar, who looked puzzled, 'You will take our sister as your wife even though you were at war with her late husband?'

Harold smiled, 'The Welsh king Gruffydd was a respected foe. Even though I defeated him, I did not kill him. His death was by his own men, not mine.' Then in order to lighten the matter, he added, 'Anyway I was not fighting Ealdgyth, that can come after we are married,' he joked.

Harold understood he could not let the northern half of the kingdom divide against the southern half. He needed their backing, as they needed his. These brother earls had the backing of a powerful army, which had been used to great effect in the past by both Harold and Tostig. Such a powerful family could easily think itself equal to the house of Harold Godwinson. However, the Northumbrian uprising, which had driven out Tostig, was in no way a challenge to the authority of the crown; it was simply a means to rid themselves of a local tyrant.

Suddenly there was jollity in the room. All men were smiling and laughing, as the door opened and Bishop Wulfstan entered the room. He saw the smiles and laughter on the faces of the five men.

'You seem happy Sire. How go things?' enquired Wulfstan.

'We have wonderful news,' smiled Edwin. 'Our two families are to be united in marriage, and Tostig will not be returning. We stand together,' he said, clasping King Harold in an arm lock.

'Wonderful. I tried hard earlier to impress on these noble lords how our country needs a united front, to face the dangers from without.' In fact, this whole idea had come from Wulfstan. It was he who had urged Harold to take this action and set about on a 'hearts and minds' campaign to win over northern support to accept Harold as king. Wulfstan, whose holiness was known throughout the country, warned the north that rebellion against an anointed and consecrated king was a major sin. In fact, he had advised Harold what to do as regards this proposed marriage.

Still smiling, Alric stood up, 'May I suggest my lords, we return to the feast, so kindly set out for us, and partake of that wonderful northern beer, in celebration.'

'Yes', laughed Morcar. 'This calls for a right royal celebration.'

Harold knew he had done the politically correct move, one that his country now required. Still his heart felt heavy for he saw the sadness this action would cause to Edith Swan-Neck, the beautiful lady who had been his common-law wife from their youth together, and the mother of his six children; but without the loyalty of Earls Edwin and Morcar he knew he would have lost the north.

The wedding of Harold and Ealdgyth took place shortly after, in the city of York. It was a hurried affair. After the ceremony, when Harold embraced Ealdgyth as his wife and the new Queen of England, she held him with a passion more than that of his own. She well knew the importance of this alliance to both families. When she spoke, her words embarrassed him. He made as though he would draw back. Gyrth laughed low and said in his ear, 'You, who fear nothing Harold, do you fear a woman?'

two weeks after the wedding, Harold set out for London, leaving his new queen with her brothers. The weather had changed, as they journeyed south; the snow had gone, but a dry bitterly cold wind from the east was still there, freezing the muddy ruts in the road. It brought watery eyes to the men, although swathed in their warmest furs, with thick gloves or wraps around their hands and hoods tied tightly around their heads, the royal procession moved south.

The girl trembled, like a moth, held in the closed fist of a man's hand, while William, Duke of Normandy ran his hands over the body of the naked girl. She was frightened and confused, but William enjoyed this pleasurable right of his, 'The Droit de Seigneur'. It was a delightful custom, he thought, whereby the duke and barons of Normandy had the right to take any newly married girl they wished, on her first night of nuptial delight as a married woman. The duke and his barons did not hold back from winning for themselves such a privilege. William had already penetrated her several times, and now he lay back resting while he demanded she performed oral sex on him. His mind was wandering off into sexual bliss, as he admired the beautiful form of the young woman.

William was much taller than most men, his large muscular frame dwarfed the slight teenage body, naked and quivering beside him. She had not dared to speak, except when he commanded her to say, 'Thank you for taking me my lord,' each time he climaxed in her. It was a little thing, but it amused him to see her struggling to say words, forced out of her, from her gut. He revelled in nights like this, and lay back with a smile on his lips. Seeing such fear in others was for him the most wonderful feeling of all. It brought him a sense of strength and supreme power, along with a lightness of the head, that otherwise came only from wine.

A sudden banging on the door disturbed his illicit bliss.

'My lord,' the nervous voice uttered from behind the closed door. 'Roger de Beaumont is here to see you from England.'

'Piss-off.'

'It is urgent, my lord.'

'I said piss-off.'

'My lord we have important news.'

This was beginning to irritate William, 'I said piss-off. Come back in the morning.'

'King Edward is dead, my lord.'

There was a long, charged silence, while William took this in. He lay on one arm, propping up his head.

'Fuck off bitch. Get back to your farmer husband,' and with that he kicked the naked girl from his bed onto the floor. She picked up her clothes, held them to the front of her trembling body and ran naked for the door. She quickly passed the men standing there outside, who were hoping they had done the right thing in disturbing their master under such circumstances.

'Close the door you fools, let me get dressed,' he snapped.

Shortly after, Duke William strode into the room downstairs, where Roger de Beaumont and his small party waited. William's strong large frame displayed his power as a great horseman and a practiced warrior. His huge square shoulders looked even larger due to the new fashion he set in wearing his hair clipped in sharply at the sides, as a step, just above his ears and forming a fringe above his eyes. He was clean-shaven, which served to emphasise his bull like neck. His hair was reddish in colour, reflecting his temper, which many had become the victims of to their lasting regret. His stern demeanour now greeted this group of men who hoped they had not crossed the thin line and upset him.

'My Lord,' Roger de Beaumont bowed his head. The cold stone floor of the sparsely furnished room inside Duke William's fortress chilled Roger's feet and spread shivers up his body 'I have travelled ahead of the rest to give you news from England as quickly as I possibly could.

William stared unblinking, as he poured himself a large goblet of wine, waiting for Roger to speak, his sharp clear blue eyes cutting deep into Roger's own.

'My Lord, King Edward of England is dead.'

'Hmmm, Edward is dead, you say.'

'Yes my lord. He died over a week ago on the twelfth night of Christmas.'

William smiled, as he thought to himself, this had started as a good night and now it was going to get even better. 'Edward was a noble and saintly king. When he was only a boy of ten-years-old and a long time before he became king, Normandy sheltered him. For twenty-eight years, we sheltered him after his family had been driven out of England by the Danish invasion there.' William drank down the wine, then quickly poured himself another. 'I remember he grew up more as a Norman than an Anglo-Saxon.'

Roger did not know how to say, what he must. He just allowed William to carry on speaking.

'We were good friends, Edward and I, and that is why he said I could be first in line for the kingdom of England after his death, if he remained childless,' then gyrating round he looked intently directly at Roger, 'I trust he kept his word?'

Nervously tightening his fingers into a fist, Roger mentally braced himself, for what was to come. 'My Lord, Earl Harold was crowned King of England on the same day as King Edward's funeral.'

There was a silence, William stood, turned his back to the small group gripping his fists together behind his back, for Roger to see.

'I take it, you mean crowned as my vassal king?'

'No, my lord, he was crowned as full sovereign of all England.'

Slowly, so very slowly, William turned to face Roger, 'He...did...what? What did you say?' Then going up an octave he repeated, 'What did you say? Tell me you worm, what did you say?'

Roger saw the huge frame of William trembling as his voice reached to an ever-higher pitch. William downed another wine in one draft.

'My lord that is why I have come as fast as I could to warn you.'

William's temper was renowned, and now it had flared up to full intensity. 'Warn me! Warn Me!' William's voice now reached fever pitch.

He grabbed Roger by the throat, 'No...body...warns... me. Nobody warns me. Do...you...hear?' There was a pause, but William's grip remained firm around Roger's throat. 'It ... is ... I ... who ... will ... warn ... them.' So saying William let go of Roger, turned and violently kicked over the chair he had been sitting on. His face had now turned crimson.

William fought for words. He clenched his fist with the index finger pointing, 'That man has no royal blood. How could this be?' he lied, for Harold's mother was from the family of the kings of Sweden, Norway and Demark.

William continued to rave, it was a fearsome sight and not pleasant to be near him at such a time. 'Am I not the dead king's cousin?' he lied again, knowing no one would contradict him, for William was in fact just a second cousin and illegitimate at that. 'Edward said I would be his successor, and now this! How did it happen?'

William stood before the dying embers of the fire, fists unclenching and clenching, eyes blazing, he walked over and bent his furious face no more than a hand's width from Roger's nose.

'I said, how did this happen? Answer me you worm.'

Roger flushed, and began to shake, 'King Edward commended the queen and the kingdom to the protection of Earl Harold and the Witan voted him as king, my Lord.'

'The Witan! The Witan!' for a moment William was speechless. 'The Witan voted for him? Who the hell are they, that they can vote in kings? It is royal blood that counts, not votes of lesser, vile, common men.'

William poured himself another large cup of wine. Roger wished he had not been so hasty to inform the duke ahead of the others. He would be glad when this moment passed and began to repeat a few payers in his mind.

'Go and bring my brothers to me. Tell them to get here in all haste. Go! Go! Get out now, you miserable wretch,' William seethed.

With that, Roger and his small party quickly made their hurried exit from the terrifying spectre of Duke William, enraged.

That night William's anger prevented him from having any rest. He tore off the linen from his bed, and thrashed around, tearing out the stuffing of his mattress with his bare teeth.

A lone figure stood at the prow of the longship as it sped across the sea towards Demark. The man's dark, sunken eyes screwed up with intense hatred, jaws clenched so tight, it hurt. He steadied himself, with one hand holding onto the base of the carved wooden figurehead of a dragon, mounted on the bow of his ship, 'The Gunhild'. It was so cold, the wind cut into his eyes, making them water. His men had been reluctant to put to sea in mid-winter. 'He is crazy', they said in whispered tones, but they dare not resist him. 'No one crosses the North Sea in February.'

The square sail was billowing full in the wind, as the crew struggled with the ropes to keep it so. They were all so cold their hands hurt, as they pulled on the ropes, wet from the sea's spray. So deep, so drawn was his temper that not one of the crew wanted to talk to him, or even approach him. Tostig's limbs trembled, his face burned with wild rage, he could not feel the cold, only the hatred, which consumed him.

When Tostig had been outlawed he took his ship with his family and some loyal Thanes to Flanders. There he took refuge with his wife Judith's father, Count Baldwin of Flanders. His wife had powerful contacts, both in Flanders and in Normandy, for she was also the sister of Matilda, Duke William's wife.

Still Tostig stared transfixed into the wind, going through the events in his mind, which had led to this. Only three years before he had been with his brother Harold on a highly successful campaign by land and sea to subdue Prince Gruffydd of North Wales, who had been encroaching on English territory. The subjection of the Welsh had greatly enhanced the prestige of the two brothers.

Tostig blamed his fall from grace on his brother, Harold. These thoughts kept going around and around in his mind: 'Where was my brother's support when I needed it? It would not have led to civil war, as he said. Why, he even agreed to the terms of the rebels and deposed me; me, his own brother. Then those bastard rebels were pardoned and Morcar took my lands as Earl of Northumbria. Those Northumbrians had undertaken this madness against their rightful earl at the artful persuasion of my own brother.'

Tostig bitterness belied the fact that his brother had nothing to gain from his ousting, except the undying enmity of his brother.

'I could wind King Edward around my little finger,' Tostig mused again to himself. 'It must have been Harold behind this.'

Tostig could see no fault in his own actions, which had led to him being outlawed and exiled. He blissfully ignored events such as the one in the year 1064, when he had a meeting with two important Thanes, named Gamel and Ulf, who wanted to complain about his heavy taxes in Northumbria. During this meeting Tostig ordered their arrest and instant execution. This was typical of his behaviour toward his people of Northumbria; but this action was strictly against English law. Similarly, later that same year he had arranged for the murder of a noble named Gospatric, who also had dared to complain to him about his heavy taxes. Yet still Tostig could see no fault in his own actions; the fault was always that of someone else. His demise was never his own fault, in his sick mind; it was always the fault of others. His was a sickness that had to be sated.

The Gunhild was now Tostig's most valued possession. In full sail with the wind behind her she was a truly beautiful sight; graceful, long, narrow, and light, with a shallow draft hull, designed for speed. With a good wind, she could make ten knots per hour. The Anglo-Saxons had copied, and improved upon the early Viking design of the longship in the days of Alfred-the-Great. Such ships were magnificent weapons of war, unequalled in their effectiveness, and the terror they could impose on any hapless costal dwellers, who were unfortunate enough to see such ships heading for them, laden with fearsome warriors.

Tostig continued to glare ahead of him, 'How dare he? How dare he steal what is rightfully mine? I am the rightful Earl of Northumbria. I *will* get it back, I *will*.' Tostig kept repeating to himself, over and over again, vowing to get his revenge. 'There must have been many who thought that I, rather than Harold, should succeed old King Edward.' His hatred had become truly obsessive. 'My sister Edith was right; I should have stood up more to Harold. Now he has betrayed me. Me! His own flesh and blood. He will suffer for this', then turning into the wind he yelled into it, 'By God, they will all suffer, I will make them pay.'

The sailors looked up on hearing his voice, bellowing into the wind, wondering what he was saying, for the sound of the sea took his words away with it. The crew looked at each other, but said nothing. They did not need to speak, for each knew what the other was thinking.

There was no way Tostig, would accept being extricated from his earldom. He was hell-bent on revenge. This voyage was heading first to Denmark, where he would seek to form an alliance with King Sweyn, and then, if necessary, onward to Norway and King Hardrada.

It had been a terrible job of work she dutifully carry out, yet she had hated every minute of it. Heaving wooden pails, which issued forth a foul stench from the substance contained therein. 'Why oh why, did her father have to be a tanner?' she had constantly asked herself. The people laughed at her and called out saying, 'Here comes the piss-pot carrier.'

Herleva Harlotta, from the Norman town of Falaise, was born a lowly daughter of a humble tanner; a trade ridiculed and despised for the evil smells their work produced. Such awful stench clung to her and all those who worked at this trade. The smell hung about in their clothes and hair. Disgusting odours, so strong that some said it even kept the rats away. Their tanning process required large quantities of dung, human urine and dog faeces. Raw animal hides were dipped into this revolting solution for a week, before the workers could use the acidic affect to scrape off the rotting flesh and hair from the animal's skin. So nauseous was this work that workshops were not allowed to operate within, or near a town or village, their work always had to be well away from where the people lived.

This had been the childhood of Herleva. An unenviable background, and yet she had been a striking girl of some considerable charm. At the age of just sixteen, she attracted the attention of the former Duke of Normandy himself, Robert-the-Magnificent. Some also called him Robert-the-Devil, for most believed he had murdered his brother in order to gain power.

Their illegitimate son was William, who inherited his father's title as Duke of Normandy, when he was only seven-years-old. After making his only son William his heir, Robert had set out on pilgrimage to Jerusalem, where he died on the return journey. Many barons of Normandy were incensed that Robert had dared to put such a base-born lad over the Dukedom of Normandy, appointing such a child as his own successor. During the boy's minority many were tempted to rebel against him. However as William grew older he violently secured his own power, even after surviving several attempts on his young life. He soon proved himself to be a suitable son of his much feared father.

William though never fully got over the shame and the ignominy of his birth. It gave him a pent up inner aggression, with violent consequences. Sometimes from the apparent, but false, safety of a castle's ramparts the defenders would mockingly call down to him and shout, 'Who is this son of a piss-pot carrier, who thinks he can stand against us?' Any who dared to challenge, or to mock his origins this way were cruelly put down by him when the castle fell.

In spite of her lowly beginnings, William's mother Herleva, had later married Herluim of Counteville having two legitimate sons by him: Odo, who became the Bishop of Bayeux and the younger son Robert, Count of Mortain. Odo became Bishop when only nineteen-years of age, allowing him to secretly benefit from the monies donated to the church. Herleva had died in the year 1050, but now her three sons between them controlled all of Normandy.

These sons were powerful, forceful men; men-of-war, trained in the latest techniques of warfare; dominant leaders of Normandy who controlled this young kingdom by fear. They were answerable only to the King of France himself.

It was a mix of family and friend, when four men now gathered in the Duke's private meeting room at his castle in Rouen. Three were half-brothers, William, Odo and Robert, and Richard Fitz-Gilbert, who after his own father's death had become the guardian of the young Duke William.

At forty-years of age, Richard Fitz-Gilbert, son of the Count of Brionne was the eldest, William, the second eldest, at thirty-eight-years, with Odo, thirty years and Robert the youngest at twenty-eight. All four men though had one other thing in common; they were all ruthless, hard-nosed fighters. Eleven years earlier, when William had been consolidating his hold on power in Normandy, he had dispossessed the former Count of Mortain, and then given his title and estates to his younger brother Robert.

Three of the four men were large in stature, Odo being the smallest. Although Odo was not very tall, he was strong and stocky, with a cold piercing eyes and terrible appearance. He had taken the title of bishop, but he was not a God-fearing man, for he was both too greedy and, as with the others, had too much of an insatiable lust for power to be called God-fearing. Little good could be said of Odo; he sought wealth by extortion and robbery; his ambitions were boundless and his morals lax. The best that could be said about Odo was that he was an incorrigible rogue.

Richard Fitz-Gilbert was of similar build to William, tall, sinewy and muscular, imbued with an air of natural authority. As the chosen guardian of William, during his youth, Richard was an active military commander. He seldom if ever smiled, and demanded implicit obedience from all under his command.

Robert, the youngest always looked to his older brothers to make decisions, and seldom spoke out of turn when in their presence, nevertheless, he had been as keen as the others, to get to this meeting.

The rain had been falling in torrents for days as these four, in sombre mood, gathered in the private chambers of William, Duke of Normandy. Several days had passed since William had been informed of events in England. Now William had commanded, that they must gather to discuss this matter. It was wild and cold outside, but the room they were in was warm, with a fire in the large grate of the hearth, piled high with burning logs. They sat around a bare oak table, with just a small barrel of wine and a set of pewter cups upon it. The rain beat hard against the windows as they sat down together. Not one of them could read or write, so no written record would be made of this meeting.

William had been quiet, deep in thought, and very moody since he first heard the news from England; no man dared venture to speak to him. He sat brooding as his brothers joined him.

'Brothers, we have a bad situation', said William as he poured himself a cup of wine. 'King Edward was my cousin. I therefore have claim to the throne of England by blood. Harold Godwinson has no royal blood and so has no legal claim to what he has taken for himself. What say you on the matter?'

Odo spoke first, 'Did you not ask Edward about his succession? Did you not ask him to state you would succeed him and inherit his kingdom?'

'I tried, when I visited him in England, but just between us, I must tell you he declined, and this was more than fifteen years ago.' This was the first time they had heard William admit such a thing.

'And did he make no further confirmation of this to you?' Odo raised his pale eyes whilst continuing to put these questions to William.

'Indeed yes, he did,' William went on. 'A message came to me through Robert of Jumieges, Archbishop of Canterbury, when Robert had been forced to return back to Normandy, after those

Saxon swine had driven him out of England putting that upstart Stigand in his place. He told me then of Edward's promise. Robert of Jumieges told me King Edward had promised me the Kingdom of England,' William looked puzzled for a moment, 'Would Robert of Jumieges lie to me?'

'Was this in writing?' asked young Robert thoughtfully; finally plucking up courage to ask what that had been troubling him.

'Writing!' snapped William. 'Who needs writing when you have the word of a king?'

'Hmmm, that's as maybe, but it would have been better if it had been written down,' insisted Odo.

'But did not also Harold make the same promise to you William?' interjected Richard.

William almost grinned, but instead, just perked his lips. 'True he made a promise, an oath, when he came to Normandy to seek the release of his young brother Wulfnoth and his nephew Hakon. He knew, not only would I not release his kin, but that I had a mind to keep him also here in Normandy'

Richard thrust himself back in his chair, so it rocked back onto just two legs, 'So he did swear to you, to give you the kingdom then?'

'Sort of! he said he did not have that authority, but we both knew it was more to get his freedom than to give me the kingdom. Is it not said, "Oaths and pie-crust are made to be broken?"'

Odo eyed William, then stood up, putting his cup back down on the table, 'So he *did* swear to help you get the kingdom.'

'It is so,' acknowledged William.

Robert, not wishing to be left out of the conversation spoke up, a little nervously, 'I understand the Witan voted Harold to the Kingship. If so I fear there is little we can do.'

'Ha!' Richard jerked his head up, almost as a rebuke. 'Robert you are young. The Witan means nothing to us. We are not bound by its findings. They are men of lower class; they cannot appoint and choose a king over our royal blood.' Richard, who of all four had the greatest knowledge among them in statesmanship, was saying what the others were thinking. 'I do not give a dog's flea for their Witan. We are royal blood, and no commoner will tell us what we can and cannot do.'

'So what do we do?' asked Robert.

'We attack them, that's what we do,' declared William thumping his fist on the table, his eyes blazing.

Odo had been deep in thought. He lifted up both his arms, as a gesture for the others to listen to him. 'Yes, yes, yes brothers, but think this through first, before we act too rashly. We will need support on any such quest, especially from the Pope and King Philippe of France.' Odo now had their full attention. 'Some may say the bloodline issue is a bit weak I fear. For in truth you were not first cousin, but the second to King Edward. The link is really through your grandfather, Richard-the-Fearless, who was the brother of Emma, Edward-the-Confessor's mother. The Pope will know you are not first cousins.' Odo lifted his arms up to heaven, 'Also Richard-the-Fearless died seventy years ago and some will say this is too far removed for you to make a hard claim due to your bloodline. We need a stronger claim than this.'

Richard responded, 'Odo may be right. If we are talking of attacking England then we will be wise not to handle this alone, we could use support. In fact all the support we can get to help us.' Richard went silent for a moment, deep in thought. Looking at William straight in the eye, he said, 'We will not get support without a stronger claim to the throne than your bloodline. France must be bought, and the most needful of all is that you send to Rome for the Pope's support.'

Odo and William nodded.

Richard went on, 'Is it not so?' he questioned, 'Do not our countrymen thrive well in Italy? Many Normans are now Saint Peter's dukes and princes. The Pope will not forget the conquest, when Normans drove out the Mohammedans from Apulia in Italy was blessed due to our Norman support. Our Norman brethren conquered it with relative ease. The apostle's banner went before them.' Then with a twinkle in his eye, he gave out a loud whisper, 'William, they say that now Robert Guiscard looks towards Byzantium for a crown. Shall he become Emperor of the East, a poor Norman knight's son at that, while you my brother sit here and fear to be a king?' Richard knew well how to goad William on.

William felt uncomfortable but said nothing, for Richard had hit home, hard.

Odo, still standing by William's side gently put his hand on his seated brother's shoulder, and cunningly enquired, 'Pray tell me William, when Harold swore to help you get the kingdom, how did he do it?'

'As all oaths are sworn; on the holy book of God, the Bible.'

'Hmmm!' Odo went quiet for a moment. 'What if he had sworn on the holy relics of a saint?'

'But he didn't.'

'Who says he didn't?'

'Wha!' William's word remained unsaid, stuck as it were in his throat. What Odo had said suddenly sunk in to them all. Odo laughed, then Richard also; suddenly all the brothers erupted in laughter as it dawned on them what Odo was saying.

'God bless my soul Odo, you are brilliant,' William took another swig of his wine. 'Absolutely brilliant; yes of course, of course. We will let it be known Harold swore an oath over the bones of a holy saint. Yes! Yes, yes.' William still laughing went on, 'So let it now be proclaimed throughout the land that Earl Harold swore over the holy relics of a Christian Saint, to give me the kingdom.'

'Which saint?' questioned Robert.

The laughter stopped for a moment.

'Oh, I am sure Odo can find us one,' said Richard beaming from ear to ear. The brothers continued laughing together again.

Still laughing Richard added, 'We must send this information to the Pope and King Philippe of France, and also send a delegation to England itself, to protest Harold's ascendancy to the crown of England, a crown that William Duke of Normandy claims as his rightful inheritance. Many will then come to our banner, especially if the Pope gives us his blessing.'

'Of course he will give us his blessing, that is no problem,' beamed Odo. 'With all the Norman knights already there in Rome as the Pope's *protectors*, he can do little else. Of course he will bless our great venture.'

Feeling very content with themselves, the quartet began to speak excitedly of the rich and excelling land that was England. They all knew England to be a land second to none, for its rich productive farmland and wool, a land of abundant natural resources of timbre, minerals and ores.

'The coffers of Canterbury are full, very full,' gloated Odo at the thought. 'They say gold paves the way to Saint Peter's Chair in Rome. Because you made a churchman of me William, when I was but a boy, did you suppose that I should be content to dwell in simple contemplation?'

'We will give you the crown of Canterbury,' said William as he slapped Odo on the back, laughing heartily. William had not felt so good for a long time.

Tears streamed down the lovely lady's face. Even now, in early middle age, she was still beautiful. Her chin was rounded and dimpled, her lips slim and perfectly formed. Her cheekbones were set high, with her arched brows forming a perfect frame for her deep blue eyes. Her long golden wavy hair, was not brushed as normal, but hung in loose ringlets where she had twisted it, repeatedly in her hands, again and again, as she absentmindedly toyed with her hair, distracted by her innermost thoughts. She was not just crying, she was sobbing, her whole body trembling with each sob.

'I had to do it,' said Harold trying to put his arm around her, which was briskly brushed off each time he tried. 'I had to do it,' he kept repeating unable to find the words he needed.

'I have loved you since we were children,' she shouted at him accusingly.

Edith, the one they call 'Swan-Neck', struggled to get her words out between her sobs. Her heart was broken. The man she had loved since they first met; the man who had fathered her children, the man who had been her husband, if not by Christian-law, but by common-law, had suddenly come back from the north of England and announced he had got married to another woman! Married! She could not believe it. This new marriage she knew, was in accordance with the requirements of the Christian church, which would outweigh her own standing. She was proud of having Harold as her partner; she had deep love for him. This new marriage would outweigh not only her personal status, but that of her children as well. This though, was not what hurt her the most; it was his betrayal of her love, that she just could not understand.

Curling up on the ground, Edith blew air through her lips. She was hurt, and she was angry. She wanted to leave him with a bloody stump where his manhood had been. 'Why?' She stammered, her tears mingling with her running nose. 'How could you? How could you?' she repeated.

'I had no choice Edith. If I had not done so, I could have lost the support of the Earls Edwin and Morcar. They were none too keen to support us at first, until I promised to marry their sister. Please understand, that without their support I could not gather a full army, to protect not only you, but the whole land.'

Edith knew what he said was the truth, but this did not make it any better for her.

'Edith I still love you, you are the one I want by my side; the one I want to always be with. It was a political marriage, not a marriage of love.'

'You still bedded her,' she screamed.

Her head bowed. She wanted only one man in her life, and now she had to share him, at least in word, if not in deed; she lied to herself. She loved him so much, and she knew that he loved her really. Her mind was in turmoil, as the same phrases kept repeating in the mind, 'Why did this cruel world make things so difficult. Why could not life be simpler? Why did things always have to be so complicated? Why? Oh, why should it be this way?'

'Whatever happens I will always look after you and the children,' Harold tried to reassure her. 'I will always be by your side. I am proud of you and of our children. Three of our boys are nearly old enough to campaign now. They are growing into fine men. They will always be ours. No one can change that.'

Edith was not listening, she could not take in his words, and instead she just bowed her head into her lap. 'We have been together now for twenty years. I know you love me really. It is just so hard to bear and understand.'

'Yes I know,' he said shallowly. 'It was not an easy thing for me to do, for I knew it would hurt you so, and I did not want that. When we met I gave you your nick-name, because your neck was as slim and white as any swans.' He steadied himself, overcome for a moment by her genuine grief. 'I loved you from that time on and still do. You have been my delight.' Yet, no matter what Harold said now, he knew the deep love they had shared together would be forever damaged.

Edith knew that Harold's new wife would now demand his attention and she would be pushed to one side. In spite of what Harold was saying. True she had been the king's delight, loved and kissed, but now she was forsaken, and soon would be forgotten; for such is the way of men, she mused.

Edith took hold of Harold's bicep in both her hands, pushed up his sleeve to expose the tattoo there, of the Golden Dragon of Wessex and England. She tenderly brought her lips to the tattoo and kissed it. Her tears were wetting his arm as she tried stoically, but unsuccessfully, to control her feelings.

Tostig's longship 'The Gunhild' was moored up in the harbour of Copenhagen, the sail neatly rolled up, but the wind still rocked the slim ship from side to side. It had been a very difficult voyage to undertake across the open sea, battling the fierce winter seas. During this time of year, most ships and crew tended to keep close inshore, rather than risk the open sea. Once safely on shore, Tostig's crew had stayed within the harbour confines, enjoying the beer and the attractive women, who would hang around newly arrived sailors, seeking the gifts and money they had to bestow.

The harbour was as busy as ever, with men loading and unloading goods from afar. They were trading in silks, spices and slaves which they brought from their raids. Also, to be bartered was amber, found in the Baltic area, then from the north and from Greenland in the west, there were furs, skins and walrus tusk ivory, to trade with the towns in Western Europe. These Danish Vikings also kept the trade route between the Byzantium Empire and the west open, by way of Kiev and Russia. There were Arab silver coins from the caliphate, Byzantine silks, Frankish weapons, Rhenish glass, and occasionally gold, all products of an extensive and lucrative trade.

The crew enjoyed their rest, gaping at such wonderful trade goods, and trying to sell items they also had come by, for this was how they made their money. Some of the men had settled down to a game of knuckle bones, initially as a pastime, but which often led to wages being placed on the outcome. They were content with their rewards for their seafaring raids. It was a profitable undertaking.

However, things were not going well for Tostig, as he wanted to involve King Sweyn of Denmark, to help him in the future fight against his brother, King Harold. Tostig had been in the presence of the King Sweyn for some time; it had been an embarrassing time for both men.

Sweyn preferred the quiet life; he was plump and was gentler in nature than Tostig.

'Why do you not raise an army yourself in England to fight for your estates there?' asked King Sweyn, irritated by the very presence of Tostig.

'My inclination is to go back to my estates in England; but if I can get help from you for that purpose, I will agree to help you with all the power I can command in England. If you will go with me to England, with the men I can muster and your Danish army, between us we can win that country.' Tostig's words were falling on deaf ears, for Sweyn was not interested. Tostig now tried a little more pressure, 'If your mother's brother, the great King Canute, could do this, then why not you?'

King Sweyn nodded, reluctantly seeking ways to avoid being dragged into something he did not want to do, into something he did not feel strong enough to carry through. 'So much smaller a man am I, than Canute the Great, that I can, with difficulty, only defend my own Danish dominions against that demon Norseman, King Hardrada of Norway. King Canute, on the other hand, took England by hard won fight, and sometimes he was near losing his life in the contest. Norway he took without even a fight.' King Sweyn looked more than a little angry towards Tostig, so he continued curtly, 'Now it suits me much better to be guided by my own slender ability, than to try and copy that great king, therefore I cannot help you in the venture you seek.'

Tostig's face hardened and he leaned back in his chair. Tostig had the trick of staring fixedly at a man, unblinking, until you felt compelled to drop your gaze. He was trying this tact now, but this time it was not working. Tostig was downcast at Sweyn's polite, but firm, refusal to help him in his quest. Tostig's bitterness now rose in his throat. Even though what he was about to say would be construed as an insult, he felt it had to be spoken. 'Your father and my mother were brother and sister; I therefore had not expected the result of my errand here to be less fortunate. I expected more, much more, from so gallant a man as yourself, seeing that I, your close relative am now in great need. It may be that I will now seek friendly help elsewhere, and find a chief who is less afraid, than you are of such a great enterprise.'

Tostig was lucky he was not dealing with a more volatile man, for Sweyn, did not reply, but merely went red in the face, with embarrassment.

Tostig saw the effect that his words had had on Sweyn, so then on reflection, and so that his journey had not been a complete waste of time, he beseeched him with a new tact, 'If you yourself cannot lead an expedition to England then let me take some of your men who will volunteer for such a mission?'

'No,' was the immediate reply, 'I cannot spare my men, for I need them here in defence of my kingdom.' Then in order to pacify Tostig and to try to curtail, what Sweyn thought to be a foolhardy mission, the King tried a conciliatory approach, 'Why not stay here with me, here in Denmark? I will give you a large Earldom and you will be an important noble. Live here in peace.'

The offer did not even tempt Tostig, for his need of revenge was the greatest force within him; 'Thank you my King, but I shall seek support elsewhere, until I have such a large army that England will regret their treatment of me; for I am their rightful Earl.'

King Sweyn stood up. Tostig's visit had upset him.

Sweyn snorted softly, 'I will have no part in this; but, not to give the impression of wishing to hinder you, I give you leave to go where you will and to see what you can do. Be warned Tostig,

I have a feeling that you will succeed only in bringing misfortune upon the whole of that kingdom and discredit upon yourself. For I know that King Harold is not so simple as to be at all inclined to let you cause trouble for him without fighting hard for his new kingdom.'

Sweyn turned to leave, but as he did so, he gave a final caution, 'Reconsider this course you have set yourself on Tostig, for I fear no good will come from it.'

Then Tostig departed back to his ship and crew. His friendship with King Sweyn, and their family relationship was now truly strained.

SPRING

The view from Mount Ulriken was magnificent; many who had ventured there thought it was like nowhere else on earth. Beginning their decent the mounted party could not help but be moved by the sheer beauty in front of them. Mount Ulriken was the highest of the seven mountains surrounding Bergen, a new trading settlement on the west coast of Norway. Wherever a man looked he could see the sea. Yet not just a straight line of coastline, like so many other places, no, in Bergen the sea intertwined itself with the land. Large fingers of water intruded their way inland, with the mountains cascading steeply down into its cold North Sea waters. As a backdrop, there was a myriad of ten thousand islands, intertwined with the sky's horizon. Bergen was the gateway to the majestic fjords in Norway, but Hardrada enjoyed the fish it produced the most.

Hardrada had seen something in the harbour, which made him quicken the pace of his horses, to get down from off the mountain.

He was a pirate of the first order. King Harald Sigurdsson of Norway preferred his nickname of King Hardrada, which could be translated as meaning 'Hard-ruler', 'Severe Councillor,' 'Ruthless', or simply, 'Tyrant'. He liked the name 'Hardrada', it made people respect and fear him more. He was nearly seven-foot tall, a giant of a man, with a long dark blond beard and even longer hair. So powerfully built was Hardrada that few dared to challenge him. Beetle browed with a prominent nose and sharp features, he was ruthless, ambitious, aloof, covetous and yet shrewd. He had such a booming voice, which he could make to be heard, wherever and whenever he wished. His huge round shield and long sword were impressive enough, but it was his battle-axe that men feared the most. He could swing it with such power, that a man could be almost severed in half with one blow. Hardrada's body was covered in many scars having spent most of his life in battle. For several years he had been in Russia, fighting in the services of King Yaroslav there. Then he went on to Constantinople, the capital of the Byzantine Empire, the wealthiest city in the known world; and there he had won many victories for the Emperor, proving his worth as a great warrior.

For twenty years, he had ruled Norway and for sixteen of those years he had been at war with Denmark. Hardrada could not sit easy on a throne; he was an adventurer and he craved the adventure which was within his pure Viking blood.

King Hardrada had been hunting in the woods above Bergen. He never tired of this, his beautiful land. Now he was returning early from his hunting, because he had seen a strange ship harboured there.

Once he arrived down to level ground he called over to a townsman, 'What ship is that, which lies by the quay?'

The man answered, 'Sire it is the 'Gunhild'; there has been a change of kings in England and this ship is full of outlaws and lawless men, whom the new king, King Harold has driven out from there.'

'Outlaws you say. By God they have a cheek.'

Not long after, King Hardrada sent for Tostig and some of his men and spoke with them, while he took his regular ale. His was not an easy presence to be in and Tostig felt his heart thumbing.

'Is this true,' the King said, 'that Harold Godwinson is now King in England, and that he drove you out?'

Tostig answered boldly, 'Aye, 'tis true alright. I know nothing good to say of him. He is a tyrant to our brotherhood. I understand that you are a better lord for men of our mind. I and my men have come to offer you our services.'

'You mean you have come to hide behind my shield and live off my generosity?' he scorned.

Tostig was taken aback at this. 'No, I do not seek to hide, far from it. For in truth I was an Earl in that rich and pleasant country. Now I wish to reclaim what is rightfully mine. I have heard it told of you, lord King, that you have conquered many kingdoms in the east and never been defeated by any odds.'

'That is true,' Hardrada acknowledged gruffly, responding to the flattery. Then his mood suddenly switched, scowling he stared at Tostig, 'But I have never yet been other men's plaything; you shall sooner serve me, than I serve you.'

Tostig thought for his next words very carefully, 'Sire, there is much wealth and plunder to be gained in England. My wish is that you should go there with a great army and win the kingdom for yourself. Then, my men and I, if we may, will help you well in this venture. If this pleases you then you will have the Kingdom of England, as did your forefather the Great King Canute, and I can look for my just reward, no more than the restoration of my Earldom.'

Hardrada did not like this man, who stood before him. He knew he was only after his own gains. However, this idea did have some merit, he thought to himself; but he would not let his visitor see that. Having been at war for so long against the Danes, Hardrada's coffers were now drained. He needed a fresh source of wealth and England was the richest country he knew of. It was tempting, but he did not want to be led by this outlaw who now stood before him.

Tostig continued to press his point, 'There are a lot of families still living in the north of England who are of Danish and Norwegian decent. They would rejoice to see you as King of England.' Tostig now twisted the truth, for although the north had large areas of Nordic decent; they now had blended with the Anglo-Saxons and were not seeking to change this.

Hardrada still did not comment, but he was taking this all in.

Tostig was beginning to think Hardrada was not convinced by his argument, so he now tried his main thrust. 'Is it not so that you yourself have claim to the Kingdom of England?' Hardrada fixed his eyes on Tostig, but did not respond.

Slightly unnerved Tostig continued with his main thrust, 'For it is known in my land that you were promised that kingdom,' he lied. Then to embroider the lie further he went on, 'Canute-the-Great ruled all of England and this passed on to his son Harthacanute. Even though he died, sadly too young, this kingdom should have remained in his family.' Tostig now had Hardrada's full attention. He now thrust his point home, hard, 'And you my Liege are of that same family. Therefore the Kingdom of England rightly belongs to you, its rightful heir.'

Hardrada pulled on his beard, stroking it thoughtfully. Tostig saw a change come over Hardrada's face. Hardrada considered to himself, 'This man Tostig may be right, here is a way I could enrich my country and pay for the wars against Denmark.'

'Thank you for coming to tell me of the death of King Edward.' His eyes flashed, 'And for telling me my kingdom in England has been usurped.'

Hardrada raised his voice so others in the large room could now hear. So far, no one had been paying any particular attention to this visitor, chatting quietly to their king. Hardrada stood up, 'My kingdom in England has been taken by a usurper,' he thundered. 'I, as a descendant of King Canute, who ruled England for sixteen years, am the natural heir to that kingdom. Harthacanute made an agreement with my father that he should inherit this kingdom.' Then, throwing his arm out from across his chest, as a gesture, exclaimed, 'Am I not my father's son?'

Others at the far end of the room laughed at their King's gesture.

Tostig had the fish on his hook. The bait had been taken.

'Tell me,' Hardrada was now very serious, 'What men and ships can you gather.'

'I can get twelve ships and men immediately from my wife's father Count Baldwin of Flanders. He is the Regent of France while King Philip is in his minority. That king is only fourteen years-old so Count Baldwin, his uncle and my father-in-law administer France.

'Ha!' laughed Hardrada, 'You talk of just twelve ships, they are hardly enough to attack England with.'

'True my King, but that is only a start. Many will come to my banner once they see it fly again from the masts of our ships.'

'We need many more men,' Hardrada repeated.

'There is much more great lord to tell you, for I hear from Count Baldwin that Duke William is also planning to invade England. King Harold's forces will be concentrating in the south, due to this threat from the Normans. He will have no knowledge of you sire.'

The more Hardrada thought of this, the more he liked it. 'England is indeed a fat prize,' Hardrada contemplated as he indulged in his habit of pulling on his long beard. 'Hmm! I could send out north to Shetland and Fair Isle and westward to the Hebrides and the Isle of Man; I can even send to Iceland. That would bring together a mighty army, an army greater than has been seen before in these parts.' He downed his ale in one gulp, 'Come we must talk more of this.'

King Harold received Duke William's deputation of protest messengers in London. They carried a rare letter, dictated by the duke himself. The letter made it clear that Duke William was now making his claim to the English throne. Harold knew now for a certainty his kingdom was threatened, for he was well aware the Normans had the largest standing mercenary army in Europe, an army that had fought many battles from France to Italy and beyond.

Harold though was content, for he also had a fulltime standing professional army. When King Canute had been king of both Denmark and England, he had introduced the Housecarls, considered by many to be the best warriors in Europe. Unlike William's forces, the Housecarls were loyal to the crown; loyal to Harold, whatever happened; money was not their motive. Normans on the other hand fought for whoever paid them the most. However, the Housecarls were only about one third of the English army; the other two thirds were made up of the Fyrd. England relied heavily on this traditional Fyrd; regiments of part-time local men, recruited to serve as the need arose. The Fyrdmen were called to arms in times of trouble. Made up of all fit free men, between the ages of fifteen and sixty, service in the Fyrd was usually for two or three months duration. All participants being required to provide their own arms, therefore a sword was often reverently passed on from father to son. Their main weaponry consisted of swords and short axes, with armour of helmets and chainmail-shirts and round shields. So that not all men were called up at the same time, there was a 'rotating of contingents', to give more regular cover from these part-time soldiers. It was important for some of the Thanes and the Fyrd to remain behind to guard their lands and those of their neighbours, when they were on campaigns against raiders; for landholders were reluctant to leave their estates and families totally undefended. Harold had agreed the payment to the Fyrdmen would be twenty shillings for each two-month period they served, on condition that this high rate of pay required a professional disciplined army from the Fyrd.

The Housecarls on the other hand other hand were a professional warrior class, drawn from amongst the wealthiest men in the country. These Housecarls were very well equipped, full-time mounted soldiers: a mounted army, but who usually fought on foot.

It was well known that King Harold had an aptitude for war, but preferred peace whenever he could. He knew though now he must prepare for war if he had to. Harold had recently inspected the dies for his new coinage and had the dies distributed to all the minting houses throughout the land. The king ordered that newly minted coins would be stamped with the word 'PAX', Latin for peace, on the reverse of the coin. By nature, Harold had always preferred talks with his adversaries, to that of open hostilities if he could, but now he knew, it was inevitable he would have to fight.

Harold sent for Alric, his trusted general of the Housecarls, and explained the letter he had received from Duke William. Alric looked at Harold's grim face, as the instructions he expected now came, 'Alric, we have to act fast. We need to mobilise the Fyrd.'

'Is it not too soon sire?' Alric cautioned. 'We do not yet know when, nor if, we shall be attacked. Mobilise them too soon and their term of compulsory service to the crown will expire before we see the enemy.' Alric was more cautious than Harold was, for he had seen how his king, sometime would act impulsively and he felt it his duty to check him in this, if he could.

'True, so I will not send for all at the same time, but half in mid April on Easter Day and half in mid June. Then if an attack is close we can recall the other half from their lands, if needed.'

'That will be difficult sire, for by mid August it would be harvest time and the men would be needed on the land, lest all starve.'

Harold dismissed Alric's concern, 'Let us trust to God Alric, this will not happen.'

Alric was uneasy with this impetuous nature of Harold. He would have preferred to wait a while longer before calling out the Fyrd.

Harold looked intently at Alric, whom he had promoted to lead twenty thousand, and more, Anglo-Saxon warriors. 'Alric, here are my instructions, note them well.' Harold then pulled out a parchment and read from it. 'This message is to go out to the entire kingdom.'

'Your King wishes to allow Earl Edwin of Mercia and Earl Morcar of Northumberland, to keep their muster in their own Earldoms, the rest are to assemble here in London. Assemble also the Housecarls to London. Mobilise the Navy. Inform all military officers we have to prepare ourselves, and our country for war. All designated free men of the Fyrd are to assemble in London.'

After reading these orders to Alric, he handed him the parchment, 'Take as many men as you need. Send messengers to all the boroughs and see all are informed.'

'As you order sire,' Alric replied willingly.

Harold then opened another parchment, and unrolled it on the table. 'This is another proclamation to be delivered in every city, every town, every village, every church, and every garrison and to the Navy. Copies must be placed on every church door.' Harold well knew that, unlike the Normans', most of the English were able to read. This was an inheritance from Alfred-the-Great's encouragement of learning for all his people.

Harold then read out the following:

The King's Call to all Free Men:
The King hereby commands all free men of military age to answer his call to arms. They are to assemble where ordered within one month. Failure to do so will result in a fine or imprisonment, also the King shall take their property and their land, as recompense. Any man who fails to answer this call, all he has shall be forfeited and it shall pass into the King's own hand.
Those Who Fall for their King:

The duty paid in arms and armour of the men who fall for his King on campaign, whether within the country or abroad, their families shall be remitted, and their heirs shall succeed to their land and property and the King shall make reward for their sacrifice.

Any Man Who Deserts his King:

Any man who, through cowardice, deserts his King, or his comrades on this military expedition, either by sea or by land, shall lose all that he possesses and will suffer execution. The King shall claim his property and the land, any which he hath owned. All he has shall be forfeited and it shall pass into the King's own hand.

Payment for Service:

All men who answer the call to arms shall be paid according to their rank, not less than four pennies per day.

This is the Word of Harold II, King of England."

Harold rolled up the parchment and looked at Alric, 'We do not know how long we have, but I fear it will not be long. You must embark the army on an intensive period of training, from now until that day dawns. Hopefully the Fyrd will just have enough time to plant their land, before they answer this call to arms.'

'Yes my king, it shall be done. As you say, we have much to do and little time to do it.' Alric knew Harold to be a great warrior, but he was deeply unsure about this action, so early.

As Alric departed Harold looked out across the valley at the young buds, just beginning to burst. Wistfully he contemplated, 'These young buds will soon bring the blaze of vivid colour, typical of an English spring.' Deep in thought, he went through all the many things that must soon be done to protect this kingdom. There are so many things to plan, he thought to himself, as he walked into the dining hall, where Edith Swan-Neck waited for him.

Still hurting, she had been busying herself in the kitchen, even helping the servants to prepare Harold's favourite food. Harold looked at what she had helped make for him, and was moved by the loving care she had gone to; also, he was truly hungry.

'Come, my King you must eat.' She chuckled at using the word 'King' for when they had been young lovers, such a situation had never entered her mind. 'I know you have much on your mind, but you must eat to keep your strength up.' So saying Edith poured him strong ale, in a silver tankard. Harold gulped down the full tankard in one go, smiled at her, his devoted Edith, and sat down to eat a fine meal of bread, capon and fish accompanied by liberal quantities of vegetables, including carrots, turnips and parsnips. All washed down by three tankards of ale.

Harold sat there, content, nibbling on some cheese and fresh bread. 'This bread is truly wonderful; I will go to the kitchen to thank them.' Harold was smiling broadly, being just a little tipsy from the strong beer Edith had given him. He put the plate down, and looked intently at Edith.

'You know you are my first and true love,' his hand reached out for her small hand. 'That will never change.' They both smiled at each other, as he stood up and walked hand-in-hand with her.

He led her into the kitchen where the women were grinding grain, baking bread and brewing beer. The women were cooking in iron cauldrons and some pottery vessels over open fires. Others were making butter and cheese. Around the room were numerous wooden bowls, from which the household would eat, and on the wall were racks of wooden spoons.

'Ah! The smell of that bread is truly wonderful,' he said again, only this time for the women to hear. 'Thank you for the good service you give me.' The women were a little embarrassed, but one of them, more bold than the others, approached him, 'Sire we have another drink recently made, if you would care to try it?'

Without waiting she reached for a cow horn and poured him a cup from a wooden barrel into the horn, it was mead, made from fermented honey.

Edith saw the glint in Harold's eye, and she knew he still loved her.

Hardrada stood, sombre by the grave of the man who had dared to question his dream.

Ulf the Marshal had been both brave and foolish. Excitement had been simply oozing from Hardrada; in fact it was carrying the King away. Now that he had cast his covetous eyes towards England, he could not contain himself. Gold, land and riches beyond his wildest dreams, were all he could think of. He was convinced he would soon establish a great empire, like that of King Canute before him.

Looking down on the fresh pile of earth over of the grave, Hardrada said, 'There lies now the truest of men and the most devoted to his king,' he bellowed, whilst standing over the grave of the man he had just killed.

Ulf the Marshal had repeatedly tried to reason with King Hardrada, 'Sire it is said that England is difficult to attack. It is very full of men-at-arms, the Housecarls are said to be so brave, that one of them was better than two other men.'

'Enough Ulf,' growled Hardrada, 'there are many in the north of England, who will run to join us once we land.'

'Sire, you do not know this for sure. It maybe now they have married on England's soil they will not want to risk their safety and join with you.'

'Be silent Ulf,' Hardrada's irritation was beginning to boil. 'I am told once they see me land in England the northern people will flock to our banner.'

'Remember,' blurted out Ulf, 'it was those same men who drove out that sly dog Tostig, and also killed his men. I do not trust Tostig; you should not listen to him.'

Ulf had failed to see he had overstepped the mark, nor to spot the anger welling up within his king.

Still he persisted, 'Sire you have much to lose, if you rush into this; I fear you will be making a mistake.'

'Ha!' growled Hardrada, 'A slave who finds both courage and a voice!' Too late did Ulf realise his mistake. Suddenly a long thin knife thrust into his neck, and silenced him forever. 'Maybe there was some truth in much of what Ulf said?' thought Hardrada to himself, 'but he had no right to try and undermine the spirit and courage of the men, before we even set out on this great venture.'

Hardrada turned away from staring at the newly turned earth of Ulf's grave, then gritting his teeth he looked straight into Tostig's eyes, with such a glare that even Tostig cast his eyes down. They had talked long and frequently together, and now he had taken the resolution, to proceed in the summer to England and conquer that country. He had sent a message through all Norway and ordered one-half of all the men in Norway to come to his call, carrying arms. He had not said why, so when the call became known there were many guesses about what might be the end of this expedition. Whatever it was, they had confidence that Hardrada was the man who could accomplish it.

All the chiefs began to gather their men and ships. Nothing was known as to the reason for the King's levy, but all men understood that mighty matters were afoot. Ships came from over the Western Sea, from Iceland, the Isles of Scotland, Isle of Man, Ireland and from Norway. All were instructed to join the host at Scapa Flow, a natural harbour in the Orkney Islands, off the northern coast of Scotland.

'This venture requires a lot of planning,' said Hardrada addressing Tostig, but still he had deep mistrust regarding this outlawed Earl's own motives. 'We have agreed to join forces, yet your own forces are very limited,' he sneered. 'Still I expect you to do your utmost to improve on your number of ships and men. If so you will get your estates returned as the Earl of Northumbria.' Then smiling through his heavy and overgrown beard, added, 'And I will get the English crown.'

'Sire, I will sail today for Flanders, meet up with the men who left England with me and then set out for England, where more will join us. Rest assured sire, we shall greatly increase our numbers.' Tostig did his best to bolster Hardrada's faith in him, but he knew only his actions would do that.

'Then let it so be,' Hardrada replied, unsure of Tostig's ability to carry out his promise. 'I will rendezvous with you in the summer and we will then combine our forces.' Hardrada glared again at Tostig, as only he could. Then threateningly added, 'But you had better bring your share of the bargain with you, if you wish to have Northumbria back in your grip. Fail in this and our agreement is cancelled.'

Tostig knew he had to succeed, otherwise it might mean his life.

Two rampant golden lions on a red background was the banner of the House of Normandy, flying proudly over the castle of Rouen, a castle which dominated the town. It displayed Norman strength, like a watchful eye, to all who saw it. Duke William had made Rouen his headquarters and was actively discussing plans regarding what action to take concerning England, with Count Richard Fitz-Gilbert, his former guardian.

William was not pleased, 'There are some barons who would seek to dissuade me from taking this great venture. How dare they? I will not tolerate such base-born cowards.'

'No, be careful, think this through. We need all the support we can get; you must not alienate the barons.' Richard always was the more rational of the two and did not want to see any division develop within their ranks. 'Rather you must ask how are we to make sure we get the support of all the barons, to take up arms against England. We must convince those who come to our call that this is a lawful venture; that God is on our side.' He gave a little smile at this suggestion. It was gratifying to have William hang on to his every word. 'I have given this some careful thought. This is what I propose: We send a delegation to Pope Alexander II with a request to support your claim to the English throne.

We state your birthright of course, but more importantly, we make it clear that Harold swore under oath, over the bones of a holy Christian saint, to give you the succession of that kingdom.'

This lie had taken hold of all the brothers, and was now being broadcast far and wide. 'We must tell the Pope that King Edward, the saintly King they call the confessor, also offered you this kingdom. Finally, we must make it clear that we will remove from office Stigand, the unlawful Archbishop of Canterbury and let the Pope appoint who he will.'

'Hmm! The Pope will support us, we both know that.' The top lip on William's face curled up as he said this. 'He needs the protection of too many Norman knights to say otherwise, and our brethren already control much of Italy.'

'True, but we have to make this as legal as we can, for all to see, so they will readily rally to our banner and not seek to dissuade us. We need to show our people that your claim is a lawful one, that we have God on our side.'

William nodded, 'You are right, as usual. This we will do, we will seek all the legal support we can.'

William still looked pensive, 'Another matter we have to consider is the actions of Tostig in exile. He could be a very useful ally to us. His messenger arrived here from Flanders two days ago. He told me Tostig had gone to King Harald Sigurdsson of Norway for support. This could be a two edged sword to us. If Tostig can draw a strong force from Norway then this could be good for us.' He looked seriously worried and went on, 'It could also be a major problem too.'

'How so?' asked Richard.

'Do we want to share England?' William spun round to face Richard, his voice going up an octave. 'Although I cannot see a combined force of Danes and Norwegians coming together, for they have been at each other's throats for far too long; but Sigurdsson, the one they call Hardrada, can call on a very large force if he has a mind to.'

'But a combined force of Normans and Norwegians could balance the large force Harold Godwinson can call upon.'

'No Richard; that we must never do. If we did then for sure we will have to share England. In addition, some of Sigurdsson's forces still cling on to the old pagan beliefs; and we are a Christian army. If we seek the Pope's support it must be as a Christian army, carrying Christian banners under the holy cross.'

Richard rubbed his hands over the neck of William's dog which had come over to him for the fuss he knew he would get, 'Tostig will want his lands back,' he said casually.

'Yes of course and if he serves us well, he can have them back. But if Sigurdsson Hardrada strikes at England first and wins his battle killing Harold Godwinson, he will claim the entire kingdom for himself.' Neither man wanted this situation. 'We must strike first.'

'We must be careful then William. So what do we tell Tostig's messenger?'

William thought for a moment, 'Tell him, "The Duke is delighted to have his support for the Duke's rightful claim for the crown of England, and if he serves the Duke well he will have his lands back." That should let him realise we are not seeking to share the kingdom with anyone and that he fights for us.'

'Good,' said Richard, 'let us hope we can strike first then, before Sigurdsson Hardrada can.'

Just then, the aged Chamberlain Walter De-Burr entered the room. His lined face was anxious, his lips pursed as he bowed low before the two nobles, and nervously exclaimed, 'The delegation to England has returned my lords and are in the courtyard below.'

'Good, send them up,' demanded William briskly.

Walter hesitated, 'Maybe it would be better, my lord if ....' He could hardly bring himself to say it, '... if, if, you saw for yourself what has happened?' he stammered.

'What on earth do you mean? Explain yourself,' said William somewhat irritated.

'The English have sent a message, for your eyes to see, my lord.'

Their curiosity aroused William and Richard followed the squire as he went down the stairs and out into the courtyard. They both stopped suddenly at the sight that greeted them. Unable to fully comprehend what he was seeing at first, the blood slowly drained from William's face, as the vision before him sank in. 'God in heaven! God damn him!' he shouted. 'He dares to treat my messengers like this?'

Richard put his hand on William's shoulder, 'This is a calculated insult William.'

William and Richard looked at the four men who had made up the protest delegation they had sent to England, and at their expensive horses. Both man and horse had been sent out from Normandy in the full ceremonial dress of the court of Duke William. Now they had returned with the horses manes' all shaved off, their tails cut to a stump and white paint daubed over their formerly black shiny bodies. The four men were no longer in their finery, but in rough peasant sackcloth, and sporting black eyes, bruised faces, broken teeth and roughly shaven hair, raggedly cut to the scalp, still with the cuts of the razor showing.

'God's breath, he dares to insult me this way?' William just could not believe anyone would have the audacity to insult him so publicly. Raising his voice so all stopped what they were doing, William's face reddened with rage, 'Not only does he try and take my kingdom, now he insults me. Harold Godwinson you will pay for this,' so saying William shook his clenched fist in the air.

William trembled with anger, 'Send the delegation to the Pope today: immediately!' then turning on his toes he stormed off back into the castle.

Two days before Easter Day, which fell this year on the sixteenth day of April, King Harold had returned to Westminster, after a second visit to Northumbria, to talk over defence tactics with Earls Edwin and Morcar; and to be seen with his new queen, Ealdgyth.

The festival of Easter arrived, with the usual excitement from the people. It had been well prepared for and eagerly awaited. There were feasts arranged throughout the country, with music from the harp, which was also used for the church music. In addition to the harp, scenes of juggling balls and knives were common. Games of dice and board games such as chess were held in public, where strong competitions ensued. Elaborate riddles were popular, as was story telling. For the wealthier Thanes and landowners, horse racing and hunting were as popular as ever.

As the sap was rising in the trees, so also it seemed to be in the people. Spring was always a time of hope, and this year was no different. The mood of the people was one of confidence. True, they may be attacked, it was the main topic of conversation, but they felt strong enough to resist any such threat. All who could were commanded by cannon law, to attend the solemn church services on Easter Day. The whole country was on its knees in prayer, confident that with God's help, it would be a successful year.

Still, Harold spent a great deal of his time deep in thought; he had so much on his mind. He sat pensively, by the fire while Edith Swan-Neck was busy with her needlework, sowing.

'Oh Edith, how I wish I could go hunting with my hawks and dogs this holy season, as I would normally, but sadly not this year.' He made an effort to bring his feelings under control. 'Maybe I shall be able to go hunting next year?'

'Be of good courage Harold; I and our children need your strength at this time. Do what must be done and God willing you will have plenty of time another day for hunting.'

Then, wistfully he added, 'I love days spent with the hawks and then to come home to a warm pottage of stew,' he gave a deep sigh. 'The word has gone out, for the Fyrd to be mobilised. They will soon be assembling and their hard training enforced. In two weeks time I shall be inspecting them to see their progress.'

The day soon arrived for the military inspection of the Housecarls and Fyrd. King Harold's horse was standing waiting patiently for its rider, by the gate of Westminster. Alric was already mounted on his own fine horse, Welland, as he waited.

King Harold and his two brothers, Gyrth, Earl of East Anglia and Leofwin, Earl of Kent came over and mounted their horses. A grin of rueful pride, spread over the handsome features of Leofwin, as they were joined by a mounted military escort. Alric took the lead, followed by the first regiment of Housecarls, then the King and his brothers, followed by a second regiment. The procession all rode out together.

Harold, Leofwin and Gyrth were natural generals. They all had a feel for war, though they would deny it. They passed the last of the low timber-framed, thatched-roof houses, on their way to the heath, where the Housecarls were gathered and the Fyrd was beginning to assemble. Many tents had been erected, forming an encampment, thousands of this army were gathering. It looked a colourful and impressive site and filled Harold's heart with joy as he looked at what Alric had arranged for this, his inspection day.

The King, his brothers and Alric were all in full military attire as they rode into the arena made ready for them. The golden dragon of England and Wessex flew proudly in the centre. As instructed, the army had assembled to order, for an inspection from their King.

'They are truly an impressive sight, are they not?' Leofwin said for all to hear.

'Sire,' said Alric with pride in his voice, 'it is said that your warriors of England made such haste to get swords of the right quality that the sound of the sword-smiths' hammers could be heard throughout the land.'

This moment belonged to Harold, so Gyrth and Leofwin peeled their horses off to one side. Harold rode straight on with Alric, then, both rode up and down the front ranks of the assembled Housecarls, who were standing rigid, as the first part of this inspection. The Housecarls all wore short-sleeved, knee-length chainmail coats, called the 'hauberk'; the sleeves were left short to enable freedom of movement in battle, some were wearing 'chausses' around their legs, stockings made of chainmail, others had their legs protected by long leather leggings or straps of leather wrapped around the legs to the knees. Under their chainmail, they wore a long heavy red shirt, which protruded below their hauberk, and covered the lower part of their arms. All wore conical helmets to help deflect blows from sword attacks; some with the back and sides of the helmet having an 'aventail' attached; a chainmail mantle to protect their necks. The Housecarl's helmet had the nosepiece as protection, but not the Fyrd, their more simple helmets had no extensions.

The Housecarls proudly displayed their main weaponry. Each man had either the dreaded long handled battle-axe, or a long spear or javelin. The main terror weapon used by the Housecarls was this Danish-style battle-axe. Their enemies feared this weapon the most. It was a large long handled axe, with a curved, honed and razor sharp edge. The wooden handle of this weapon was three to four feet long. In battle it would be swung from side to side; it had the ability to cut down a mounted soldier and his horse in a single blow. It was truly a fearsome weapon.

Their spears were made with a seven-foot long ash shaft with an iron head. It would be mostly used to jab and thrust and was seldom thrown. The javelin, on the other hand, was much shorter and used mainly for throwing. The javelin had a longer iron shank than the spear, designed to bend when it hit a shield, thereby rendering the shield too heavy to hold up high for long, and bending so that it could not be returned and used against the thrower.

Each Housecarl had a double-edged sword, with a shallow grove running along the blade on both sides to make it lighter. Through use in battle, and in constant training, a warrior's sword became a personal attachment, one that he used instinctively and with great skill. It became like an extension of his body. Improved developments in sword making had come from the Danes; a process of forging twisted bars of iron together, to give a more durable implement.

Swords and daggers were held in a baldrick, a leather strap suspended around the waist of the Housecarl.

Whereas the Housecarls had the long, leaf-shaped Norman style, shields that protected the lower part of the body as well as the upper, the Fyrd had the traditional round shields of the Anglo-Saxons and Danes. These shields were made of lime-wood, three or four-feet in diameter, being covered in metal or leather, with a large heavy iron 'boss' in the centre. This 'boss' could be used for deflecting blows and for thrusting into the face of an opponent and knocking him off his feet. Lime-wood being the preferred wood for shields, for it is not very dense and is lighter in the hand, also it is not inclined to split, as oak would, also the fibre of this timber binds around blades preventing the blade from cutting any deeper.

Many of the Fyrd had little armour, other than a helmet and shield, many having no more protection than a leather tunic, but they expected to collect their armour from the fallen dead in battle. As the Fyrd lined up, it was plain some had already collected chain-mail coats from previous encounters, but they were a minority.

The small number of archers had no armour at all, save that of leather tunics and a helmet. They were employed for their skill rather than for close up combat. Many frowned on the archer, considering him not so brave, as those who took part in hand-to-hand combat. It was not a position many aspired to.

Still mounted on their horses, King Harold and Alric proceeded to ride up and down the front ranks of the Housecarls. 'Without doubt Alric, these are the finest warriors any king could have,' noted Harold as he moved away from the Housecarls and over toward the Fyrd.

'Sire the Fyrd are still arriving from their towns and villages, but daily they are flocking to your call.'

'Good Alric,' Harold saw the pride in these part time warriors, their chests welled up as he approached, 'you must see to it that these men are trained to the fullest and highest standard,' then added, 'and with haste.'

'Sire they already train daily with the Housecarls. All now have a demonstration to perform for you after this inspection.'

Harold nodded his approval as he entered amidst the ranks of the Fyrd.

The round lime-wood shields of the Fyrd were gaily painted, some with just one colour, others with a red cross on it, and others with the colours quartered.

Satisfied, Harold pulled his horse to the front of the assembled army, all of whom were still standing to attention and intent on hearing what the King had to say. Harold's brothers now brought their horses over to either side of Harold and Alric.

'Warriors of England,' began Harold, 'Our kingdom and our homes are threatened from without. We await a possible attack from the Norman, Bastard Duke William, who would call himself King of England.'

'No! Never! Never!' was the spontaneous united cry from the ranks.

'We do not know where and when they will strike, but we must be ready. Be ready to protect our homeland and our loved ones. You are a noble army, a proud army; there are none like you anywhere.' A loud cheer went up.

Harold now paused, drew his sword and laid it gently onto his left hand. 'Look well after your weapons, not only because your lives depended on it, but I, your King will dismiss you from these noble ranks, if armour and weapons are not the kept in the best condition. Your weapons are powerful, but they are not as strong as your spirit. When the time comes, this army must act as one body. You must be one body,' he again emphasised. 'You must be of one body of solid armour, one body of solid defiance, one body to instil fear into our enemies, one body against an enemy who would seek to destroy us.' More cheering arose. Now the army was devouring every word coming from King Harold.

'Look yonder,' Harold pointed to a spinney of trees nearby. 'See there, the leaves of the trees and how they are bursting into life. This is a bountiful and pleasant land, willed to us by our brave warrior forefathers; will you protect it?'

'Yes!' came the loud reply in unison.

'I ask you again; will you protect it?'

'Yes, yes, yes,' was the tumultuous response.

Alric rose up in his stirrups, drew his sword and pointed it to the sky, facing the massed ranks, 'For God and King Harold.'

'For God and King Harold,' was the instant shouted reply, 'For God and King Harold.'

Harold, his brothers and Alric turned their horses and went over to the canopied chairs situated on a wooden stage built for the occasion. There the brothers sat down, while Alric remained mounted on Welland.

Alric ceremoniously presented his sword in salute to the King, 'Sire with your permission we will now demonstrate some of our training.'

'Carry on.'

Alric signalled to the army commanders. The Anglo-Saxon war drums started their rhythmic beat, the sound of which had brought terror into many an opposing army. A trumpet sounded and several hundred Housecarls ran out into the arena in front of the King and his brothers.

These men stood in close ranks, eight men deep facing the King. There was an expectant silence.

'Shield wall!' yelled Alric.

With a sudden thrust and a loud simultaneous bang, the front row abruptly locked their shields together in front of them. Each shield overlapping the other. It was in such precision unison it almost came as a surprise. The wall looked solid.

Gyrth and Leofwin both turned to Harold. Gyrth was exuberant, 'By God what a wonderful sight. Alric has trained them with commendable precision.'

'Fyrd form up!' With that order, an even greater number of the Fyrd ran to take up their positions behind the ranks of the Housecarls.

'Spears out!' was the next barked order, from Alric.

Several hundred spears immediately lunged out of the shield wall, some horizontal, some at a forty-five degree angle and some vertical. The wall was impenetrable to anyone on foot or on horse, seeking to break it, for horses would be impaled on the spears bringing down the hapless rider.

'Forward!' the lines of men moved slowly forward, stamping their feet hard in a rhythmic movement, and shouting, 'Out, out, out,' as they advanced, in time with their stamping feet. This was a chant always performed when readying to attack an invader.

'Halt! Reform!' The ranks lifted their spears, turned and ran back to their original formation.

'Shield wall!' Then, just as quickly, the troops turned again to reform their shield-wall, in unison.

There was an air of expectancy, for as impressive as this display had been, all knew, there was more to come.

'Boar's snout!' Fifty Housecarls moved very quickly to obey this next order. At running pace, stamping their feet as they went, gathering to one side away from the shield-wall. They formed a

triangular wedge shape, with shields locked together and battle-axes raised at the ready.

Harold addressed his brothers, 'See the boar's snout. If we are hemmed in at any time, the sheer weight and momentum of such a wedge charging will drive straight through an opposing shield wall, turning the battle in our favour.'

He did not have time to finish what he was saying when Alric issued the next order.

'*Arrows!*' Alric hollowed at the top of his voice.

Thereupon, a second row of defensive shields along the shield-wall was immediately held above the heads of the front rank and above the heads of those behind, forming a protection against an imagined arrow attack.

'Wonderful, well done Alric, well done,' Harold's voice betrayed his excited pride in what he had just witnessed.

'Your military knowledge is considerable, brother' smiled Leofwin.

With the demonstration now finished the men of the 'boar's snout' retired back to their ranks. Alric rode forward again, 'Sire the Housecarls would now like to demonstrate a new technique they have been learning.'

'Interesting Alric, let us see it.'

Alric nodded to the commander.

Four rows of Housecarls ran out, two rows facing the other two rows. Each row consisted of one hundred men. One group of men were called the 'Hawks' and the other the 'Doves'. The front rows of Hawks and Doves faced each other and took up the stance of a mock battle; swords in the right hand and shields in their left. They proceeded to sword fight with practice shots at each other, pushing and parrying with the shields; performing this action deliberately very slowly, so that to Harold and his brothers, it looked almost like a dance.

'*About arms!*' was the next asserted command.

Upon this command, the second row of the Hawks moved forward to replace their former front row. These second row of men had their shields in their right hand and their swords in their left. The effect was immediate. The left-handed men of the Hawks were able to lock shield to shield with their Dove opponents. Doing this pushed shield to shield and exposed the opponent's unguarded right side of the Doves. The Doves fell down in mock death.

Alric rode up to the King, 'Sire this is a tactic which would surprise and take the enemy off guard. We have used naturally left-handed men where we can, but some right-handed men have sought to master this surprise manoeuvre.'

'This is well done Alric. This tactic must remain a secret until the time comes to use it. You have done well with the training; we are pleased with what we see, thus far. Make sure, as more of the Fyrd answer the call to muster; they are brought up to the same standard as displayed here. My watchword to our army is, "train, train, train." See that they all understand this. I can have no weakness in England's proud army.'

'It shall be done my King,' and with that Alric drew his sword, and raised it in front of his face, in a salute to his King.

'This is indeed a good day,' Harold beamed contentedly to his brothers as they and their escort mounted to make their return to Westminster.

There was still one area that greatly troubled Gyrth, he had raised it before, and now would do so again. 'Harold I have been talking with Leofwin,' he ventured, 'we wish you to consider making a regiment of cavalry, in the manner of the Normans.'

Harold would have none of it; he had heard this before and rejected it. 'You would have us become Normans?' he tried to joke. Then his smile quickly faded, 'Yes I have heard all this before, but I am not convinced. You saw how strong our shield-wall is, no cavalry could get through that. No my brothers; why waste good horses on the end of a spear? The Housecarls will use horse to get to the field of battle, but after that, they will fight on foot, as we have always done. It has seen us through this far and we have won many battles using our shield-wall. Is it not rightly feared for its impenetrable strength? I see no need for cavalry.'

Harold was irritated by Gyrth raising this issue again, for he could see no use for cavalry.

Harold's brothers were not convinced though. Harold's impulsive and dismissive approach to the use of cavalry had been of concern to them. They were determined to approach the matter again.

Many Norman knights had been ordered to attend an assembly with Duke William. They were to hear of his preparations, and to witness the return of the delegation sent to Rome. In addition, he wished to instruct the knights personally, to see their training was up to standard. Each Norman knight was the leader of an attachment of soldiers. Usually only the sons of a noble or a knight could train to become one. Their hard training had begun when they were just boys, from the age of seven. Every boy who was to become a knight was required to go to live in another noble's house. During this time he was trained how to ride and fight in war. He was taught to use a bow and to practise swordplay, then, when he was about fourteen-years-old, he would be apprenticed to a knight. As such, he would sometimes ride into the battlefield with his master. If all went well he would become a knight around the age of twenty-one. Knights had to furnish their own horses, men, and equipment. Some of the more wealthy knights also agreed to provide ships.

All the knights of Normandy gathered before Duke William, as the delegation, which had been sent to Rome, returned and now presented themselves to the duke.

The four men of the delegation bowed low together, then standing, one offered the duke an open letter, 'My Lord, we bring good news from Rome. Pope Alexander II has approved your claim to the throne of England. The blessing he offers you is due to the Norman's support in Italy to his holy office. For through Norman support, in southern Italy and Sicily, Godly Christians have repelled the Mohammedan's aggression. They won back those lands from the grasp of the infidel, for the Church of Rome. Because of this, not only will he support you, he has also sent you a consecrated banner.'

The delegate walked over to a table where an embroidered cloth lay, covering an object. The delegate carefully removed the cloth to reveal a four-foot square banner held in a carved wooden frame. The banner was plain white, with a simple bright red cross quartering the square.

'This banner', continued the delegate, 'was blessed by the Pope himself and sprinkled with holy water. This he did, so that you may carry his banner before you into battle with your enemies, as a symbol of Christ's judgement.'

Duke William smiled, which is not something he did very often. 'Excellent! Excellent! Now we can move things along quickly,' William sat back in his elevated chair, feeling very pleased. 'This Papal support will also help protect my borders from the French during my absence,' he mused to himself.

'My Lord,' the delegate went on, 'Pope Alexander has sent you a tooth of Saint Peter the Apostle; which you may carry with you into England, for your protection.'

'We are well pleased with this. Go take your reward from the treasury.' William stood up, clapped his hands, 'Inform my brothers, all barons, nobles and generals, they must assemble at Lillebonne for a Council of War.' William could hardly conceal is delight.

William thought the delegate had finished, but he remained where he was, not moving, 'There are two more things my lord. The Papal Court wishes you to know, that if God blesses your mission, you should remove the Anglo-Saxon upstart Stigand from his illegal position as Archbishop of Canterbury.'

'That will be a pleasure. You may inform his eminence.'

'Finally, my lord,' declared the delegate, savouring his moment. 'Emperor Henry IV of the Holy Roman Empire also gives you his full support.'

William stood up, grasped the delegate by the shoulders and embraced him. Then he turned and signalled to his attendants. 'Scribes write this letter. Issue this proclamation throughout all Norman territories:'

> *The Norman forces must now amass at Saint-Valery-sur-Somme. All who attend me, Duke William of Normandy, on this our holy mission to England, a mission blessed by God, will be given lands and titles. This is an order no man must negate, to disregard this mission now will be met with just punishment. It will mean prosperity to those who come with me, and for his family for generations to come, for England is a rich country; this land will be given to those who come with me, to help secure my kingdom.'*

William now became effervescent, bubbling with excitement, as he issued his orders, 'Send all ship builders to me; we have many new ships to build and to build them quickly. Get the timbres ready. Send to the barons to inform me how many ships and men they will have for this mission. Let them know, the more ships they send me, the more reward they will receive. I need ships, as many ships as we can build, and as many ships as already are built. Let this be known throughout all Normandy and all Norman territories, we are invading England in God's name.'

A great cheer went up from all the assembled knights who heard this gladsome news.

William had known this support was coming from the Pope; hence the main reason he had assembled his knights. He now stood and solemnly addressed them all, revelling in the moment.

'It is now more than one hundred and fifty years since our ancestor Rollo landed on these shores, from Norway.' William braced himself, for he wanted to issue a clear message to all who now stood listening intently before him. 'We are descended from the proud Vikings who settled here in northern France under the great leadership of Rollo. Since his time, we have prospered well, and built on the warlike reputation of our noble ancestors. The Norman knight is the best-trained and best-equipped soldier in Europe. You are the most feared warriors and we will *take* what is rightfully ours. The rewards, in English lands, to those who live, will be commensurate with each participant's rank and contribution. He, who may die in this service, will receive the reward of eternal paradise in heaven, which is more than compensation for his service.'

William had arranged this well, for now the leaders of his army were keen to follow him and to serve him unto death, if need be, but the promised earthly rewards was the greater motivation.

'You must now practice your art of war. See that you ride well, for your horse is a fighting machine that many will fear, use the spear as a lance, for we will have need of this. Now pray to God daily, for now we have the Pope's blessing, this is a holy war.'

William had his men, just where he wanted them, ready to serve him or die in the attempt.

'They are saying it is a bad omen,' Edith Swan-Neck was nervous as she clung tightly to Harold's arm. Both were gazing up at the evening sky from their London home. Crowds had been turning out every night to gaze at this new phenomenon; but often the English clouds obscured the view. Tonight though it was clear, the town's folk were all in the streets, fearful of this strange sight in the sky. It had first appeared on the twenty-fourth day of April and had remained there for several days now. Throughout all England, this was a portent in the heavens, such as men had never seen before.

'What is it?' Edith asked with fear in her voice. 'Has God sent it?'

'It is a new star, one with a tail. Some are calling it a comet. No one recalls ever seeing such a thing before.' Harold was alarmed, but did not want this to be shown.

'It frightens me,' Edith confessed, pulling even tighter on Harold's arm, 'I think it means trouble for our kingdom. Elmer a monk from Malmesbury says it is the sign of great changes coming and maybe the end of the world.'

'Do not worry Edith; it shines on all men not just on us. Why should it be a bad omen only for us? It could equally be a bad omen for others instead.' Harold tried his best to reassure Edith, but deep down he did not like the disturbance this new star was causing to his people.

'Do you think it is the same star which led the wise men to Jesus at his birth?'

'Maybe,' he admitted. 'We will find out if this longhaired star is God's will, or not.' Harold was none too pleased with all this. The last thing he needed at this time was superstitious fear gripping his people. They stood together on the small darkened balcony, outside of their private chambers, as they continued to watch this apparition for some time. Harold felt a deep sense of unease, which he had not known before.

Night after night, this star remained fixed in the sky like a mighty beacon, whose unusual light reached out across all the country and beyond. Fear gripped the people and many were saying it was a symbol of destruction.

'Nettles mean good soil lad, but it is hard work to get these roots out. Better to do it now, before they grow tall.' Ricbert struggled, swinging his clawed fork, over his head and bringing it down hard on the tangle of nettle roots. His two oxen stood by quietly waiting, tethered to the plough. Ricbert and his eldest son Wilfred tackled the nettles, while his second son, Dunstan gathered up the roots. Short and stocky in stature, Ricbert had farmed this land all his life. He had permanent ruddy cheeks and nose, due to his constantly working outside, in the elements of wind, rain, sun and frost, which had all left their mark on his face. Whatever the weather Ricbert would be tending to his farm.

His farm was near the River Trent outside the town of Nottingham. It was far enough away from the regular flooding of the river, but not too close to the town. From his several strips of land, he could see the great outcrop of rock, close to the town, which cast a long shadow down the valley. The children of the town would many times climb up to the top of this hill to play.

'Don't go near that cliff face,' he severely warned his four younger children. He was fearful of them getting too close to the edge of the cliff face and falling to their certain death. In Roman times, a lookout post had been on the top of this hill, but that had long gone, with just a few ruined stones now remaining. In the taverns of Nottingham, some would say this hill with its sheer cliff face would make a good stronghold, for a castle, but no one had felt the need to build one.

The crops Ricbert grew were mostly wheat, oats and barley. The barley he used both as a cereal and as the base for his beer. He had been pleased with his crops of vegetables last year and hoped now this new crop would be the same. There was a plentiful supply of fruit, when it was in season on his farm, such as apples, blackberries, raspberries and sloes. Near to the fruit, he had hives for bees, to collect his only sweetener, honey, which he also used to make mead. Pigs were his major food animal, although he also had some cattle, goats, and sheep. He had raised the oxen himself; they were very good for heavy farm labour and for transportation. Even so, he found it difficult to grow enough food to keep many of his animals through the winter, so when each winter approached more than half of the animals would be slaughtered and the meat salted, to keep them fed through the long cold months. The daily work for Ricbert and his sons was considerable and heavy. Five days a week, he and his sons would toil on the land, except on the Sunday Sabbath and the Fyrd Day when he and Wilfred would report for their weekly training practice, as did most men.

He was glad to live near the town of Nottingham; it was so convenient for him. He could harness two oxen to his cart and travel on it to the market, where he could barter and trade his products. There were many things to buy in Nottingham, from the smiths manufacturing ploughshares, swords, nails and axes; or from the potters, weavers, carpenters, soap makers, millwrights, wheelwrights, bakers, butchers, and many other tradesmen and craftsmen. There was everything he needed there. He had recently brought his wife a comb, finely made from bone.

The chief topic of conversation in the town had been the appearance of the comet. It had worried most of the people, but they had all prayed to God, and it was now gone Ricbert was glad it had gone, for it had troubled him to see such a sign from heaven, he wondered what it could mean.

Nottingham was a lively town, situated as it was in the Earldom of Mercia, at the south end of the great forest of Sherwood. Much of Mercia was covered in dense forest. Ricbert had not travelled much, but he had once travelled north to the village of Edwinstow, in the heart of the forest, when the Fyrd were called out by Earl Edwin, but by the time he arrived, the disturbance had been settled. He would not have like to travel alone through that great forest, gangs of robbers made it too dangerous, and there were still some wolves around, but thankfully, most of those had been driven out.

Wilfred and Dunstan had returned to the oxen to get the plough moving again, while Ricbert sat exhausted from the efforts of digging out the clumps of nettles. Something made him look up; it was a rider, heading for the town. He didn't know what it was, but something about the rider made him feel uneasy, for the rider was dressed in fine attire and seemed to be in a great hurry.

It was still dark, two hours before dawn, the scent of sweet May blossom filled the air, as the longship 'Gunhild' rowed quietly into the large inlet of the river Medina, to the south of the Isle-of-Wight, leading the way for the ten other longships to follow. They were deathly quiet; no one spoke as the oars gently lapped into the still waters. On board was an expectant crew of men from Flanders, led by their commander, Tostig. The Flemings had been promised much plunder from this island off the south coast of Wessex, which was tantalisingly close to King Harold's heartland.

Tostig's Lieutenant was Copsig, a ruthless man who was always ready to carry out the wishes of his superior, whatever they may be. He was an unattractive man of medium height, with a balding head, yet long straggling side hair, which served only to emphasise his baldness. His body was heavy and ungainly; in his sneering face his wild brown eyes lay deep beneath a frowning forehead. Sometimes, when his men had had too much beer, they would quietly joke together, so as not to be heard, 'He has a face only God could love.' Then they would do their best to hide their sniggers. In public Copsig affected dignity, although he had little education to mellow his rough manners.

Copsig had spent the winter in the Orkneys and had come to join Tostig ahead of his personal main fleet, which were to join him soon. Copsig, a Saxon outcast like Tostig, had deployed two ships to guard the entrance to the inlet, while he captained the last ship of the convoy proceeding inland. The convoy made a beautiful, yet sinister sight as they hove-to, in the inlet.

Tostig's ships were all of traditional Viking design. These ships typically drew only about three feet of water, and the Danes and Norwegians, who had settled in Northumbria, had taught their trade well, they were experts at sailing up rivers, allowing these Viking warships to travel deep inland. Their favoured tactic was to find an island where they could moor their ships, the better to protect them, and then to spend some days or weeks raiding the surrounding countryside.

This, during the first week of May, would be the start of Tostig's planned revenge on his brother Harold. It felt good, very good, as he observed the sleeping town, which was completely unaware of the threatened danger.

With the ships made fast, guards were stationed by them. About three-hundred men stealthily fanned out around the sleepy harbour of a new port recently built, close to the small town of Carisbrooke. No one spoke, for all knew what to do. Several merchant vessels were moored by the quayside fully loaded. It had been the information about these vessels, which led Tostig to select this new port for his raid. The small garrison in Carisbrooke had been made even smaller by the call-up of the Fyrd, leaving less than two dozen men to guard the town, and all were sleeping, including the guard on duty outside the garrison's enclosure.

A dog, tethered outside one of the harbour houses, started barking. It roused the sleeping guard, just in time for him to see the knife flash in front of his eyes, as it sliced into his throat, so that he fell back with a choking cry. By the time the dog had raised others from their slumber, the first shades of light of a new day were beginning to appear. A wooden shutter of a ground floor hatch opened from the Harbour Master's house, the occupant gazing outside, cursing the dog. Slowly he saw the dim outlines in the water below, betraying the presence of the longships in the inlet. The sudden shock and horror of what he saw quickly set in.

'To arms, to arms, we are under attack,' shrieked the startled Harbour Master, as simultaneously an arm reached in through the hatch and pulled him forward, onto a waiting sword.

Men of the garrison began to appear and soon small pitched fights were breaking out. The element of surprise was the key factor, those few who tried to defend the town died quickly doing so. They were hopelessly out-numbered; the whole area only had about thirty families. Within a few minutes, most of the Anglo-Saxon Fyrd were either dead or wondered; it was hardly a fight, just a massacre. No one had been expecting such a sneak attack.

The terrified towns' people were quickly rounded up, old men, women and children, herded into a tightly huddled group, surrounded by heavily armed Flemish raiders.

Copsig was strutting like a peacock, up and down in front of them; shield in one hand and drawn sword in the other, 'Who will speak for you?' he demanded.

An old man was pushed to the front, 'I will,' he said.

The old man went spinning to the floor as Copsig stuck him hard with his shield. 'When you address Earl Tostig you call him "Lord", you wizened cur.'

'Y-y-yes my lord,' he spluttered as the old man's lips burst forth in blood, and teeth fell out of his mouth.

Tostig looked at the man as he struggled to get to his feet. 'We need all the money from the trading going on here and provisions; all the provisions we can carry. Try to hide anything from us and we will kill you all. Understand?'

'Clearly my lord,' replied the old man, fearing for his life.

Looking at the group of captives, Tostig walked over to them, 'Copsig sort this mixed bag of rubbish out. Take who you will.' His eye fixed on a group of girls crying, their arms holding tightly around each other. 'You can take first choice Copsig, and then your men may take who they please.' Tostig wanted to make sure these captives would benefit his purse, 'Do not kill them or draw blood, I want them undamaged to sell as slaves later. There will be a goodly price in the market for them.' Tostig looked at Copsig and gave a wicked smile, 'But first Copsig, they will keep the men happy this night,' then he added with a smirk, 'and while on board ship.'

The men laughed, delighted at the prospect of using these girls for their own pleasure. The terrified girls were beyond crying, they were transfixed and sorely afraid of what awaited them.

'Alright men take what you want from this town. We have all day before we need move, enjoy these women, but stay on your guard.' Copsig walked straight to the group of girls, and stood still for a moment ogling them, saliva began to dribble from his mouth. He then closed one nostril with one finger and blew the contents of the other to the ground. Smiling he reached out and roughly pulled one of the terrified girls to him. 'This one is mine,' he laughed, and marched off with her to a nearby empty house.

The repeated rape of the women, the burning and looting of the town went on all day. The ships were loaded with the stolen provisions and all money that could be found was handed to Tostig. Toward evening, the raiders settled down to drink the local beer, which had been found in large quantities in one of the warehouses. Soon the raiders became very drunk; the bodies of the slain Anglo-Saxon Fyrd were thrown into the river inlet, as well as the bodies of some of the women who had died from the excessive abuse at the hands of these raiders.

Amidst the drunken revelry, the wooden buildings were set alight. The whole of the new port was burning, which gave the opportunity for some of the captives to escape from the mayhem, away into the darkness, but several of the poor ravaged girls and women, marked as slaves, were not as fortunate, as they lay bound in the hold of a ship awaiting their fate.

By mid-morning on the following day, the convoy was again at sea. They were heading for the port of Sandwich in Kent, but Tostig wanted to make his presence felt as much as possible, and so raided any town or hamlet along the way that took his fancy. As he sailed he made sure to do as much damage, everywhere along the seacoast wherever he could, until they arrived at the port of Sandwich. he was hitting his brother where he knew it would hurt him the most.

Standing in front of yet another burning house, observing the occupants and their goods being loaded on board his ships, he conferred with Copsig.

'Copsig, you say your fleet will join us as we head north to Northumbria?'

'Aye, that they will, they have their orders to join us, as you say.' Copsig had told his fleet to keep close inshore and to sail only during the daytime.

Tostig was thoughtful, 'Tomorrow we enter Sandwich. By attacking along the coast, as we have, we will be stretching Harold's forces, for he does not know where we will attack next. It is possible that King Hardrada will not be ready to attack until late summer, I therefore will force my cursed brother to call out the Fyrd and spread them as thinly as possible until that time.'

Tostig brought his forefinger to his nose, in an all-knowing gesture. 'By attacking Sandwich, I seek to strengthen our forces, even more than by your ships alone. Then we will move up the coast to Northumbria, where I will truly make them regret what they have done to me. Yes by God, they will rue the day.'

'So how will our forces be strengthened by attacking Sandwich, and before my fleet arrives?' inquired Copsig, who mentally revered Tostig's educated mind.

Tostig smirked, 'There are many ships there, it is a muster for some of Harold's navy, but they are not well protected, as we have seen so far. We have enough men to seize the town, take the ships and enlist all the men we can.'

'If they are Harold's men, how can we enlist them?'

'Is your mind so weak it cannot think of ways to do this?' Copsig gave a knowing smile.

The news of the attacks from Tostig's fleet soon reached King Harold in London. Alric was immediately sent for and now stood before his King. 'Alric, send one thousand troops down to Kent; Tostig has chosen to raid the shores of his homeland.' Harold was trembling with rage, 'I have ordered the navy, moored here in London, to set sail for Kent. I know my brother, I am sure he will be heading for Northumbria, where he may try to seize back his Earldom.' The news of the raids had shaken Harold; he had not thought his brother could muster a force strong enough, so early in the year, to harry the English along the coast.

Alric tried to reason with Harold's impulsive nature, 'Sire this could be a diversionary tactic to weaken our forces, so that a stronger force can attack elsewhere. If we are spread too thinly then we will be too weak if Duke William attacks.'

'True,' acknowledged Harold, 'but Duke William will not be ready a while yet, I think, we must protect our people from my brother.' Harold had been torn within himself, how to respond to this, for he knew full well, it could be a diversionary tactic. 'I have given this a lot of thought Alric. I will make our base on the Isle-of-Wight for the summer, so that our navy can be ready to repel any ships William sends to sea. Our main forces must now be concentrated on the south coast, while Earls Edwin and

Morcar concentrate on the north. We have to protect our coastline with all the force we can muster.'

Harold turned sharply to stand face-to-face with Alric, 'We will gather greater naval and land forces than any king in this country has ever gathered before.' Harold knew he had to do this. 'I am credibly informed that Duke William will attack somewhere along our south coast, so we must be ready.'

It was a difficult decision for Harold, as to where his forces should be based, but the south coast seemed the most likely, so he intended to concentrate his forces there.

'If we move our navy now, as its heads for the Isle-of-Wight, it should be able to meet Tostig and drive him off. Our navy must try to intercept Tostig's fleet, while on the way to setting up the base on the Isle-of-Wight. If we can, Tostig will regret his actions against us.'

Harold pondered over these thoughts and mused to himself, repeatedly. 'What is Tostig up to? What *is* he up to?' He knew Duke William was plotting an attack, but he did not know of King Hardrada intentions at all; nor his brothers' involvement with that King.

'Sire,' Alric slammed his fist, in frustration, into his other hand, 'These raids will force the Fyrd to use up their service time and our resources. Curse the man.'

'Tostig has chosen his targets well,' nodded King Harold. 'These attacks are a personal affront against me. He has attacked on the estates of the Godwinson family, on *my* own estates. Honour has made it now impossible to ignore these raids. I shall seek just vengeance for what he has done.'

The smoke rising from the fire in Ricbert's house escaped through a hole in the roof. Sometimes this smoke made the family's eyes sore, but this time the tears in their eyes were not from the smoke. In the winter, it was a warm house having a wooden, rather than a dirt floor; now though it was warmer weather so the door and window hatches were open. The one large room had a split-level at one end, where the family would climb up either one of the two ladders there, to get to their beds. Now it was spring and the weather was warming, yet the children shook, as if cold. They, and their mother, Mildryth, were upset.

Ricbert was standing on a bench, normally used as a table, to reach up into the framework of wooden beams holding up the roof. Between the thatched roof and the single floor there was no ceiling, it was all open. With reverence, Ricbert lifted down his sword, from where it was normally kept, high up on the beams. Also, his round shield was unhooked from the rafters and passed carefully to his eldest son, Wilfred.

The messenger Ricbert had seen riding in his fine clothes, had brought the news that all members of the Mercian Fyrd in Nottingham were to report to Earl Edwin in the capital of Repton.

'Don't go daddy,' Leola his five-year-old daughter begged. 'Don't leave us daddy,' she cried.

'Daddy has to go, so that you will be safe, my sweet.' Ricbert struggled with his own emotions.

'We are safe daddy, don't go.' Her tears ran faster as he picked her up into his loving arms.

'No we are not safe Leola, the Orcs are coming.'

'What are Orcs, daddy?'

'Sit down children. Let me tell you the story.' All Ricbert's six children and his wife, Mildryth, gathered around him and sat down. They loved to hear his stories, told to them many times throughout the long winter nights, but they were not so sure they would like this one.

'Orcs are foreigners, monsters, not from this land. They are more like demons than men, and they do evil things. Where we live, we are happy, but these people do not like us being happy, it makes them angry when they see we are happy, and they want to take our happiness away from us. Where we live, people call it "Middle Earth", because above us is heaven and below us is hell, and we live in the middle of the two. Orcs are always fighting and now they want to fight us. They are coming from across the sea, from a land called Normandy, where they live, so we must go and fight them to stop them coming here and taking our happiness away. Our fight with them will be a fight for our Middle Earth, so we must drive them back, back to hell where they came from.'

Ricbert put his sword across his lap, and gently pulled it out of its scabbard. 'This is the most valuable thing we have. It belonged to my great grandfather, and soon I will pass it on to my eldest son, Wilfred. It is incredibly expensive to buy one of these, more than we could afford now. That is why I look after it. Sometimes we can find new ones when we have fought a battle, and take them off the dead there. With this sword I will fight to drive out the Orcs, so that they cannot come and hurt you.'

Ricbert looked thoughtful for a moment, as all his family listen to his every word. 'If Wilfred was just a little older, I would let him have this sword now, but at sixteen years-old, he is just a bit too young. I would be happy to use just my bow, for I am a very good shot with it, I don't really need a sword and a bow. The bow is my chosen weapon.' The bow always hung by the door, where it was kept ready for hunting, or killing foxes, and he always took it for regular practice on the Fyrd training day once a week.

'For God's sake look after him,' demanded Mildryth, tears still in her eyes, and clutching hold of their eldest son, Wilfred, 'He is only sixteen.'

'I am old enough to fight, mother,' Wilfred protested. Both his parents looked at him with concern. Wilfred's face was just beginning to grow whispery stands of hair, which to him denoted his new manhood, but to his parents showed only his youth.

'Well I don't know about that son,' countered Ricbert, 'but you can certainly help us.'

'How will we cope with the farm?' Mildryth asked, worried how she would feed her children.

'Dunstan, is fourteen, he will be in charge while we are gone. We also have Ceadda who is twelve and Edsel who is nine, these three boys will work hard to keep the farm going while we are gone. The two girls Leola and Ealdgyth are too young to help their mother, but they will learn.'

'When will you return father?' asked Dunstan pleased at his newly found authority.

'It should be sometime around the end of July,' then added quickly, 'before the harvest sets in.' Ricbert then solemnly fastened the family's sword to his belt.

Tostig watched as six of his longships carrying Copsig, and three-hundred and fifty men sailed out of sight, leaving him with five ships and nearly three-hundred men behind. It was already daylight; surprise was not what Tostig wanted this time. The warnings of Tostig's presence had gone well ahead of them, all along the coast of southern England. As a result, the coast was alive, with nervous expectation. Soon the war horns and drums from the port of Sandwich were sounding, with troops rushing to the harbour estuary to meet the oncoming raiders from the sea. The Sandwich Fyrd consisted of over two-hundred men lined up ready to meet these hated raiders. Copsig held the ships close offshore, while vehement exchanges were shouted across the water to each other. Both sides whipped up the aggression, as taunts and obscenities were hurled at their foes. Some of the English defenders started to wade into the water, demanding that the raiders come ashore and take their punishment.

A group of the raiders held up one of the girl captives, taken from along the coast. Her distress and abuse was clear for all to behold. Copsig ran his rough hand over her exposed breasts, then, pulling on her loose long hair, he forced his foul smelling mouth onto hers. Howls of hated filled the air from the English military. Arrows were fired from the shore, but they were easily knocked to the side at that range by the shields of the raiders; which further infuriated the English. Swords beat a rhythm on their round Anglo-Saxon shields, but still the invaders ventured no closer to the shore.

'They are cowards,' was the general cry. 'Come on to the shore you sons of pigs, if you dare.'

While all onshore were watching this spectacle, a sudden shriek from behind them made the English defenders turn around. A large group of women and children, on the slopes of the hill behind the defenders, were being pushed forward in front of a mass of raiders. Those at the front were the families of the men now defending the harbour. Dumbfounded, the English did not know which way to turn. One boy suddenly broke away from the herded group, running quickly away as fast as he could, only to be brought down with a throwing axe, thrown by one of the raiders. Screams rent the air.

The figure of Tostig pushed through these traumatised people, and strode to the fore. Holding up his hands he shouted, 'Silence!' A dull rumble came from the surrounded defenders.

'I am Tostig, rightful Earl of Northumbria.'

The English defenders looked on as they saw the raiders holding firmly onto their women and children. Many of the women were being held with a knife at their throats; also, Tostig's archers had their bows drawn at the ready, all pointing at the huddled mass of frightened humanity.

Half turning and pointing back toward the captives, Tostig shouted, 'Either these will die, here and now, or you will obey my orders.' The English fell silent, now only half-aware of the men on board the ships beginning to wade through the surf ashore.

'I have more than five-hundred men here, who will obey my every order. Do not think they will not. Your brats and women will die now unless you do as I say.'

'Never!' shouted one man. 'No never,' shouted another. Then a terrible howl came up as a battle-axe chopped through the toes of the latter, leaving him rolling on the ground in agony.

'Bring her to me,' commanded Tostig, pointing to a teenage girl. Grabbing her hair and pulling her backward. 'Does she die, or does she live?' screeched Tostig as his knife brought a drop of blood from the girl's throat.

'No! That's my daughter,' shouted one of the English defenders, dropping to his knees. 'Please sir I beg you have mercy.'

'All will live if you obey my orders.'

'What are your orders then?' an angry Englishman asked, upset they had been so easily tricked.

'The sailors among you and those around this district are to make all ships in Sandwich ready to sail. You have until tomorrow mid-day to do this. You who are sailors will take these ships to join with my fleet.'

'My Lord, that is nearly thirty ships, we cannot get them ready in that time.'

'Who are you?'

'I am Geffrei Gaimar captain of this command.' Geffrei was a middle age man with red hair. The freckles on his face were well hidden by his thin straggly beard. He was in full battle dress, holding a spear and holding his shield high.

'Step forward Geffrei Gaimar, and leave your shield and spear on the ground.'

Geffrei Gaimar did as instructed and faced Tostig. 'Well captain, either you do as I command, or you can watch while they die,' Tostig sneered as he pointed at the captives. 'What say you?'

'We will do as you say,' Geffrei Gaimar reluctantly agreed, knowing he did not have a choice.

'Tell your men to lay down their weapons and get the ships ready.' Tostig felt relief that his plan was working so smoothly. Then turning to his men, he ordered, 'Now get those snivelling wretches housed in a compound where we can keep close eyes on them. Place fifty men around them. The rest of you disarm the English, make ready the ships and round up every sailor you can find. Any who resist, put to the sword immediately; every man who can, will sail with us, if they want their families to live.'

Geffrei Gaimar and his men went reluctantly down to the harbour to do as they were instructed. They would have to bide their time for any revenge.

The fire gave the main source of light. Shadows flitted in the dark corners. Smoke curled along the high beams of the ceiling. Many of the Viking warriors sat on the long narrow benches along the sides of the protracted wooden hall. This was the King's hall at Solunds, just north of Bergen, in Norway.

Within this long wooden hall, a celebration was taking place, for the reuniting of the first forces to come to King's banner. King Harald Sigurdsson, Hardrada, was drunk. He was a fearsome sight when sober, but he was a terrifying sight when drunk. He could consume beer at an immeasurable rate; jug after jug he frequently poured down the contents of, his seemingly insatiable throat. After gulping down each jug of beer, his bellowing voice got louder, at the same time as his eyes became more glazed.

'What you doing over there?' Hardrada pointed to a group who were equally as drunk as himself, who were in the far corner of the room.

Surprised that the King had seen them, one inebriated man struggled to get to his feet, 'I was showing Gudrun my scars from the battles fought in your service sire.' Svein was a braggart who had always done something better than others had. His opponents in battle were always bigger than any had seen; his feats of daring were better than others could even dream about. He was known for his exaggerated tall stories; but his scars were real enough. A ragged gash under his ribcage, received from a glancing spear, had left him with a discoloured medal of honour, which he was proud of having and repeatedly would show it off, whenever he could.

'Ha!' scorned Hardrada, as he downed yet another tankard of ale. 'Be that as it may; but what about this for a scar?' He fumbled to untie the crossover tapes, laced to bind his leggings. Unable to coordinate his hands while bending over, the King stumbled to his knees.

Someone laughed; then quickly stifled it. Too late!

Hardrada, on all fours, slowly pulled himself to his feet, one of his leggings hanging loose and falling over his foot. His eyes glared. Spittle ran from his mouth.

'Who dares to laugh?' he questioned in an unnaturally quiet and cynical voice. No one answered. A nervous silence greeted his question. 'Who dares to laugh?' he now thundered eyes bloodshot with so much beer.

'No one my King,' Styrkar the Marshal of King Hardrada's forces strode forward. He was a gallant and brave man, Hardrada listened to him more than most. 'It was simply a fart from someone not used to so much beer.'

'A fart you say? Ha! We recruit farts now do we?' All the room broke into laughter. 'Let us drink to our farts men,' and with that all downed more ale. 'Fill your jars and cow horns men and drink to our attack on England, so we can all fart on it.'

'I, that we will sire, and we also drink to England's new King, King Hardrada,' shouted Styrkar.

'To England's new King,' echoed all in the hall.

Hardrada slumped back down in his carved chair, his leggings still around his ankles, and his loin underwear exposed. 'Let us see your scars men. Proudly show what wounds you bear for the King of the Northmen.'

Soon all the men were showing each other the scars they bore. Those who had none were soon feeling left out of it, and that somehow they were lesser men for not having any. Laughter erupted when one man stood in front of them all, naked from the waist down. 'Sire my rump carries these scars, a truly painful wound.'

'That will teach you to turn your back to the enemy,' thundered Hardrada, his fist thumping on the table.

All were now in hysterical laughter. Glad that the King's mood had been so changed.

'Captain Gyrd,' Hardrada shouted across the room, to one of the captains of a ship. 'Gyrd, bring in the two women slaves you took from Spain,' Hardrada's eyes now glinted. It was not long before the two terrified girls were pushed into the room and onto their knees in front of Hardrada. 'What say you men, of these dark haired beauties?'

'Sire we used them well on the voyage back to Norway,' said Gyrd wondering if he would ever be able to sell them at all now.

Hardrada looked at them, cocking his head to one side, 'Pay Gryd well you devils, for this service. Use them as you will, form a queue and enjoy yourselves.'

Hardrada slowly stood up, clumsily still trying to fasten his leggings, then, he staggered toward the door at the end of the room. He slowly and unsteadily approached the door, to leave. All eyes were on him, no one moved. As he reached the door he stopped, then in a flash, stuck his knife into the throat of Einar Jonsson. The startled look on Einar's face brought a twisted form of satisfaction to the king. 'That will teach you to laugh at me,' and before the man had hit the floor, Hardrada stormed out.

The youth stood nervously, yet full of hatred, with his head bowed, in front of Duke William. 'You long haired layabout. You look more like a dammed Saxon than my son,' scorned the duke. He was angry with his eldest son Robert, who though only fifteen-years-old, already had a rebellious streak. Robert had taken to growing his hair long, which was too much like the Saxon style for his father to accept. Not only that, Robert spent nights carousing with a rough crowd of aristocratic thugs, who had begun to swarm around him, to elevate their own weaker positions. His brother, nine-year-old William Rufus was Duke William's preferred son, he had the same red hair as his father, but both boys were already getting out of control and both, like their father, had violent tempers. Robert had deliberately formed the habit of wearing his blond hair long, which sent his father and the priests of the church into outrage.

'You will not bring disgrace on me by looking like a Saxon,' William shouted, as his hand struck hard into the face of young Robert. 'I will not have it.' William struck him again. Robert stood steadfast, his hate for his father burning through his eyes. 'Do you hear me?' The third blow knocked Robert to his knees, but still he said nothing and did not cry. Secretly, Duke William was proud of Robert's fortitude, but he would not let him see that. 'If you do not do as I say, you will not accompany me when we invade England. Now go, and in future you will present yourself more like a Norman than a Saxon dog.' His son remained standing, still with his head bowed, so that his father could not see the fury in his eyes.

Just then, Richard Fitz-Gilbert walked into the room, 'Do not be too hard on your son, William.'

'What!' William's temper raged. 'He is short, fat, impulsive and unstable. How can this short-arse be my son? Look how small he is.' His eyes glared as he continued to fume. 'Yes, that is what I will call him. Robert Short-Arse. He will never be like me.' William pointed to the door, 'Now get out of my sight Robert Short-Arse and get your hair cut.' With that Robert left, the hatred for his father more intense than ever, a hatred that would never diminish.

'I like these jaunts with De-Beers,' Richard sought to change the subject and calm his brother down. 'I have been to De-Beers farm, where he has such a charming new wife.' Richard's eyes glinted.

'Yes I hear tell,' agreed William, his temper suddenly cooling. 'Did he offer her to you?'

'Why else would I go there?' Richard laughed. 'She certainly knows how to please a man.'

'Well soon we will have many English women at out beck and call. We will of course oblige them to follow our Norman custom, for a man to offer his wife to a Norman noble.' William sat back in his chair smiling. 'Yes that will be fun.'

'You know the old saying good brother,' Richard rubbed his hands. 'A woman, a dog, and a walnut tree, the more you beat them the better they be.' With that, they both laughed aloud.

Both men poured out cups of wine. 'That is not why I came here brother,' Richard took a long drink, placed his cup on the table, and went on. 'Your orders have been carried out. Your marshals are busy recruiting and collecting your feudal levies and hiring mercenaries from all parts of France, Flanders, and the

Norman territories of southern Italy. Now I invite you to see the fleet being built and assembled at the mouth of the River Dives.'

'Good,' smiled William. 'We shall visit there soon. Our plans must be well made and thoroughly carried out,' William sat back in his chair, pressing his finger tips together, laughed and said, 'Now how do we get to De-Beers?'

Meanwhile William's son, Robert, watched his hair fall away in clumps as the barber cut away at it, gradually exposing the shape of his scalp. When at last it was finished, the barber looked at him, smiled and said, 'What big ears you have.' Robert was mortified. He felt the sting of tears in his eyes and wondered how and when he could avenge himself against his tyrannical father? He knew his revenge on his father would not come now, but one day it would, sometime in the future, surely it would; he vowed to himself to make it so.

When Tostig heard that King Harold was on his way to confront him at Sandwich, he had quickly sailed away, taking with him men from that port, some had gone willingly, but most unwillingly. Tostig ordered that they should sail eastward from Sandwich, around Kent, then he turned north with all his fleet of sixty ships. His fleet was now made up from the eleven ships he had from his father-in-law in Flanders, plus those stolen from Sandwich, plus Copsig's fleet of seventeen additional ships which had joined them. Copsig's fleet had successfully rendezvoused with them, as planned, north of the River Thames estuary.

Copsig's fleet had sailed down from the Orkney Islands, off Scotland. These islands were part of King Hardrada's kingdom. Hardrada's permission had been forthcoming for these ships to harry the coast of England, prior to his own planned enterprise. All sixty ships were in full sail heading north to Northumbria, full of high expectations.

Tostig's grim determination would now be bringing him closer to his personal enemies, Earl Morcar of Northumbria and his brother Earl Edwin of Mercia. It was the middle of May, as Tostig's fleet sailed into the mouth of the River Humber.

'The raids along the Norfolk coast seem to have given you little pleasure, my lord,' Copsig saw the dark mood that radiated from Tostig. Both men stood at the prow of the ship looking intently at the looming headland they were fast approaching.

'Huh!' snarled Tostig, 'Why should we rejoice over such minor triumphs? They are not the reason we are at sea. A few towns and villages burnt and destroyed will not give me back my inheritance.' He forced a smile, then added, 'I do though, gain some satisfaction knowing it will cause Harold some mischief. Most men fled inland when they saw our sails, the few dozen English we put to the sword will not decrease Harold's army much,' Tostig paused, while thinking. 'However, if we burn York and Northumbria, then by God, they will know we are here.' Tostig gripped the side of his ship, his eyes flashed with hate. 'I was informed that King Hardrada's army of Norsemen will not be ready until the end of the summer. So by these actions we will seize the initiative and weaken England's defences for later in the year.'

'So why so glum, soon we shall be setting foot on your own soil of Northumbria. Look there is the coast and the district of Lindsey. How green and rich this land is.' So saying Copsig looked out from the ship toward the estuary, where he saw a dozen distant riders along the banks of the wide river.

Tostig turned and looked back toward the helmsman at the rear of the ship, to issue an order, 'We will sail further inland, to where there are long sandy banks at low tide. We can beach our ships there in the lea of the headland.' Tostig felt an unusual contentment in seeing the coast of his homeland again.

It was only the next day when Earls Edwin and Morcar struck. The Earls had been privy to the planned attack by Tostig and Copsig, knowing of Tostig's raids they had stationed lookouts along the coast, expecting Tostig would not resist an attack on his former Earldom of Northumbria. It was all too obvious to the brother Earls, so they had waited in hope, and now it had paid off.

Tostig's men had been led on inland, by the feigned running away of the Englishmen, of Mercia and Northumbria, in front of their advance. Several thousand of the brother Earl's men lay hidden in dikes and behind hedges, ahead of the advancing raiders, awaiting there to allow Tostig's marauding bandits to put enough distance between the invaders and their ships. They continued to advance toward what they thought were local farmers and tradesmen.

Suddenly the English ran out from their hiding places. Row upon row of very angry men, all heavily armed, ran across the path of the advancing Tostig. These local men had heard of the rapes and murder of their fellow country-folk, by these invading Flemish bandits from across the sea and they wanted revenge. The Anglo-Saxon drums of war began to beat a sinister, fear inspiring rhythm. The marauders now came face to face with professional Anglo-Saxon Housecarl soldiers, standing in battle array, in full armour. For a while, both sides silently looked at each other, the invaders were unsure of what to do next. The Earl's army then locked shields and began to move forward, slowly, but determinedly, stamping their weapons on their shields in time with the beat of the drums.

Tostig ordered his own men to lock shields. Gradually he made order from the confused panic of his men and awaited the clash of iron and steel. There was a sudden movement from his left wing, which made him look up. The men from this wing were running away, parallel to the lines of men, making a wide space between Tostig's men and themselves.

Tostig gaped in dumfounded horror, as a voice shouted across the void between the two lines of men. 'We are for King Harold and England.'

Tostig froze as he recognised Geffrei Gaimar leading the men he had hi-jacked from Sandwich. 'We are King Harold's men,' Geffrei again shouted as he and his men now swung round running in a large arc to join with Earls Edwin and Morcar.

A loud cheer went up from the ranks of the Housecarls, as they saw this new support running to join them.

'Bastard,' screeched Tostig. 'You and your families will pay for this, by God they will.'

Suddenly Tostig realised he had lost nearly half his men before even one blow had been dealt.

'Close ranks,' ordered Tostig.

With that the first onslaught from the Mercian, Northumbrian army and the men from Sandwich, struck Tostig with all the force they could muster. Battle-axe swung against shield and sword. Tostig's men were panicked. Men were falling, cleaved open with deadly blows from the English battle-axes. Flemish shields smashed. Within minutes it was clear Tostig must make a fighting retreat, if anyone was to stay alive. To run away would have been fatal, for any who took that road of escape. Men were dying all around Tostig and Copsig, some with their faces caved in, others with wide-open wounds, to their legs and arms. So desperate were the living to get back to their ships, many fell backwards over the bodies of their dead and dying comrades. Gradually they made order from the confusion, as the pace of their retreat quickened.

The Earls struck again, simultaneously at both ends and centre of Tostig's retreating wall. Defenders already stretched were forced to split into smaller units, to meet this fearsome attack. It was desperate fighting. Soon they were running. Against all the disciplined control Tostig had demanded to see from his men, they were now in full flight. Frantic efforts were made to get to the ships. Those who did manage to get back to the ships selfishly started to pull on the oars, some with only five or six men on board.

Slaughter took place on the sand banks of the river, as the English closed in on the remaining raiders who had been left stranded. Geffrei Gaimar, in full fury plunged his sword into every hated raider, who through some mishap had stumbled in his panic. The few, who had stood to fight, were soon cut down. Many who lay dead, even so, were still pierced by spear; sword or dagger, so great was the rage of the English.

Of the sixty ships that had so boldly sailed up the River Humber to attack this piece of Northumbria, only twelve made their escape to the open sea and of these, not one was fully manned. Tostig lay gasping for breath over the rail of the ship, as he stumbled into the vessel. Grabbing an oar, he forgot his rank and pulled with the other survivors, with all his weakened might to move the ship into deeper waters, away from the wall of steel, which now lined the riverbank. Copsig had also made his escape, but in a different ship, glad to be away from the increased resentment which he knew would madden Tostig in this defeat. Where now, were the reinforcement demanded of Tostig by King Hardrada?

The slaves, taken by Tostig's raids along the English coast, had been in the slower merchant vessels, captured from Sandwich. The support ships of the English Earls soon had most of these merchant vessels back in English hands. The female slaves had been spared a life, said to be worse than death.

In spite of this reversal, the remains of Tostig's ships, which now limped north, were laden with the plunder from the unfortunate English, who had suffered at the hands of these raiders. 'At least this plunder will help quieten Hardrada, once he knows how many of his ships are lost,' pondered a breathless Tostig as he pulled on an oar. He could not help but tremble at the thought of Hardrada's anger once the King knew how many of his potential ships had been lost, due to Tostig's own impulsive behaviour.

Tostig took his remaining battered raiders and headed his depleted fleet of ships north, to Scotland, where he knew he would get a welcome from King Malcolm III. King Malcolm had become a good friend of Tostig, when King Macbeth of Scotland had driven him out, forcing him to seek refuge at the English court of King Edward. Tostig knew he could wait there the whole summer if need be, until King Hardrada could rendezvous with him, for the larger invasion to come.

SUMMER

All stood with mouths agape, as they entered the nave. Words were lost to them while they arched their necks to look up at the high vaulted roof, almost oblivious to the trumpets whose call heralded the entry of Duke William and his Duchess, Matilda; the daughter of Baldwin, Count of Flanders, and sister of Tostig's wife. They took centre stage, but what a contrast of form this noble couple made; Duke William, tall and muscular, whilst his Duchess, Matilda, was small and plump, being only four-foot eight-inches tall; yet both commanded a fearsome respect from all. What Matilda lacked in height, she more than made up for with her tongue. She would berate any, and all, who crossed her, or who simply upset her. The force of her tongue could make warrior men cower.

The assembled crowd was awestruck; what a wonderful sight, what a wonderful building this is, so huge, so high, so much space. How could such a roof and of such a weight, be supported? 'Surely there is none finer than this building, in the entire world,' were the unspoken thoughts of those who stood there, silenced by this wonder.

All the great magnates of Normandy had been called to attend this dedication of his wife Matilda's new abbey at St Etienne, in Caen, on this the eighteenth day of June. It was truly becoming an eventful year. The abbey had a beautiful facade with semi-circular ornamental arches, ending in two large symmetrical square-shaped bell towers at the front of the building. The vast nave was supported by parallel rows of arches from floor level, with more arches on top of them. Few who were there this day, had ever seen such an immense space under one roof.

Outside, the magnificent cloisters looked out onto restful gardens. Herb gardens, studded clumps of flowering shrubs and herbaceous borders, carefully set out to be both ascetically pleasing and useful for their medicinal properties.

In 1049, when Duke William was only twenty-two years old, he had married Matilda of Flanders, his cousin. The Pope, who initially would not permit the wedding of cousins, finally had given his permission, but only when William and Matilda agreed to build two new abbeys. This was the first one, in which the women of holy orders would serve God; the other abbey, for the men, was still under construction. This was a lavish endowment of Matilda's new foundation of this new order. Both of these abbeys were to atone for their 'sinful marriage', in the eyes of the Pope.

Present in this new abbey, were the leaders of the planned expedition set to invade England. Carrying out this last solemn act, would, they believed, place the enterprise under divine protection. After the priests had carried out their service to dedicate this edifice to God, a silence, pregnant with anticipation hung over the congregation whilst Duke William mounted the rostrum.

William slowly surveyed the congregation, 'I, William, rightful King of England, Duke of Normandy and Maine, have had this wonderful building completed in honour of God and of the blessed Saint Etienne, in the town designated by the name of Caen. This building is for the salvation of the souls of my wife and my children, and to the glory of Normandy.' William paused, looked around, then raising the pitch of his voice continued, 'I call for the blessing of God on our just and rightful quest to claim the Kingdom of England.' A loud cheer arose from all those assembled. 'I call on God to bless our invasion plans.'

William again waited for the murmurs of excitement to subside, before continuing, 'There are those among you, who tried to council me against this great venture.' Nervously some of the barons realised this was aimed at them because many of them had become alarmed at the risks of this whole enterprise. 'Some tried to dissuade me.' William hit his chest with his fist as he said this, 'I will not tolerate any dissent, nor any hesitation in this our just and holy venture.' William now raised his voice to a shout, 'Yes! hear me oh God, this is a holy quest,' his voice echoed around the abbey. 'Has not the Pope of the holy church of God, blessed our plans? 'Has he not sent us a banner to fly in the faces of our foes? A banner consecrated by the Pope himself.' More cheers came forth.

William pointed to a solemn procession now entering the nave and walking slowly forward to where he stood. Four fully armed men surrounded the bearer of the Pope's holy banner, held high, as they made their way to the front of those assembled. The banner was square of shape, with a simple red cross on a pure white background, which quartered the banner into four equal sections. William waited, then took hold of the banner and held it up, as high above him as he could reach. 'This holy banner will go before us, so all will know our actions are the will of God; what more could we ask?' Wild shouts of joy echoed throughout the abbey.

'I listened to those who would seek to dissuade us. So I sought a Great Council of the Duchy,' William's eyes were glaring now, staring intently into the eyes of those barons who had dared to question his actions. 'And what did this great council decide?' His huge fist hit the rostrum with such force it cracked the wood. 'They gave us their general assurance of support. Our quest is blessed by God and man.' William waited for the cheers to subside. 'I will vow to you now, all those who fight with me on this holy venture will be rewarded. No matter how lowly they may be, they will receive rich rewards for their efforts in this holy cause. Lands, estates and farms will be theirs, if they draw their swords for me.'

Now the congregation was elated with joy. 'Nations are flocking to our cause,' he smiled, nodded his head and went on. 'Every day we are getting volunteers to join with our Norman arms, from Brittany, Maine, Flanders, France and Aquitaine. How can we lose? How can we lose?' Then for emphasis, he again shouted, 'How can we lose?'

The rapturous cheers and support echoed in their ears as Duke William and Matilda made their way out of the abbey, into the gleaming sunshine of this June day. She turned to look at her husband, proud to see men honour him like this with their praises.

In the long evening twilight of a June day, Alric accompanied Harold as they inspected the defences constructed around the Isle of Wight. Both men were struggling within themselves at the news that King Harald Sigurdsson of Norway, Hardrada, was planning to attack the north of England, with the help of Harold's own brother, Tostig.

'Alric, these long summer days and very short nights of an English summer are truly a great gift from God.' King Harold said wistfully, as he gazed out across the hay meadows, which were now in full flower.

'Indeed they are Sire. It gives us more daylight to prepare ourselves.'

'That is not what I meant Alric,' was Harold's sad reply, 'but you are right.' Harold, now speaking through clenched teeth, went on, 'This news from Northumbria is very grave indeed. I feel that on such a beautiful day as this, no one should have such news.'

'Indeed,' acknowledged Alric, 'it is very grim news; but I am glad the released captives from Sandwich were able to warn us, otherwise we would have been taken unawares.' Alric was struggling to reassure himself, as well as his king.

'How did we miss Copsig's fleet?' Harold mused, not really listening to what Alric was saying. 'Our fleet sailed south from London towards Sandwich, yet Copsig had somehow joined with my brother and their combined fleet slipped past us.' It vexed him to think of missing the chance to stop these coastal raids on his kingdom.

Alric did not want to dwell on what might have been and endeavoured to concentrate Harold's mind on the positive, which had come from his brother's raids. 'But at least we are now aware of Hardrada's intention to attack us in the north.'

Harold's mind was in turmoil, 'If we divide our army, we will have two weak armies. If we keep them together, where do we base them? Shall it be in the north or in the south?'

Alric was worried with the way Harold's thoughts were going. 'Sire, we cannot divide our army. We are strong enough to take on both of these devils. We can beat any force sent against us, but we must not divide the army, for that will weaken us.'

They now arrived at the King's chambers; Alric escorted Harold to where the war cabinet had gathered, in the great hall. This meeting King Harold had arranged.

It was with a sluggish step that King Harold entered the hall, the heavy and magnificent oak beams spanning the gathering below. Harold's brothers were there, Gyrth Earl of Essex, Leofwin Earl of Kent, as was Hakon, the King's nephew and Ordgar, General of the Fyrd.

Ordgar had estates near Shrewsbury, not far from the Welsh boarder; he was a stocky, agile, golden-haired Thane, known for his fiery character. He had rebelled against Edward-the-Confessor before this year, when he had seen Edward aligning with the Normans. Ordgar's men were long familiar with this firebrand of a general, who had been placed over them. It was this passion in Ordgar, which King Harold had found to be just what was needed in the character of a general, especially in this the hour of England's greatest need. All were now joined by Alric, General of the Housecarls, and King Harold II, Supreme Leader of the English army. The tension was plain to see on the faces of all as they sat down, with their king.

'You all know,' Harold began, 'we now could be facing two armies at opposite ends of the country. We are here to seek your wisdom, and God's direction, as to what actions we should take, where any action should be taken, and when.'

Alric gazed upon the scene, aware much was now at stake for them all, 'Sire, we may be facing two armies this year, although as yet that is not certain, as one may come this year and one next: we have no way of knowing. I urge you though, not to divide our army,' yet again Alric impassionedly put forward his fear. 'If we do, we will have two weak armies and both could fail.'

'True', nodded Leofwin in agreement, 'but if we do keep the army as one whole, we could be in the wrong place when an attack comes.'

Mutters of agreement came from the others.

'Let the navy guard the south, while the army guards the north,' Ordgar suggested, eager to enter the discussion.

'There is some merit in that,' agreed Harold.

'Then what?' butt in Leofwin, 'We will still have our forces divided.'

Harold felt agitated, 'We must be ready to face the invasion fleet of William. Already he is building a fleet, mustered at Rennes on the Normandy coast. We cannot let him land unopposed. He will be at his weakest when he lands. That will be the best time to drive him back into the sea.'

Alric tried to put the obvious question before them, 'Sire do we have any idea when these attacks will come, and which will come first?'

'Alric is right,' Gyrth supported. 'Which of these, our enemies, is the one most prepared, the one most advanced and ready to attack?'

Harold entwined his fingers before him, across his chest, almost as an act of prayer. 'William needs to build more ships, whereas Hardrada already has most of them.'

'So we go north then,' Ordgar said impulsively.

'I think not,' insisted Harold. 'Alric, how say you?'

'Sire, we must be ready on both fronts, but we cannot divide our army. The main roads of England are generally good, so we could set relays of couriers on fine horses, from York to London; and set fires on the hills as methods of signalling. All this we can organize. If we centralise our land forces we can then use our fleet; some ships to patrol our southern seas to give advanced warning of any action from Normandy, and some to patrol the north. Not only will this keep our forces in a state of readiness, it will give us early warning from both the north and the south.' Alric's reasoning seemed sound to all, except Ordgar.

'If we could miss Tostig's fleet, and let it slip through our fingers, we could miss these others also,' Ordgar flashed his rebuff.

'We must be more alert and patrol the seas more thoroughly,' countered Alric. 'Then set up a rapid set of mounted couriers. If we do this, any warning of an invasion can travel the country within two days.'

'But what about the army?' Leofwin's frustration was getting the better of him. 'We cannot move an army that quick if it is at the wrong end of the country when an attack comes. Then what do we do?'

A silence suddenly hung over the room. All knew they had very little choice.

King Harold sat back in his chair, and looked up at the rafters, 'It is evident we need to keep two armies on standby during the summer and into the autumn. We have no choice.' Harold looked glum, but Alric even more so.

'The Housecarls are mounted,' Alric stated the obvious. 'They could travel the country in a few days if need be. It is the Fyrd which is the problem, most are not mounted.'

'Bah!' Ordgar felt insulted at such a statement. 'Many have their own horses and they can bring more from the farms of their districts, for those who do not have horse. These the King can requisition, by an official order.'

'Cart horses?' scorned Alric. 'Such horses are more used to pulling the plough.'

'Damn you,' Ordgar thumped the table. 'It is better than nothing. Better than walking,' Ordgar fumed.

'Alric, do not disparage such horses,' Gyrth spoke up. 'They are able enough to carry a man great distances, and most Fyrd have access to such.'

Harold held his hand up for silence. 'Save your anger Ordgar and Alric, for our enemies. I will command the Fyrd to bring as many horses with them as they can muster, we must have at least two horses for each man. Also carts. Every village must donate a cart. We will need carts to carry the army's provisions, and their weapons; also to carry those without a horse. Those of the Fyrd, who are already at their stations and live not too far away, can return to their homes, to gather what horses and carts they can. We must be ready to be as mobile as possible.' Harold pause knowing what he had to say would not be what most wanted to hear. 'The Housecarls and Fyrd, who are already in the north, must stay there under the leadership of Earls Edwin and Morcar. The majority of the Housecarls will remain here on the Isle-of-Wight. If either army is attacked, the other must move swiftly to be by their side, preferably before full battle is struck. Delay any attack by harrying them, if you have to, until our full forces can be joined.'

The words and their meaning sank in to those around the table. No one spoke. It was at a time like this when a leader had to lead, and sometimes his decisions were hard to make.

Gyrth broke the silence, 'The fleet and army are all in a state of readiness. We will stay this way throughout the summer and autumn, if need be.'

'Gyrth,' Harold continued his orders, 'position some of the fleet and force at Sandwich, at the western end of the channel, where we can rely on the tides and prevailing wind to speed them to confront any attempted landing from Normandy.'

'We are forgetting one thing,' Ordgar raised his eyes to meet the others. 'Many of the Fyrd will want to return to their fields for the harvest, by late August. It is in their contract and oath to serve, that they return after two month of service. Otherwise we could have mass starvation within the country.'

Harold was all too aware of this major problem, and sought to side step the issue for now, 'I pray we will see action well before then, gentlemen. We are mobilising England on an unprecedented scale, never before has England been mobilised to such an extent.' Harold smiled to himself at the thought. 'We are ready for them, by God yes, we are ready for them.' Harold rose to his feet, 'Gentlemen, may God bless us all. Whatever the future holds, we will meet it with heads raised and swords drawn. We will fight to the end to protect this, our dear country. If we fall against our enemies, we will have spent our lives well and die in a noble cause protecting our people.' The full weight of Harold's words sank in to all there. 'We have been swept up by the wind of great events, but we will not be found wanting.' Harold now repeated, 'We must do all we can to protect this, our beloved country, and those we hold dear. Do your work well, for much depends upon it.' With that, Harold turned and walked out, his brow deeply furrowed.

The young slave hated this job. He stood in a deep pit, pulling on a long crosscut saw, while his master, the woodsman stood on top of the tree trunk in the fresh air. Each time the long saw was pushed by one, and pulled by the other, downward; thick chocking sawdust fell all over the slave, stifling his breathing, clogging his hair, his eyes, his nose and ears. He could hardly breathe. It was such hard work; he was wet through with sweat. Every muscle in his body ached. There were dozens of similar sawpits and all were full of sawdust. Each pit had two men pushing and pulling their long saws the full length of a tree. Others collected this sawn wood to make planks for the sides of ships by skilfully using an iron adze. The wood was carefully divided up, some to use as planks, some for long keels to make the foundation of the ships and some for the all important mast and mast-housings.

Everyone was so busy. All were hard at work. Hundreds of men toiled throughout these long summer days. The air was full from a cacophony of noise, from the sound of shouted orders, and the sound of saws on wood, of axes and adzes, the sound of hundreds of blacksmiths, beating out rhythms with their hammers. Woodcutters were leading their wagons, laden with timbre. Still others heated up the tar that would be placed between the planks of the clinker built hulls, to seal them from the sea; upon which they would soon be sailing. Large masts were cleverly honed into the precise shape required for their purpose. Others worked skilfully with their adzes to make the sawn planks smooth. Blacksmiths had their forges blasting out more heat, on an already hot day, while the sweating smith forged his iron, for the making of thousands of rivets, chains and weapons.

There was now no trades more profitable in Normandy, than that of the ship builder and armourer. Many a Norman warrior was seeing to it that the links of his chainmail coat, the 'hauberk', were strongly fastened together, as were the 'chausses' stockings, and an 'aventail', to cover the back and sides of his helmet. All had to be just right.

This scene was being repeated all along the shore of Normandy; in all shipyards, the noise of shipwright's mallets was constantly heard. The hemp-fields had had their borders enlarged, which caught the eye quickly with their brilliant green leafage, as the need for ever more rope was demanded. Everyone had a job to do and all were busy at it. The women provided food and drink for the men, none of whom had the time to leave their site of work. Rough tents were erected to accommodate the brief sleep period; which was allowed only during the very short time of midsummer darkness. No rest was made for anyone. All knew they were involved in a major project and none wanted to be seen, or dared to be seen, slacking from this great work, which was now to hand.

The invasion fleet was being prepared and readied at the mouth of the River Dives and neighbouring ports. William, together with his brothers and Matilda, surveyed this scene with satisfaction, as they sat on their horses, which had been regally regaled for the occasion. Matilda had a beaming smile on her face, for she had come to present her husband with a present, a present paid for from her own substantial fortune. They stopped at the top of a slight rise, William's party looked down on the harbour at the finest and largest longship, they, or anyone else, had ever seen.

William turned to his brothers, scarcely able to conceal his pride at what they now viewed. Pointing his finger with hand outstretched, William flushed with pride, 'That is a gift from my duchess. Have you ever seen a more magnificent sight my brothers?'

'No, never, she is the most beautiful thing I ever did behold,' Odo's mouth drooled with saliva, as his eyes stared in disbelief at the sight they had all come to see.

'My husband, the Duke, should only have the best there can be,' Matilda had not stopped grinning since they had suddenly come upon the sight which now transfixed them. 'This is truly fit for the Duke of Normandy, is it not?'

Odo was almost in a trance and said nothing, as they all rode down to the quayside.

Robert broke the stunned silence, 'William she is more than magnificent; she is truly glorious. All will now know they are in the presence of a great man when they see this. It is a fitting accolade for the Duke of Normandy.'

Odo recovered from this initial awe-inspiring sight, 'What will you call her?' he inquired.

'The Mora,' Matilda couldn't wait to get her words out, 'The Mora,' she again repeated. 'For it means "*mansion*" and no duke ever had a finer mansion than this. This will be Duke William of Normandy's flagship, the finest ship ever built. It will carry the Pope's holy banner to England.' She could not contain the pride in her voice and a tear of joy sprung to her eye. They all dismounted and walked over to the ship.

'The Mora' was over one hundred and thirty feet long, with thirty-six oars. The stern was decorated with a golden gilt figure of a child, a herald, whose right hand was holding a flag, pointing to England and whose left hand was pressing an ivory war horn to its lips. At the prow of the ship was an ornately carved head of a lion.

William pointed up at the red cross on the white background, fixed to the top of the mast; there was an affected tone to his voice, 'From the highest point of the mast will hang this framed banner from the Pope.' In his usual show of aggrandisement, he put his right hand on Matilda's shoulder, 'Once I set sail all men will see I am on a holy mission, blessed by the Pope and riding in the finest ship ever put to sea. It is a fitting tribute to my mission.' William stood transfixed, both clenched fists thrusting into his waist, gazing upward at the elegant mast. 'Once the sail has been unfurled, it will show the two rampant lions of

Normandy. This crest I will make the symbol of England, in place of the Golden Dragon of Wessex.'

'Lord Duke,' Robert beckoned to a man to come over, he had been standing close to the noble party. 'Let me introduce you to Stephen Fitz-Erard, he will be the captain of the Mora.'

Stephen Fitz-Erard bowed low, as William turned and smiled at him. 'Well captain, what do you think of her?' asked William.

Unlike most Normans, Stephen was bearded, a man of middle age, with a belly larger than most, 'My lord she is simply wonderful. No man ever, was the captain of a finer ship than this,' He was a happy man at the prospect of commanding such a vessel.

'Then see that she serves my course well captain,' William suddenly spoke harshly and with force. 'We must be ready to sail by August. See to it that all other captains know this. We sail the first week of August.'

'Yes my lord. It shall be done as you say.'

William and his party remounted their horses, and pulled to ride away. As he did so, William turned to Stephen, and shouted back to him, 'Serve me well captain and afterward you will be exempt from tax for evermore.'

Stephen bowed low again, hardly able to believe his luck.

During the month of August, the weather in England had turned foul. As so often can happen in these northern latitudes, summer does not necessarily mean good weather, and the sun of spring and early summer had given way to rain and storms. King Harold gazed out at the relentless rain.

His arms felt like lead, after all the hard training he had gone through with his men, for Harold made a point of it and would not shirk from such physical exertions.

Harold was troubled, he felt as though the walls of the castle, on the Isle-of-Wight, were hemming him in. Unanswered questions constantly raced through his mind. How much longer would he have to wait? Who would come to attack his people first? Where would they attack? He had brought the main strength of his forces here to the Isle-of-Wight, but there was no enemy in sight.

Harold had seen men face death before in his battles with the Welsh, so he knew they must be well trained to face men who would kill them if they could, without even thinking about it. He knew his army would not let him down, but somehow though, he had to keep their spirits up. He knew the men would take their confidence from his own manner; so he constantly kept up a good spirit with them, and as a result their camaraderie was high. When though, the rain prevented too much activity, he then let his own thoughts dwell on what lay ahead. The unknown unknowns; there were too many questions that would not leave his mind. 'If only I knew where and when they would strike,' he kept saying to himself.

Horses and men were constantly drilling in the castle yards, every Housecarl, Fyrd and Thane had heeded the call and gathered to the service of their King, two-thirds to the Isle-of-Wight and one-third to the Earls Edwin and Morcar in Northumbria. The daily wearing of the soldier's chainmail was weighing heavy on them. Through the winding country-lanes went troops of footmen and mounted horsemen. All summer long, armed men were collecting at Harold's headquarters from every part of England, wherever his summons had wakened a favourable response. The mutual respect between Harold and his army deepened as the months wore on. A respect and love, that only soldiers truly understand, when they must entrust their lives into the support and protection of their comrades.

The churches had become crowded daily as men went to pray and the priests urged God to protect England. War was on everybody's mind.

The pink and white wild roses, of England, which each year festooned the hedgerows of early summer were now all gone, the wild sweet blackberries were ripening and the harvest growing on a pace. It was already late summer and the young apple fruits were getting larger on the boughs.

Harold was beginning to feel hamstrung by the limitations of the Fyrd. They were duty bound to serve, but only for a limited period. Once the harvest time came they would want to go home to gather it in, otherwise they, and their families, could face starvation during the coming winter. In addition, the supplies to feed all his large army were getting very low. 'Please God, let them attack now,' Harold prayed. 'Let them attack, while we are strong.'

But they did not come, and the summer days started to grow perceptively shorter; they had only a few more weeks of summer left.

Ricbert and his son Wilfred had followed Earl Edwin's call, along with hundreds of other Mercian men. All the fighting force of Mercia had moved north to York, joining with those from Northumbria. It looked such a strong force. Young Wilfred had never seen so many people before; York was much larger than Nottingham. He was quite excited by it all and daily came to tell his father what he was learning. He had been given an Anglo-Saxon war drum, with which he beat giving off a deep tone: he was being taught the signals for the troops. There were so many of these to learn, but he took pride in doing it well.

Ricbert was glad to see his son so happy, and secretly delighted that as a drummer-boy he would probably not be in the thick of any fighting.

As an archer Ricbert had taken a lot of jibing from the others, because his skill with the bow was not thought so well of. Those who swung the great and deadly Anglo-Saxon battle-axes, in daily training, thought themselves to be so much better for having this skill and streangh, than those of a mere archer. They looked down on someone who did not get close up to the enemy, who simply sniped at them from a distance. 'You can't even see who you are killing, with that thing,' they joked; but did so with a sting in their tone.

Still, Ricbert also had his sword and shield, which he practiced with daily, and when he was not practicing, he was honing its edge, or yet getting more flights for his arrows. All of the army would daily sharpen and hone their weapons, until the edges were so sharp that just running a finger gently along it could cut through the skin. He could not help but admire the feared battle-axes and the men who swung them with such ease. It made him wonder how anyone dared to face up to such a weapon.

Ricbert constantly worried about his wife and children on the farm. There was so much work to do on the farm and he was not there to see it done. He knew his wife and children would try, but equally, he knew they must struggle. What worried him most was the harvest, it was now late August and the harvest should be starting soon. Would his wife, Mildryth, know not to get the grain in if it was wet or even damp? It was frustrating knowing all the work he knew needed to be done at his home, and yet here, in spite of the daily training, there was still a lot of time when they were doing nothing. In fact, all this waiting was getting to him, nothing seemed to be happening; where was this enemy?

Many of the men were beginning to get bored. Most of them were used to working very hard every day at home, and they could not get used to the idea of having some time on their hands; and now, the summer had turned so wet, every day it was raining.

It had all been so very urgent and exciting at the start of this campaign for Ricbert, but that feeling had now passed. All he wanted now was to get this over with and return home.

'God curse this wind,' Duke William looked up to the sky, with his brother Odo. 'How long must it blow from the north? This is summer,' he sarcastically exclaimed, 'or rather, it is supposed to be. We cannot put to sea with a north wind against us. We will be blown back to our own shores.' William shouted a prayer to God, into the wind, 'Dear God, hear my plea. Send us a favourable wind, one to blow our fleet to that accursed isle of England. They have put forth an Archbishop, not approved of Rome. Let them suffer for their sin. In the name of Christ, hear my plea.'

It can't continue like this,' Odo sought to reassure his brother.

'It is already mid August and we should be at sea by now.' William's frustration was making him constantly irritable, this along with the stress of organising such a large invasion force. 'This army is ready to sail now, yet just as we are ready to go, this wind has started to blow against us. We need to get this fleet to sea.'

William paced up and down in vexed irritation. Both men had been careful not to let their frustrations be seen by the armed forces. For their men, 'This was all part of the plan;' except that it was not.

William looked up at the banner by the weather vane on the church tower; it was rent and tattered by the raging wind. He sat down and took his head in his hands. He was dismayed, 'To fail Odo, will make me the jest of all Christendom. If Rome is with us, why does God hide his face? Our preparations have been complete now for some days.' William paced the floor, 'We have five hundred war ships and six-hundred supply ships all ready to sail. God grant us a favourable wind.'

'Well it could be to our advantage, bother,' Odo thought it wise to raise William's spirit. 'If Hardrada attacks before we can, it will weaken the English.'

'I'll not hear of that again, you bloody fool,' William erupted and turned on Odo in fury. 'We must attack first. If Hardrada wins the battle then we are faced with the possibility of a split and shared kingdom. If Harold beats Hardrada then Harold will be viewed as the stronger and thousands more will flock to his banner. We must attack first, we must.' William was becoming gravely concerned that all his plans could be wrecked and the vast sums of money spent would be lost. He well knew that to fail now would be his downfall.

The Viking army of Northmen, which King Hardrada had assembled, was extensive. It included his main battle hardened force from Norway, together with forces from Iceland, the northern Faeroe Islands, the Shetlands and the Orkney Islands. He also had men from the Isle-of-Man, as well as many from highland Scotland. Men had even come to join him from the towns on the east coast of Ireland and from as far away as Greenland, with still other volunteers, or mercenaries from Denmark and Sweden. Men, from all these Viking lands, had given their ships and crews willingly, to become part of Hardrada's great fleet.

Many said Hardrada was Christendom's best warrior. The Icelanders in particular loved their King. He had been of great help to them, ten years earlier, when their country had suffered a hard famine; he had sent them food and timber, so now they would happily fight for him.

The fleet had sailed from the Solunds, just north of Bergen in Norway and now, on the first day of September, it was anchored in the harbour of the Shetland Islands. Hardrada's fleet was to head next for the Orkney Islands, where Tostig's fleet of twelve ships would be joining him. All told, when the fleet would be fully assembled at Kirkwall in the Orkneys Islands, the Norwegian King would be heading a fleet with a total strength of three-hundred ships, carrying between ten and twelve-thousand men. The very best of all the Norse warriors were within this invasion fleet.

It had taken two days to sail from Norway to the Shetland Isles. In open sea the winds had been very favourable, blowing straight down from the north, thus enabling a great turn of speed to be had, as they sailed due south. The largest ship in this fleet was Hardrada's flagship the 'Long Serpent', which, similar to Duke Williams', could house thirty-six rowers. The sail had on it Hardrada's emblem, the black raven. From the mast flew a pure white triangular banner, also with the fearsome black raven emblazoned upon it. All knew this emblem well.

On board his flagship with Hardrada were most of his family, his wife, Queen Elizabeth, his two daughters Maria and Ingrid and his youngest son, Prince Olaf. Hardrada knew that northern England had a large population of Scandinavian settlers from past campaigns, who he hoped would give him their allegiance. This was to be no ordinary raid, no indeed; this was going to be a full invasion. Hardrada had brought along his family, because he intended to stay. His oldest son, Magnus had been left behind in Norway and declared King of Norway, by his father. All was set for the full and total occupation of England by this Viking army.

Alric was uneasy. Ordgar stood there with an ashen face, embarrassed and anxious, in the presence of his King and Alric, General of the Housecarls. 'Sire,' Ordgar fumbled for his words, 'It is the first day of September. The harvest is ready to gather in and the Fyrd have been in arms all summer long.'

King Harold nodded, but said nothing.

'Also sire, our food and provisions are getting very low. The men should be allowed to go home.' Ordgar was trying to justify what he himself did not really want; but the law said the Fyrd could return to their land, once two months had been served in the Kings' service, and they had already served much longer than that.

'And what if we are attacked?' Alric glared, unable to conceal his wrath. 'What then?'

King Harold acknowledged the inevitable, 'True they have served us well and trained hard throughout this summer.' Then through a thin smile, said, 'I do not think we will be attacked now. The season for war is about at its end. The English winter is not a time when a foreign army will want to campaign in the open. It will be too cold and wet. The roads will be deep in mud, their men will become wet and frozen in the open, baggage trains will not progress and food will be difficult for an army to find.'

Alric looked dumfounded. He knew what was coming.

Harold went on, 'Bastard Duke William will not risk crossing the sea now, when the storm season is about to start.' He looked Alric in the eye, 'And we have heard nothing of King Hardrada. I feel they will also wait until early next spring, when they will have the chance for a full campaigning season.' Harold sat at his table, with half-eaten food on it. He put his chin in his hand, and then uttered his heart-rending order, 'Ordgar inform the Fyrd they may return to their homes eight days from now.'

'No!' Alric stood up knocking over the stool he had been sitting on. 'No, you can't do this my Liege. There is still a month of campaigning left.'

'Alric we have no choice, the men must go home to get the harvest in.'

'Sire the women have been working the fields, and they can continue doing so. We must keep the men here.'

'Do you really think they will attack now, with just one month left of the campaigning season left?'

Alric hesitated. In his heart, he knew it was still possible, for at least one of the foreign armies to attack, but he could say nothing to prove it. 'Yes sire I really believe one or both may still attack us.'

Harold's mind was in turmoil, what should he do? He stood behind the table, placing both hands heavily downward upon it, 'Then send riders to all parts of the country. If we are attacked we will recall the Fyrd.' Turning to Ordgar he added, 'The Fyrd may be disbanded on the Nativity of Saint Mary, the eighth day of September, eight days from now; until the spring: unless that is, we need to recall them. They may leave our Isle-of-Wight base on that day.'

Ordgar could not bring himself to look at Alric. Turning away, he left the room, to inform his men. Harold had now committed himself, only time would tell if this was the right decision to take.

Alric was left standing there with his mouth agape. Harold shared the same unease as Alric, but he was hamstrung by the law of the land. Unmoving and still with his hands placed firmly on the table, Harold continued, 'Alric, after the Fyrd have left, move the Housecarls to London, on the twelfth day of September, and I will sail with the fleet that day to meet you there, in London. Our English army will then wait in London to meet whichever army comes first; if come they will.' Harold slapped the palm of his hand onto his forehead. 'It is seldom an army will attack a foreign land, this late in the campaigning season.' However, both men, so experienced in war, knew this was a calculated gamble they were taking.

The large sweeping bay of Kirkwall in the Orkney Islands had never before seen so many ships at anchor there. This small but important town was abuzz with excitement. Kirkwall's importance was due to the residence of the Norse Earls of Orkney being situated there. The people there were used to seeing regular trade visits from Viking parties from far afield, but nothing like this had been witnessed before. Not only were they hosts to the largest fleet anyone there had ever seen, their King and his family were with them as well.

There was trouble and tension inside the large hall of residence, wherein lived the joint Earls of the Orkney Islands, Paul and Erlend.

'What in the name of hell do you call this? Is this all you have gathered to join our fleet?' King Hardrada's voice bellowed out, and reverberated around the hall, he was not pleased to see Tostig and Copsig standing before him, in this, one of his Norwegian Earldoms. His face reddened, as if about to burst,

'You bring me just twelve ships, manned by Flemish and Scots. This is all you have! This is all?' Enraged he yelled his words at the two men standing before him. 'Where are the men and ships you said you would get me from your former estates?' Hardrada did not wait for an answer, 'Where are they?' his voice now reaching an even higher pitch. Everyone, justifiably, felt terror when Hardrada was angry. The hall kept silent, no one willing to become the target in Hardrada's maddened state.

For a moment, anger twisted Tostig's face. He took a deep breath, and bowed low; he felt he had done a lot to stretch Harold's forces across the country. If he had not raided the way he had, then Harold could have been able to concentrate his army more than he had done. As it was, Tostig felt he had at least kept much of his force together, by fleeing for the summer to Scotland, to the court of King Malcolm.

Tostig struggled to compose himself, 'Sire we had sixty ships and men we were bringing to your side, but bad winds and treachery took them from us,' he lied, to cover his embarrassment.

Copsig turned and beckoned to his men waiting nervously at the back of the long room, 'Sire we have brought you much plunder to offer for your cause, all taken from the English.'

The large, long wooden hall was thick with smoke from two blazing fires. At the end of the hall, the doors opened and several large wooden chests were carried in and placed before the King. The King remained impassive, pulling intently on his beard, as he did when he was angry. Hardrada sat impassively awaiting to see what Copsig would bring before him. Hardrada was seated at the top table together with his queen, his daughters and his son. The chests were all opened to reveal, coins, silverware, gold and bronze, taken from the harbours, civic centres and churches of England; all victims of Tostig's raids. It was displayed before the King, along with many swords, daggers and war axes. Copsig scooped up large bundles of this looted treasure and placed it in a heap at the King's feet.

There was a visible change in Hardrada's countenance. 'Well this is something,' he grumbled, not wishing his pleasure to be seen, or even suspected. He looked and waited before speaking again. Hardrada knew he needed the inside knowledge from Tostig, of the rivers and tides along the coast of Northumbria. 'Your treasure allows you to keep your command,' he again paused, his glaring eyes staring intently at Tostig before continuing, 'even though you lost us so many ships,' he sneered. Then with a dismissive action, to humiliate Tostig further, he ignored the treasure laid out before him, turned to his son, seated by his side and asked, 'Prince Olaf, how many ships and men do we now have out there in the bay?' He gestured with a sweep of his arm.

'Father we have three-hundred ships and ten-thousand men,' smiled Olaf. A cheer went up from those assembled, who until now had not been sure which way Hardrada's feared temper and his displeasure, would take him. They had all seen men die for less than what Tostig had done to Hardrada's cause.

'We will rest here for a few more days, prepare our weapons well and then we sail for England. The wind is perfect, blowing from the north. It will take us due south, straight to England.' Those gathered were glad the tension had been broken and sought to lighten the dark mood, which had pervaded before. Fists thumping on the tables raised the noise of the assembly to a crescendo. Hardrada lifted his hand for the excited warriors to quieten down. 'This venture is not be one to take women on, so I will leave my wife, Queen Elizabeth and my two daughters, Princesses Maria and Ingrid behind, here in the Orkney Isles. My son, Prince Olaf, will stand with his father in the face of battle.'

Prince Olaf beamed with delight, 'It will be an honour to fight by your side father.' With that, Olaf drew his sword high above his head and shouted, 'For King Harald Sigurdsson of Norway.' Anticipation shone in the eyes of the warriors, and then Olaf shouted again, 'King Hardrada.' Cheers, stamping of feet and the thumping of tables filled the long Viking hall.

Paul and Erlend, the joint Earls of the Orkney Islands and subjects of Hardrada, were seated at the same long table with the King and his family. These Earls were subjects of Hardrada. The King now turned to Earl Erlend, a young man, keen to prove his mettle, and eager to fight alongside his King, 'Many Orkney men have been keen to show their prowess and join with us. This is an Earldom I am truly blessed with, it would please me to offer one of my daughter's in marriage to you upon our return.' Further cheers echoed around the rafters of the hall. 'More beer all round,' he demanded. Men, who had been troubled by Hardrada's possible reaction to Tostig, now dropped their guard and started to gulp down more beer, as the foaming flagons were carried into the room.

This act of betrothal had not been entirely unexpected, as this arrangement had been discussed before, quietly and in private. However, this news was greeted with glee by the people of Orkney, who believed this marriage would bring them great security and prosperity.

This was on the twelfth day of September, the same day on which King Harold of England now sailed with his fleet from the Isle-of-Wight to London, and the same day where events now began to move, across the English Channel.

Duke William felt seasick. This great invasion fleet had gathered at the mouth of the River Dives, but the weather refused to cooperate with William, who had been trapped by unfavourable Northern winds for a month. These

149

same winds that were now helping King Hardrada were also hindering Duke William from leaving port.

Stephen Fitz-Erard, captain of the Duke's flagship, the Mora, had not wanted to sail. 'My lord, the sea is too high, the wind comes in from the north, we will be blown back to shore,' he pleaded; but his plea was to not listened to.

'Captain Fitz-Erard,' retorted William, 'It is already the twelfth day of September; we sail now! There is too much at stake to risk further delay.' William was in charge of a multi-national force of restless warriors, who would not want to wait around too long; they could soon turn into a problem for him, if he could not deliver on his promises to them.

The day was grey and dull with no break in the heavy, angry clouds; even so, once Duke William had commanded it, the fleet had put to sea. The horses were difficult enough in normal times, trying to control them in these open ships; but now it was becoming impossible to hold them in a safe position on board the ships in such a rough sea. Even though the horses were blindfolded and roped into holding bays, they were open to the weather and did not like the pitching and rolling of the sea. The animals became frightened, stamping their hooves. Some began to kick out, straining on their leashes. Frantically the men struggled to keep them calm; but it was soon evident they were failing.

Several ships' crew soon began to lose control of their horses. High-spirited warhorses did not take kindly to the pitching and rolling of the sea, and neither did many of the men. Some of the horses eventually broke free; then in their panic tried to jump into the sea, unhinging the delicate balance of the ships. It was not long before a dozen or so ships were floundering under the extreme difficulty of controlling the warhorses. Shouts and squeals of the men mingled with the terrified neighing of the horses as several ships carrying them began to capsize. Many horses were now in the water, aimlessly swimming in the foaming sea, hopelessly trying to find somewhere to go, even trying to climb back onto the ship, with the crew having to fight them off. Men were drowning, being quickly sucked under by the weight of their chainmail armour.

'William, we are losing men and ships,' shouted Richard above the wind, rain now stinging his eyes. 'We must seek shelter; we cannot afford to lose any more ships and men.'

William squinted up his eyes against the wind and rain. 'The bells of hell are ringing against us,' he acknowledged to his close friend. 'God damn this weather.' William uttered a curse against the elements, which could hardly be heard by others. 'We have the holy banner and relics blessed by the Pope, and yet God still does not smile on us.'

'It could be that he wants us to wait,' Richard concluded.

Duke William was thoughtful. A great deal depended on the success of this mission. If he failed it would be a signal for others to rise up against him, and because of the money already spent on this invasion, his country would become bankrupt. No one would fund another such venture. William knew he had to succeed; he dare not fail. Already there were ships and men to be replace; he could not afford to lose any more. All these thoughts went rushing through his head, as he now used all the power his voice could muster to shout out an order, 'Captain Fitz-Erard, turn about, head for the estuary of the River Somme, head for Saint-Valery-sur-Somme.' Wet through, William slumped back onto a chest containing his expensive clothes.

The Mora turned so it was now with the wind, and headed in the direction ordered by William, but other ships were not so fortunate. As they turned and tried to follow their flagship, more ships succumbed to the panic of the horses, the pitching and rolling of the sea. As they turned sideways into the wind, they became unstable and simply rolled over. Norman warriors were flailing about in the water; many unable to swim became doomed to a watery grave. Still other ships were now well out of sight and they had not seen the Mora turn, with no way to know what was happening, so a few continued to sail onward.

Looking forlorn and bedraggled William and Richard felt despair. Duke William's invasion plans were now very close to becoming a total disaster.

FALL

For three days, the weather had been calm and quiet. Summer had ended and it was the beginning of autumn. In these northern climes, the fall often sees warmer and better weather than that of the summer, and this year was to be no exception.

The sixteenth day of September dawned with a terrifying sight for the people of the town of Scarborough, on the Yorkshire coast of north-eastern England, part of the Earldom of Northumbria. The sweep of the large south bay was full of Viking longships. The largest ship had the banner of the black raven flying from its mast. They had arrived during the night, and now all three-hundred ships, of King Hardrada's invasion fleet, were either anchored or beached, in the lee of the huge headland, jutting out into the sea, giving them a natural shelter.

The town of Scarborough was built on the steep south-facing slope of the headland, beneath an old Roman lookout tower, which still stood on the highest point of this promontory. From this vantage point, a viewer overlooked both the north and the south sweeping bays of the sea. The English garrison and inhabitants, of Anglo-Saxon and Danish origins, looked up with dismay at the normally peaceful hill towering above their small town, for now it was swarming with Vikings. The town only had about fifty homesteads, all of them built of wood with straw-thatched roofs. Around the town was a wooden stockade, atop of an earthen ditch. Vikings were assembling on the beach in front of the town, while many others had climbed the steep hillside above and were now looking down on the town's people below. About two-hundred English manned the stockade, preparing to defend themselves.

'I don't believe this,' said Tostig as he formed his men up along the beach. Shocked by the sheer audacity of the English, he turned to face his men with a fixed smile on his face, 'They think they can fight us?' The Viking warriors laughed, and beat their shields with their swords.

The giant form of Hardrada towered above Tostig, 'For God's sake, they do not really believe they can fight us, do they? Tell them who we are,' he thundered, 'and demand they submit to me as their King.'

Tostig and Copsig strode forward toward the English defences, 'I am Tostig your rightful Earl. I have come with King Harald Sigurdsson of Norway, King Hardrada; he has come to rightfully claim his English throne. Submit to him now, and join with us.' Tostig waited. It was evident some discussion was going on behind the stockade. Irritated by this delay in giving any form of response, Tostig repeated his command, 'King Hardrada demands you submit to him now.'

'Piss off you traitor,' was the sudden and unexpected response, from an Englishman with a strong northern accent. 'We had enough of you before, when you misruled Northumbria. We'll not see you back here among us. Go back from where you came; you stinking traitor.'

Tostig nostrals flared wide open, his face reddened. To have such an insult in front of his men was unforgivable. 'Who dares to talk to me thus?' demanded Tostig. Copsig stood transfixed by his side, with mouth agape.

'Go back and tell your King, the people of Scarborough shit on his claim. And tell him Thorgil, an Alderman and Thane of the Council of Scarborough, who speaks for our town; say to him we refuse his illegal claim.' Thorgil and all who stood with him knew these words could be their death-knell, but they would rather die than submit to this alien invasion.

Tostig was rooted to the spot with anger. Looking straight at the defenders, he slowly brought his thumb and forefinger to his nose, lifted his nostrils slightly, and then blew a ribbon of snott, onto the ground in front of them.

Incensed, the Vikings began to form into a regiment of three-thousand men, all with shields high and weapons ready. Suddenly with deep, guttural yells, they ran at the stockade. Into the deep ditch, they jumped or fell, then in frenzy tried to scramble up the other side. It was difficult for them to get a hold, so steep was the climb. Many slid back down; others managed to get a grip on the stockade only to have their fingers chopped through with an Anglo-Saxon battle-axe. Ladders were carried quickly forward. Dozens of scaling ladders were placed against the stockade, yet each time one man managed to reach the top, his head was cleaved open by a blow from above from a long dreadful battle-axe. As Vikings fell into the ditch, arrows rained down on them from the stockade, killing and wounding many more. Another wave of Vikings followed, but with the same results. Soon it was impossible for them to get into the ditch without standing on the bodies of their fallen comrades.

High above the town, the Vikings on the hillside had begun to roll rocks down on the town below, but most of these rocks just stopped in the ditch before they could even hit the stockade. However, this action gave Hardrada an idea.

'Enough of this,' barked the loud voice of Hardrada above the mêlée. 'Pull back. There is a better way than this. They will suffer for their resistance.'

There was now some confusion, and they all looked to their King for orders. 'Take anything that will burn and build a great pile high on the hillside above the town.' Hardrada was going to burn them out. Throughout the rest of the day, a steady stream of men could be seen walking up and down the steep hill above the town, until several huge bonfires were established up there. An alarming silhouette, as the sun was setting.

Other Vikings had been eagerly gathering in fresh food from around the district. The harvest from the land and the sea had been freshly garnered, so now there were good pickings for these invaders.

It was a long night for the English defenders, wondering what the next day would bring, but knowing it would certainly bring a fight. As the sun broke the following morning, the great fire, high above the town, was lit. Soon it was blazing. Then, using long wooden forks, made for the purpose, heaps of this burning material was pitched forward, rolling it down the hillside, onto the helpless town below. Within minutes, the stockade was ablaze, as were several houses. After an hour or so, the whole town was an inferno, with many defenders dying in the ensuing conflagration.

When it was evident the peak of the fire was beginning to die down, the order was given, 'Now you can attack,' laughed Hardrada.

And attack they did. Running down from the hillside above, the Vikings swarmed through the ruined stockade, and on into the town, where they slew all, and any they could. No quarter was given, young and old alike had a sword thrust through them or were cleaved open with a blow from a battle-axe. Copsig dived into the thick of the fighting; not wishing to be left out of what had now become nothing more than butchery. Copsig saw a defender putting up a gallant resistance. With the defender's back to him, Copsig slid his blade along the defender's chainmail and into his face, cutting deep into his cheek. It was not long before the remaining exhausted defenders of the town surrendered.

'Bring them to me,' said Hardrada quietly, in sharp contrast to his earlier shouted words. Those who knew him, understood, only too well, when he spoke in soft tones like this, that Hardrada was at his most dangerous and most angry. It was this, the quiet tone of his, which many feared. The bedraggled group who stood before Hardrada included the outspoken Thorgil.

Blood caked his mouth and his right eye was swollen shut. Thorgil had known worse, from the Welsh wars, when he had joined with Earl Harold. He was proud of the way the others had refused to show fear, in the face of this Viking attack. He watched as Hardrada strode purposely toward him.

'So, you thought you could deny me did you?' Hardrada's eyes blazed. 'You have cost me many good men. Now you will pay.'

Thorgil and the remaining defenders were all stripped down to their loin clothes. Bare-chested their arms were bound behind them. Then they were hoisted upside down by their ankles, and tied to the frames of the doorways, which had remained unburned and still standing. For what seemed like an age, they hung there until a dozen or so, were similarly trussed up, awaiting their fate. Screams suddenly pierced the air, as a knife was thrust into the stomachs of the hapless victims, opening up a large gash through which their intestines were roughly pulled out, to hang down over the victim's chest and face. Death would not be quick.

'Leave them there like that,' Hardrada ordered through gritted teeth. 'Let them know why they are dying, and let others learn from this.' Hardrada then walked away from the grizzly sight, leaving them in writhing agony. He reached the beach where the captive women and girls had been taken. Terrified, they had all been herded together. The men looked at Hardrada expectantly. He responded, 'Enjoy their bodies my men. Do with them as you will.' With a sickly smile on his lips, he made his way through his gloating men, who were all keen to obey this order. 'But we will take none alive from this town. Let this serve as an example to any who choose to resist us. There is little ship room for them anyway. There will be time for you to take more women when our fighting is done.'

Hardrada hoped that the news of this atrocity would make Englishmen realise there was nothing left now for them, if they would preserve their lives, but to submit to him King Hardrada as the King of England.

Later the next day, the eighteenth day of September, Hardrada's invasion fleet sailed further south. Scarborough was still burning and the bodies of their many victims lay unburied. Early on the morning of the nineteenth, this vast fleet turned westward toward the mainland of England, under the protection of Spurn Point, at the estuary of the mighty River Humber. Tostig was now in his home waters and knew the tides and the areas of danger very well. On board his flagship and under the banner of the black raven, Hardrada held a war council. He had listened carefully to Tostig's directions so far, but now he was concerned.

Hardrada discussed his thoughts. He knew if he made a wrong decision now, things could go seriously wrong. 'If we disembark here we are protected from the waves of the sea, but still subject to these fierce tides.'

Tostig looked at him, for the first time he realised Hardrada's age was beginning to give him a little more caution than he had hitherto displayed. At fifty years-old, Hardrada had already reached an age beyond that of the previous six Kings of Norway.

Now, looking concerned Hardrada continued, 'We cannot leave our ships beached, high and dry for six hours at a time. To be stranded on the shore like that will limit our movements. We need a place where our ships are safe, and where the tides will not leave us stuck on sand or shale, twice a day.'

'Sire,' ventured Tostig, 'I have long considered this situation, and therefore have reconnoitred the area well. There is a place ideal for your grand fleet. It is both secure, and safe from ambush. There is a town called Riccall, far inland from here on a tributary of the River Humber, called the River Ouse. By using the fast flow of the tides, we can make five to six knots each hour. Riccall will make a good base from where we can strike at the city of York, which is your expressed desire.'

This was what Hardrada wanted to hear, 'If you are wrong in this, there will be a price to pay.' He tilted his head and looked sideways at Tostig; to be sure, that he had understood this intended and sinister warning. Hardrada then acknowledged Tostig's advice, 'York then will be our target, which will become our stronghold for the winter.'

'You will not regret it sire. The river is long and has many turns, but it is wide and I have often sailed it without mishap.' Tostig's confidence was infectious. He went on to explain, 'At Riccall there is a safe way to leave the fast moving currents. The River Ouse takes a sharp turn there, to the south. This has created a swampy hinterland, with a lake, a safe area of large water, well away from the main flow of the river. It will require navigation to be skilfully carried out when leaving the main river, but I can explain this to your captains.' Tostig was very satisfied with himself. For his own security, he knew he needed make himself a great asset to this Viking army in order to stay alive.

'Good. So be it then.' Hardrada stood up, 'The warships will go now, and the supply ships can follow as soon as possible. We will put riders on both banks of the River Ouse to protect us from ambush and to discourage those who would seek to forewarn of our coming.' Then turning to look backward over his shoulder, he looked fixedly straight at Copsig, 'Copsig, and see to it. You will ride along the banks of the river.' Hardrada knew, very well, that if any English were encountered along the banks of the river, it would be Copsig that would be killed. He did not like, nor trust this man, and considered him to be expendable.

Before long, the invasion force of ten-thousand men navigated inland along the River Ouse. As ordered, riders headed by Copsig, were dispatched along both banks as the fleet made its way to Riccall near York, in Northumbria. Tostig was gleeful.

Now at last he could destroy those who had evicted him from his Earldom, just ten months before.

The proud old city of York had closed its gates and a sombre mood hung over the city. A thick pallor of smoke, from the many cooking fires of the dwellings, hung in the still air, because for once, there was no wind to blow the smoke away. The stillness of nature, added to the air of expectancy pervading over all. The brothers Earl Edwin of Mercia and Earl Morcar of Northumbria had already received news of the sacking of Scarborough. Now they had another messenger standing before them, informing them of the fortification of Riccall. 'Unassailable', had been the messenger's considered comment on the situation there.

Edwin rose to his feet, his mouth agape in disbelief, 'How many men did you say? Ten-thousand?' He could hardly grasp the reality of the situation. 'My God!' He was lost for words. 'Ten-thousand Norse near York,' he again repeated, and began to pace up and down with his hands held tightly behind his back, muttering over and over again, 'Ten-thousand! Ten thousand!' He just stared open eyed at his younger brother.

Suddenly he shook himself, as though getting free from an invisible grip. 'Thank God Alric set up this new fast communication system of riders to the south. 'Send a message to King Harold in London, tell him ten-thousand Viking Norsemen have landed in Northumbria, under the command of King Hardrada of Norway, and they are heading for York.' He paused for a moment, clenched his jaw and then went on, 'And tell him

...,' he paused, unsure how to say this, his lips curled upward, 'tell him his treacherous brother Tostig is with them.' He could not hide his contempt for Tostig. Both brother Earls knew the name only too well, and hated the very mention of him.

The messengers ran out from the room to take this grave news to King Harold as quickly as possible.

'What do we do brother?' Morcar asked. 'Do we go out and attack them, or wait for them to get to York?'

'There is merit in both,' Edwin acknowledged. 'If we stay in York, it can be well defended. This will give us time for King Harold's army in the south to get here. However, this Norse attack is larger and fiercer than anyone expected. This must be the largest fleet ever to sail from any Norse port, they could overwhelm us before King Harold arrives, and that would then give York into the hands of Hardrada. If Hardrada takes York then our King would have an even greater problem, for ten-thousand Vikings could not be easily beaten, if they choose to defend York.'

Morcar nodded, 'By letting them penetrate this far inland their lines of communication are long. Better to harry them along this line now before they reach York.'

'We can do more than that Morcar. We can stop them in their advance on York.'

'Where? How?' Morcar was keen to know the answer.

'We have only four thousand men, not enough to meet them on an open field of battle. We need to find a narrow position where we can stop Hardrada's progress.' Edwin's military brain had been wrestling with these thoughts for some time. He now confided in his younger brother, what he thought was an answer. 'We need a choke-point, of restricted space which we could effectively block with the few troops we have available.'

Morcar smiled grimly and nodded.

Edwin now outlined his plan, 'Just outside the city of York, between York and Riccall, is Fulford.'

'Yes I know it well,' agreed Morcar. 'The ground there is always wet and marshy and crossed with many streams and ditches.'

'Exactly,' smiled Edwin. 'The gap there between the river and the marsh at this point is narrow, a smaller army can hold off larger numbers there. They will be trapped between the river and the marsh.'

'And there we will stop their progress to York,' said Morcar seeing the wisdom of his brother's reasoning. 'Then Fulford it is. We will hold them there.'

Both brothers were grim faced, knowing the enormity of the task now facing them.

The twentieth day of September dawned with Earls Edwin and Morcar at the head of their two armies from Mercia and Northumbria. Unsure of where attacks would come from, nearly half of Edwin's forces had remained in the midlands, while Edwin himself headed this northern contingent.

Ricbert and his son Wilfred were with this, the Mercian army, and although Ricbert could not see his son, he could hear him. Ricbert, as an archer, had been placed to the rear, but Wilfred was one of those now beating on the traditional Anglo-Saxon war drums, near the head of the column, inspiring the English as they moved south. Ricbert felt apprehension for his son, knowing this would be his first battle and no amount of training, or talk, could ever prepare a man for his first battle, in the face of a violent and malevolent enemy.

As the English forces reached Fulford, a few miles south of the city of York, they began to form a solid shield-wall. It was an excellent place for defenders to hold off an advancing army. Where they stood, the ground was firm and they overlooked any who wanted to attack them. In front of them was a deep ditch gouged out by a fast running brook, known by the name of Germany Beck. Attackers would have to cross this first and then fight up a slope toward the defenders. Their flanks were secure. Earl Edwin had the right flank, which was protected by the River Ouse and by the side of this river was a swampy marsh. Earl Morcar had the centre and the left flank. The left flank had further marsh to their side, thereby preventing the attackers from getting around either side of this shield-wall. These natural elements provided significant obstacles for the attackers to deal with.

The only weakness in all this for the defenders was that the lay of the land did not allow the two flanks to see each other.

The Earl's shield-wall of Housecarls was spread out, as a solid body of heavily armed men, for a length of over one-thousand feet. This line stood four ranks deep, with the leaders and experienced warriors in the front, behind them stood the men of the Fyrd, equally ready to give their lives to defend their country. It was a formidable force and they held the better ground.

Ricbert was to the rear, on the right flank, close to the river, while Wilfred, nervous but proud, was close to Earl Edwin, ready to transmit any signal, by drum as may be required.

The Viking base of Riccall was seven-miles further south than Fulford and Hardrada was feeling elated. He was never more effervescent, than at the thought of battle. Hearing of the Earls leaving York had made him ecstatic; he did not really want a long siege against that city, while being forced to look over his shoulder in case King Harold's army should suddenly be upon him. This was just what he wanted. He was laughing and smiling constantly at the prospect of a battle. He ordered his son, Prince Olaf to stay and guard the ships and ignored his protests. Hardrada's great booming voice could be heard all around, shouting orders and greeting commanders. He had not felt so happy for a long time.

'What a wonderful day for a battle,' was his consistent greeting to anyone, everyone and no-one in particular. His force was marching quickly northwards, and was now close to the encounter. They could hear the Anglo-Saxon war drums beating a constant thumping out of their menacing rhythms. These drum beats were countered by the shrill sounds of the Viking horns. Hardrada's excitement rubbed off on his men, there was a spring in their step as they drew ever closer to the sound of their enemy. 'We will make short work of them, while their King Harold amuses himself on the Isle-of-Wight.' He was unaware of Harold's true position, but believed him to be still on that island, awaiting Duke William. 'We'll cut through them, like piss through snow,' he joked.

The dreaded banner of the black raven could now be seen by the English, as Hardrada's huge forces suddenly came into view. It was a fear-inspiring sight. Wilfred's heart missed a beat, and in his trembling he nearly lost the rhythm of his drum, when he first set eyes on these terrifying invaders from the sea. 'So these are the Orcs,' he thought to himself, unable to take his eyes away from their savage appearance.

Hardrada and his commanders now saw the shield-wall and the natural defences around it. All of the shields were painted in an array of bright colours, some plain, but most with two or more colours, some with the Christian cross prominently displayed. All the shields overlapped, so that no gap could be seen. The whole wall was bristling with weapons; spears, swords and the long handled Saxon battle-axes. 'Clever,' muttered Hardrada. Then he gave an order. The sound of the Viking war horns filled the air. Immediately his men began to spread out jogging along the opposite bank of the Germany Beck brook. As his army manoeuvred into position, a great deal of shouted insults and taunts came from both sides, until they came to rest in equal length to that of the English.

Hardrada wore a helmet of petrifying appearance. His eyes and cheeks were framed to make him look more like a demon than a man. His neck was covered in the long chainmail 'aventail', a mantle attached to his helmet. The double headed two-handed battle-axe was his main weapon, with a long sword by his side.

'Sire, you have no shield,' Tostig saw how Hardrada was preparing for battle, without a personal shield. Seeking to protect the man he had invested so much in, he shouted across to the King, 'Sire, please take this one.' Tostig made a great show, of handing to Hardrada, one of the finest shields from his own stock.

'Bah!' was his curt response. 'This double headed axe is my shield. I need no more than this against these weaklings.'

A cry went up from the ranks of the English when they saw Tostig perform this rejected action. Now, they suddenly recognised their most hated of foes. 'Tostig dog, Tostig dog,' the cry became a chant. 'Tostig dog, Tostig dog,' it went on and on. Tostig did not know how to respond. 'Tostig dog,' they repeated in rhythm, as they also now began to slap their weapons into a pulsating beat upon their shields. Then the another chant erupted, 'Kill, kill, kill the bastard,' and simultaneously all of the English in unison started to thump their weapons on their shields, creating a crescendo of shouts and noise.

Many of Tostig's foes now facing him, were the same ones who months before had deposed him as Earl of Northumbria and banished this tyrant from their midst. Eyes stared across the brook at the man all English hated. A wag from the English ranks shouted out, 'Horseshit has more honour than you do, you traitor.' Laughter erupted from those around him. If he did not know this before, he knew it now: Tostig was a marked man, and would be fighting for his life.

'I see your people are giving you a warm welcome back!' Hardrada sneered through his teeth.

Less than one-hundred feet now separated the two armies. Any Vikings in the front row, who felt some trepidation at the awesome sight of this English shield-wall before them, soon had his fears allayed as more and more Norsemen assembled in line behind them. Yet, the sea of mud between the two armies concerned many.

On the right flank, where Earl Edwin's Mercian regiment stood, the ground was at its softest. Here the mud merged with the several streams making the Germany Beck brook into a delta, a morass. Earl Edwin's men were more thinly spaced here. No Viking warrior would be able to attack at this point, for the mud would grip his legs up to his knees, making him an easy target for the few bowmen the Earls had within their force, who were used mainly as snipers to pick off the unwary. This mud was no place for warriors to fight. Still, Edwin signalled the archers to be ready, just in case the enemy tried to attack there. Therefore, as ordered Ricbert moved forward with the few other archers, to be immediately behind the shield-wall.

The continuing stream of Norsemen arriving from Riccall began to trouble the young Earl Morcar. His men were becoming impatient after what seemed like hours of waiting for the Norse to arrive. Both sides had been firing some arrows and sending stone slingshots to each other, but this was more of a hindrance, than a real problem.

By now, Hardrada had had enough time to form a plan in his mind. He was a man of great skill in warfare, which he hoped would soon become evident. He considered the men from the northern isles, along with Tostig's men, the Flemings and Scots, to be his weaker troops. They were not so tried and tested, as were his men from Norway. He commanded these weaker troops to take up their position in the centre of the Viking army. His hardened Norwegian warriors with years of warfare against the Danes were undoubtedly his stronger force; these took up their positions on the left and right flanks. The English Earls were now facing an army led by a great leader, who had more thirty years fighting experience behind him.

Morcar, unwilling to wait any longer, and not wanting to see even more of Hardrada's forces join the centre ranks, which he now faced, now made the first move.

'*Advance centre!*' was the order. Morcar's men moved slowly forward toward the Germany Beck brook in front of them. The long line of the shield-wall was tight and solid.

'Dear God, what is he doing,' thought Edwin to himself when he saw his brother's move. 'Why leave your stronger position?' If he could have cried out to him to stop, he would have done, but it was too late.

Bravely Morcar led the shield-wall forward, as they moved into the depression in the land in front of them. Javelins were hurled from the English line into the packed ranks of Hardrada's men. Some found their mark, others stuck into the shields held by the Norse, thereby rendering the shield too heavy to hold for any length of time. The weight and length of the javelin's shaft added so greatly to the weight of the shield it rendered the unfortunate's shield almost useless.

The combined weight of Morcar's men on the soft banks of the Germany Beck brook suddenly made the bank give way below them, forcing the English quickly down the steep side of the embankment and over toward the other side. This enforced sudden charge was met by Tostig's men. Screams and yells now filled the air. The shields of these warring opponents crashed with great force and noise into each other. Morcar's men pushed forward with all their force, straining forward in an effort to find a space in order to strike a blow. It was now when a man needed all the strength he could muster. It was now when all his training would prove worthwhile. Weaker ones would be pushed over and fall, to a certain death. This was why they had trained so hard to increase their muscle power. Morcar still had his spear as he thrust it forward into the eye of a yelling Viking. His scream drowned out within the noise of the melee. Spears were used by the men behind the shield-wall to thrust as a stabbing tool, one man would jab half a dozen warriors fighting in the Norse lines. Some of these spears had hooks curling back from the point, which were used to hook on an opponent's shield and pull it away. Battle-axes held by those in the shield-wall now began to swing, crunching into the heads and shoulders of the Norsemen. Men were falling beneath the feet of the onward thrust of the English wall, pierced and clubbed to death by the Fyrd behind. As the wall moved forward, the expansion it created began to force gaps within it.

'Close the wall!' was the constant cry from the English commanders as they pressed forward. The shield-wall held. Swords were now flashing, used as stabbing weapons into the bodies of those bowled over beneath the feet of the onward thrust of the English. Every gap in the English shield-wall was quickly repaired. And all the while, with every fibre of his being strung tighter than a bow string, Wilfred kept to the steady beat of his drum and tried not to see the carnage around him.

Morcar was terrified, and for an instant the urge to turn and run seized him. Then the horror of showing fear in front of his men checked his feelings and he welcomed the cold chill of fright that raced through him, keyed up every muscle and every one of his senses, in readiness for the imminent need to kill, in order to live. He assumed his position in the middle of the front ranks and took an even firmer grip on the two handles of his shield, thrusting his sword into the body of a fallen Viking as he strode over him.

His shoulders were aching, as he pushed and stabbed in a swirl of constant motion. The small valley of the brook was churned with mud, blood and dead or dying men. Morcar now fought with insane intensity, cutting his way deeper and deeper into the enemy column. Morcar's men eagerly followed their leader as the Viking's centre began to give way. The English were now inflicting heavy casualties on the invader's central ranks. Slowly but surely Morcar's men penetrated into the dense mass at the centre of Hardrada's army.

Exactly what Hardrada had wanted!

The brook curved into an ark sweeping away from the English position and they were being drawn into it. The further they advanced; the thinner became their extended line.

Now Hardrada made his move.

Earl Edwin's smaller force from Mercia had remained stationary, holding the right flank by the side of the River Ouse. Neither Ricbert nor Wilfred had moved. Where they stood, the flow of the brook broke up into many smaller streams before tumbling into the river. The ground was a morass, deep, broad, and full of water.

Morcar's advance had stretched the English line between these two distinct sections. Hardrada at the head of his elite Norwegian forces now attacked this weakened area like a man possessed. Swinging his long double-headed battle-axe wildly about him he led the charge straight to where the two halves of the English army were at their weakest. As he ran forward, his men protected him with their spears and shields. He ran at his enemy with the force, strength, and fierceness few men had ever attained. Hardrada hacked and swung at anything that moved. The English to the right of Morcar's advance, either had to pull away, from Hardrada's charge, or be were cut down where they stood. The giant size and strength of Hardrada was inspirational to his men as they ran straight at the English. Hardrada's axe flashed and chopped into the necks and collarbones of Edwin's men at such a rate they began to fall back. Fallen English were crawling on their hands and knees in the deep mud, in an effort to escape this maddened assault, only to die by a sword or spear thrust into them by those following quickly in the wake of their King.

Edwin quickly saw the danger, Hardrada's attack was cutting the two armies of Morcar and Edwin in half, penetrating between the two regiments.

'Reform the shield-wall!' Edwin cried at the top of his voice. However, King Hardrada now swung his attack away from Edwin and drove into the weakened English line between the two armies of the English. Here the ground was firmer and took

the Norse across to English side of the brook, to the rear of Morcar's advancing troops. Elated Hardrada's men pressed on forming a 'U' shape around Morcar's army and cutting them off from Edwin's forces. The open side of the 'U', for Morcar, was marsh and swamp. Morcar was effectively surrounded.

Morcar could not see what was happening, as the men on his far right now were hit by the storm of Hardrada's charge. Steadily the outflanked line yielded to Hardrada's superior force. Suddenly Morcar realised the Vikings were upon them from behind.

Edwin told the drummers to signal a forward advance, but as they tried to push forward, it was soon evident that his troops were far too few in number, and could not reach the mass of Morcar's men in the centre. Edwin could make no progress.

Not wanting his troops to be cut down, Edwin ordered the drums to sound the *fallback*. He knew he had to move his army safely back toward York, or die in the attempt. As long as Edwin could hold his shield-wall, the Vikings could not defeat them. They had the river to their right, which gave protection from that direction, and marsh ground to their left affording protection there. Edwin was now working a fighting retreat.

Ricbert was not so much angry, as disappointed; apart from shooting a few arrows, he had seen no action at all. His son Wilfred, he was relieved to see, was now *beating the retreat*, and keeping safely behind the solid Mercian shield-wall.

There were now three main battlefronts at Fulford. Morcar's frontal advance, Hardrada's attack from Morcar's rear and Edwin's fighting retreat.

'Disengage!' was Morcar's new order. 'Fight a retreat along the brook. Form a protective shield-wall.' Fear and anger in equal measures flooded in Morcar as he realised his predicament.

As Edwin began his retreat from the right flank along the bank of the River Ouse, Morcar formed a protective wedge and started to move the left flank the opposite way, along the brook into the marsh area. Morcar's Northumbrians had inflicted a heavy toll on the centre of the Viking army, but now they were in retreat. No amount of bravery could save these defenders of York.

After fighting for hours and now wading through heavy mud, many Northumbrians were exhausted, unable to move or dodge blows. Ever larger groups of these dishevelled defenders became isolated and easy prey. Many others just drowned. The English lost about a third of their numbers at Fulford; the Germany Beck brook ran red with blood. Many of the dead had received multiple wounds, including a high proportion delivered while the victim was in the prone position, stuck in the mud. It had been a killing field.

Later as darkness fell, Ricbert and his son consoled each other, behind the closed gates of York. The Mercian's could see Earl Edwin was safe, but no one was sure what had happened to the brave and noble Earl Morcar. What had been a strong Northumbrian army, was now, little more than a few blood soaked stragglers, desperately hoping to get back to York, where they could seek some refuge.

Since his failed attempt to cross the sea on the twelfth day of September, Duke William's feared temper had raged for days on end, for all to hear. He had had men hung, and left there to dangle in the wind, for some perceived failure, or some imagined delay to his plans. No one dare approach him, not even his brothers, so great was his rage. Frantic efforts were being made to replace the lost ships and men. William was incandescent when heard that some ships had been intercepted and taken by King Harold's navy, which had sailed on without him, after he had turned back to France.

Everyone who had work to do, did so vigorously, and made sure to keep his head down, so as not to attract the Duke's wroth, or even his feared gaze. Daily, William stayed with the fleet, that was waiting at Saint-Valery-sur-Somme. The winds were now good, but the repairs to the damaged fleet were still incomplete. 'How can this be, if God is with us?' William would scream at the sky.

Some of the barons were beginning to wonder if a postponement would be the better option, but no one dare approach William about this. He was transfixed on his goal to invade England, and no event of nature, nor any person, was going to deter him from this. Due to his single purpose of mind, the repairs were being made at an unbelievably rapid rate.

Each day, with much show and pomp, William went to the Abbey of Saint Valery where he would make a public display of saying his prayers to God, he and his captains made generous offerings at the holy shrines there. The monks came out in solemn procession bearing their sacred relics, and the Norman host knelt devoutly and did homage, beseeching God to grant them victory. Each day William constantly watched the weathercocks for any sign of a change. He had to move soon, and desperately did not want any more foul weather to spoil his plans.

One day when William was leaving the church, a messenger rode up in great haste, dismounted and bowed low before him.

'News from England my lord,' he declared.

William looked very grave, his staring eyes unwilling to take any more bad news. 'Now what?' was the thought, which raced through his mind, as the messenger approached him. Bracing himself for more bad news, the Duke acknowledged him, 'Continue,' he ordered curtly.

'England has disbanded the Fyrd, my lord. They have been released from their duty to serve and have returned to their homes.' The messenger became nervous at the silence that followed. What should he do? Should he say more, or keep quiet? He remained quiet, on one knee.

The Duke smiled, for the first time in days. Then his smile broadened, and then he gave way to a laugh. No one could remember hearing the Duke laugh like this before. His laugh continued. Soon others were joining in, also laughing. They did not know why they were laughing; but if the Duke was laughing then that was good enough for them. His laugh became infectious, and now everyone was laughing. He gave a gold coin to the messenger, 'God is with us, now we will attack,' he shouted. Laughter and cheering echoed in his ears as he mounted his horse and rode away, still laughing. 'Now we will attack,' he shouted back to any who could hear. 'Now we will attack.'

The impulsive, but magnificent attack on the Vikings, by Morcar and his Northumbrian army had not been entirely without affect. Many Vikings had died in the battle. Morcar had lost the greater number of men, but he had finally managed to drag himself back to York, by using the fighting retreat battle tactic. It had been a costly retreat and the death rate had been high. Too high, for now, Morcar's army was in no state to reform and many of Edwin's forces were still scattered south of York.

It was the middle of the night before Earl Morcar and the remnants of his army, staggered into York, bloody, with many carrying horrific wounds, but alive. Both Edwin and Morcar were well trained to the arts of war. Their ability to keep their defences as they retreated all the way back to York had proved this.

Edwin embraced his bloodied brother, when they finally met up again, and sought to console him, 'True, this battle belongs to Hardrada, we may be beaten, with many drowned in the marshland, yet there are many left who can still swing a sword and King Harold will surely come to our aid.' Morcar was too weak to respond, but just looked blankly through his blood stained eyes, at his brother. The deep gash to his head and a broken arm were now his main concern.

Although Earl Edwin's Mercian army was still largely intact, he could not allow it to now fall into the stronger hands of the invaders. Early on the day after the battle, on the twenty-first day of September, the order was given for Edwin's army and the remnants of Morcar's to immediately leave York, knowing they could no longer fully defend it. They quickly headed southwest to Tadcaster; and along with them went Ricbert and his young son, Wilfred.

Whilst at Tadcaster the Earls met a messenger from King Harold. The messenger had arrived in that town the same day as the Earls. His message was to inform them not to engage Hardrada until the southern army could join them. Though the messenger had arrived too late to prevent the battle, it was not too late for the messenger to tell Edwin of King Harold's intention to move north.

'All is not lost, brother,' said Edwin to Morcar who now lay on a bed, with his wounds well bandaged. 'There is new hope.' Yet within himself, he now wished the messenger had managed to reach him before the battle, instead of after.

One thousand years before this eventful year, Ermine Street had been built by the Roman conquerors of Britain, in order to move troops across the land quickly. Now a new army headed north along the entire length of this road, from London to York. They had set out on the twenty-first day of September, the day after the battle of Fulford. News of the defeat at Fulford had not yet reached this southern army. It was enough for them to know of the slaughter at Scarborough.

In a hurried council of war, it had been their considered opinion that Duke William of Normandy would not now be attacking England, for they had heard of Duke William's failed attempt to cross the English Channel and it was already late in the campaigning season. Some of King Harold's navy had intercepted and defeated an isolated group of William's ships, which had been scattered by the storm on the twelfth day of this month. The council concluded that William was in no state to launch an attack this late in the year. Therefore, the logic now was to concentrate their forces on the enemy already here and move the entire English force north as fast as they could.

King Harold of England, together with his brothers Gyrth, Earl of Essex, Leofwin, Earl of Kent, also Alric General of the Housecarls and Ordgar commander of the Fyrd, headed this large English army northward. The golden dragon of Wessex and England flew proudly at the head of this magnificent army. Other banners were also held high on this long and proud march north, including the white dragon of East Anglia, the double-headed silver eagle of Mercia and the white horse of Kent. All would be rallying points at the time of battle, but the King's golden dragon of England was the one most revered and honoured.

Alric earnestly wanted to engage these invaders and Tostig in particular. He felt an intense excitement within him, even joining in with the talk of many of what they would do to this enemy.

King Harold had ordered every man should travel forty-five miles each day during ten hours of travel. Thereby, he said, the one-hundred and eighty miles from London to York could be covered in just four days of hard travel. However, he knew full well, that to do this would entail one of the greatest marches in military history. Even so, he was confident it could be done. It had to be done. He had to protect his beloved country. Harold inspired his men; they knew him well as their leader. They readily moved north, eager to seek revenge; their heads were held up high, enjoying their ability to cover large distances in a few days. They were proud of their King and his generals.

Together with the baggage train, the line of men stretched for miles. All the Housecarls rode their own horses, they were proud, determined and in unison. 'Such a fine body of men,' exclaimed Alric, many times over. Behind the Housecarls came the Fyrd. Most of the Fyrd were mounted but those who did not have a horse to ride were being carried in horse drawn carts. Many such carts had been requisitioned in the King's name, to help with the fight that lay ahead. All carts had spare wheels and many had extra horses. Any cart which lost a wheel, was quickly pulled off the road, out of the way of the progress north, with the men under orders to, not only repair the wheel, but to make up any time they lost in the process.

Many of the Fyrd, who just days before had been sent home, where now flocking back to join their army as the march north progressed. Some were hurrying up from the south, behind the main column, to catch them up; others from the West Mercian and East Anglian Fyrd were waiting by the roadside for them to arrive. As the army moved ever further north, so it also grew in size and strength. This was an elated force of men, they were glad, at last to be able to combat those who had invaded their land. Spirits were high.

It was early on the third day of this long march, as they headed toward the city of Lincoln; that the news of the battle at Fulford finally reached King Harold. Harold and his generals spoke together as they rode onward. They knew now they had a fight on their hands, a fight for the very sovereignty of England. The news enraged him and his army so much they stepped up their pace, along this long road for the rest of the day, until eventually they sighted the city of Lincoln in the distance.

The support from the population along the way for their army, had been constant and infectious. 'Another welcome for us sire,' Alric pointed ahead along the road leading into the city, where groups of women, children and old men had come out to greet their army, as it headed north to protect them, and their country.

'It is a gladdening sight to see,' King Harold acknowledged, as he waved his hand in response to the cheers and applause of the crowd. 'I see they also bring food and gifts for our men as so many have done since we left London.' Harold was overjoyed at the reception he had been receiving. 'I would stop and greet them if I could, but we must press on.'

'Yes indeed sire,' Alric nodded in reflective response. 'Your orders for ten hours a day to march north are being carried out, with no unwarranted stops along the way. I know of no other who could inspire his people so.'

Harold in deep thought was as tired, as the rest; it had been an exhausting three days. Entering the city, he turned to look at the long line of men and equipment following him. 'Such a march has never been done before, but this does not mean it cannot be done.'

'Yes sire,' Alric grinned, 'and do it we will.' He pulled his horse Welland to the side of Harold's horse, stood up in his stirrups and looked back with Harold at the long line of men behind them, 'Just look at the determination on the faces of your men. They know the protection of their families is at stake. They will do it alright, by God they will.'

King Harold smiled at this reassurance. From Lincoln they would continue along Ermine Street to Tadcaster and finally to York itself. King Harold had inspired his people to do what have never been done before. They were all, grimly determined.

Due to the relative success of Earl Edwin's forces, in making a fighting retreat from Fulford, it was a few days later before King Hardrada and Tostig entered York to accept its surrender, knowing that there were still many of Edwin and Morcar's heavily armed men around in the district. Because the brother Earls had fled York, the city was now back in the hands of the hated Tostig. This was Tostig's reward for taking up arms with Hardrada. Three days after the battle, on the twenty-third day of September, King Hardrada held a great feast in Riccall for his victorious army. The next morning, on the twenty-fourth day of that month, Hardrada and Tostig entered York, with a parade of the victorious Norse army, to accept the submission of that city.

It was a hot day, hotter than it had been in mid-summer, a frequent weather pattern for these northern September days.

There had of course, been much crying and sadness from the citizens of York, at the loss of so many of their men. Tear-stained, red-eyed, bitter and sullen, they now gathered in the city centre as ordered by King Hardrada.

Pulling himself up to his full giant size, he addressed them, 'You are now my subjects and I am your King,' he began in his usual loud roaring voice. 'We will not plunder your city if you submit to me as your King.' Hardrada waited. There were many within the crowd who were of Nordic and Danish origin, whose forefathers had settled here during the last two hundred years. He expected them to be joyful at his conquest; yet they were silent.

Angry at their silence, Tostig spoke up, 'Accept King Harald Sigurdsson of Norway, King Hardrada, as your rightful King or your city will be raised to the ground.'

A reluctant, mumbled and stilted, 'God save the King,' came from those gathered there.

'If you conclude an abiding peace with me this day,' Hardrada went on, 'you will be left in peace. Be warned though I will only conclude this peace, if you, who are able, march south with me to secure and conquer this realm.' This was Hardrada's plan to recruit extra men to replace his own, who had been injured or killed, and to replace them with Norwegian and Danish stock from the settlers here in northern England. Yet it was not as simple as that. The loyalties of these settlers were now divided, they had families who were of mixed Anglo-Saxon and Danish stock, and their true loyalty belonged to their own King Harold and the brave Earl Morcar, but they had been beaten and were now hearing the terms of their victor.

King Hardrada had not finished, 'I further demand from you one-hundred and fifty sons from your leading families to be taken as my hostages. You will deliver them to me tomorrow at the new camp I am setting up at Stamford Bridge.' The look of shock and horror on their faces was plain to see. Their beloved children would now have to be handed over to the Norse as hostages. 'You will also provide livestock and food from your harvest, as much as my men demand, to sustain them through the winter.'

Stunned silence greeted these harsh demands from Hardrada, as he stepped down from the platform, where he had stood to watch the parade of his troops and accept the surrender of the city. 'Tostig, as you are now the reinstated Earl of Northumbria, see to it that this city provides all that my men need, and to give help for our many wounded.'

Tostig was jubilant, he had achieved what he had set out to do, and was now reinstated as Earl of Northumbria.

Hardrada's smile beamed through his thick beard, when in a loud voice for all to hear he joked, 'Earl Tostig, what will your brother be doing now?'

'Running around in panic, I don't doubt,' was Tostig's equally loud and flippant reply. This brought forth laughter from the Viking warriors, as was the intension.

'Sire, how long before our armies meet?' asked Tostig. 'It will be some time before Harold can make his way north. Do you intend to go south to meet him?'

'No,' replied Hardrada, 'let him run round in panic a little longer,' Hardrada's smile was more of a smirk. 'We have strong defences here in York. Let the cur come to us, if he will. Now, I am returning to Riccall and then later I will go to make a better base for us at Stamford Bridge. As we agreed our warriors will not despoil this place, your city of York, for the city is now yours. We will move to take the south in the spring.' Hardrada felt content with the success of his mission, so far.

The following morning, the twenty-fifth day of September, the weather continued to be hot and sunny in northern England, which made the Norsemen uncomfortable. They were not use to such high temperatures and many had removed their heavy chainmail armour. The weather was so warm, some had even stripped off their clothes and were casually walking around bare-chested. The main body of Hardrada's army was taking their ease on the east bank of the River Derwent, near the village of Stamford Bridge, situated approximately seven miles to the east of York, on the eastern edge of the Vale of York. Two or three hundred Vikings had made a separate camp on the west side of the river, away from the main body of men. Also, about one-third of the Norse army had remained at Riccall, due mainly for the need to repair their armour and weapons after the exertions of Fulford. Much of the equipment requiring repair, had been taken on board their ships moored at Riccall, awaiting a favourable time for such work to be carried out.

Hardrada, Tostig and Copsig, sat together on the grass of the meadow, close to the river, near Stamford Bridge. They were glad of the opportunity to relax a little after all the work and preparation for this invasion and the physical excursions of the battle. They were all very happy with the way things had gone for them, so they settled down waiting for the hostages to be brought to them.

'This is why I recommended this place as a base for you, sire,' Tostig was in the process of extolling the virtues this site. He had recommended it as a suitable base, in much the same manner as he had recommended Riccall, for the point of disembarking of the Norse army. He was proud of his success in recommending these two suitable places for this vast Norse army. 'You see,' he went on, 'over there we have ...' He did not finish his sentence, but looked intently into the distance.

All three now looked in the same direction. 'What is all that shouting about,' Hardrada demanded to know, rising to his feet to see what all the noise was about. 'What is it?' he barked.

'I'll go over and check sire,' offered Copsig in a confident manner.

When Copsig did not make an immediate return, Hardrada stormed over to a group of his men who were pointing to something on the far hillside.

'Copsig. What is all the fuss about?' he demanded, but thinking nothing in particular about it.

'Sire over there – look.' Copsig's eyes squinted at the strong sunlight.

A mile to the west he could see a rise in the ground and cresting the top of this ridge a glint of sunlight was reflecting off something. Then there was another, then another. Hardrada's mouth dropped open, as he realised the sun was reflecting off the steel armour of a vast army.

'It could be the escort for the hostages you have demanded sire, or the tribute they are ordered to bring,' ventured Tostig, in the hope that it really was so.

Hardrada did not take his eyes off the ridge; he glared intently at this rise in the land, which was now full of men. Squinting his eyes against the bright sunlight, he saw it; scarcely able to believe what he was seeing, – a large banner. The Golden Dragon of Wessex and England, flying high above them.

Hardrada's face reddened. Then, snapping out of his trance-like state, he roared the order, *'To arms! To arms! Sound the horns.'*

Men started to run everywhere. Frantic men, with a look of panic on their faces, desperately began looking for their armour and weapons, which had been so casually laid to one side just a short while before.

'How? How could they?' Hardrada stared at Tostig. 'How could they get here so quickly?' he demanded to know. 'Running round in panic was he?' he sneered, his anger now raging toward Tostig. In full voice he barked, 'Well how in hell's name is he now here? You godforsaken bastard, you fool,' he screamed at Tostig as he ran to form up his men. 'This is not possible. To arms you fools, the English are here, the English are upon us.'

King Harold's army had arrived at Tadcaster the day before, on the twenty-fourth day of September. His epic march north had been achieved quicker than any man had thought possible. They had managed an incredible average distance of forty-five miles a day, for four days. In Tadcaster King Harold had met up with Earls Edwin and Morcar, who informed him the bulk Norse army was only eight miles away at Stamford Bridge, and even more importantly, that this army was now divided with one third being at Riccall.

With Morcar wounded and Edwin exhausted from the recent battle at Fulford, Harold had ordered Morcar to stay in Tadcaster, he would have to wait for another day for revenge. However, Edwin's Mercian army was now at full strength and had joined with Harold's troops as they advanced from the south. Ricbert and Wilfred were still with Edwin's troops, both feeling gleeful at the prospect of being a part of this vast army.

Before leaving Tadcaster, Harold had sealed off the road, and placed guards at other strategic points on the way to York. Secure in the knowledge that his presence in the area was unknown and that he had taken all necessary precautions to keep it that way. He allowed his army to rest and recuperate in the meadows around Tadcaster for the rest of that day, while he continued to gather intelligence. Earlier in the morning, Harold had ordered his army to march through York, where he was well received, and to continue on to within a mile of Stamford Bridge. The order was for a silent march; no drums to be sounded, and no shouts of any kind, they were to move quietly and quickly. Arriving at Stamford Bridge, they kept well hidden below the rise of the land.

Now at midday, King Harold lined his army up all along the ridge for all to see. Wilfred and the other drummers received their orders to start up the deep rhythmic beat of the war drums. The sound echoed all around for miles. These dreaded Anglo-Saxon war drums now began to beat an intense, fear inspiring rhythm. The deep low boom, boom, boom, didi boom, of the penetrating sound from these drums, brought the sound of war to all ears. They were designed to bring fear to the enemy and courage to the English, which was exactly what they now were doing. The noise they made echo around the hills and made the pulse of the warriors thump faster and faster. The English army now began to move forward toward the river.

'Send riders to Riccall,' barked Hardrada. 'Tell my son, Prince Olaf to stay on board ship and that Eyestein Orre is to lead the charge here. I order our men at Riccall to get here as fast as they bloody well can.'

Not only Prince Olaf, but also Earl Paul and Earl Erlend of Orkney, who was betrothed to the King's son, were also at Riccall, along with a third of the Norse army.

The Viking war horns all around were sounding the *'Call to Arms!'*

'Tostig!' ordered Hardrada, with his voice booming above the confusion. 'You are second in command until Eyestein arrives.' Then in a quieter mode, he lowered his tone so as not to be heard. 'Tostig we cannot form a full shield-wall. We are outnumbered. They will easily sweep around our flanks. We will have to form "the boar's snout", with this triangular wedge we will be able to cut through their shield wall; until help arrives that is.'

'As you command sire, it shall be done.' Tostig had an unexpected and excited elation at being made second in command.

Hardrada continued to speak quickly, in an excited talkative mood, 'Our men are still hung-over from the feast and celebrations we had last night. Many are carrying wounds from our last battle and some of their chainmail armour has been left at Riccall. The beer has befogged our heads. We should have given more thought to this and protected ourselves better.'

Tostig noted that when blame was being apportioned, his 'I' had now become 'we'. Even so, King Hardrada could now see that he had relied too much on the council of Tostig.

'Hold the bridge while we form up,' Hardrada was looking toward the wooden bridge some half-mile distance from his army. This was the bridge crossing the River Derwent, which gave name to the nearby village of Stamford Bridge. King Harold's army was on the opposite side of the river to that of the main Viking army. 'Send in the Berserkers to hold the bridge and buy us some time for help to arrive. Where is Marshal Styrkar?' Hardrada yelled. 'I need him here now.'

'He is on the other side of the river, sire,' was the unwanted and unwelcome reply.

Styrkar and the Vikings were on the west side of the river, the same side as King Harold's forces and were now running towards the bridge. They needed to cross the river and join with the main body of their army on the other side, before the English could get to them. The few who had armour were frantically trying to put on their chainmail, at the same time as trying to flee; others were looking for their weapons, so casually laid down Earlier.

Alric had anticipated all this and was now in full gallop with five hundred of his Housecarls down the slope of the ridge and toward the isolated Vikings. In a long sweeping action, Alric led his men as they galloped between these Vikings cutting them off from gaining access to the bridge. A feeling of elation swarmed over Alric, it was the feeling of a victor over that of the vanquished. Styrkar and this band of invaders were doomed. The Housecarls charged straight into this confusion of ranks; it was an easy target. Swords flashed at the running men, who were wearing little or no armour to protect themselves. Heads were targeted, as were shoulders and backs. The upper torsos of these men received multiple wounds and quickly succumbed to Alric's charge. It was not long before all Norse there lay dead, or were dying.

Hardrada and Tostig looked on in horror at the carnage the other side of the river. Turning to his men, Hardrada sought to concentrate their minds, 'Order Fridrek the standard bearer to set up our battle standards,' The standard bearer promptly hosted up the large standard of the black raven, in the centre of the Viking army. Tostig's own banner was also set up in a separate section, where both Tostig and Copsig stood.

Sweat ran down the face of Alric as he returned his regiment of Housecarls to where King Harold waited and watched. 'Who are those who stand at the bridge?' Harold asked of Alric.

'Berserkers sire,' Alric grimaced 'They are chosen for their size and fierceness. They are wild men, who will never surrender. They are trained to be merciless killers, whose strength grows with battle. Some say they are fuelled by a drug known only to them.'

'They certainly seem a wild bunch,' Harold acknowledged. Dressed, as they were to terrorise and intimidate, with fearsome looking helmets, and wearing animal fur sleeveless jackets, hung with all sorts of macabre and gruesome symbols from earlier encounters. Their naked biceps, of incredible size, glistened with sweat, holding a doubled headed battle-axe with a short two-foot long handle in one hand and a small round shield in the other. Harold let out a slow breath, 'They will welcome the blood they seek to shed. They wish to slow us down and give time for the Norse to form up in battle array. They obviously know nothing of the Roman ford a little way upstream from this bridge, about which the men of York told us. The foot soldiers shall engage them by frontal assault; while you're mounted Housecarls go across the ford and come at them from the rear.'

A hundred foot soldiers then moved forward toward the bridge. No more men could be used in this action, as the width of the bridge did not allow for a wide front. The encounter was savage. No English could get near to these powerful men, so spears were thrust forward from behind their shields, held high. The Berserkers' battle-axes then crashed with power, and cut through the shafts of the spears. The English were hacked at and dismembered in horrible fashion. Soon Harold's men began to fall back, as the Berserkers held the bridge.

Ricbert lifted his bow, for the King to see, waving it as a gesture for him to be allowed to use it. Harold though ignored him. Ricbert felt mortified.

'Alric, to the ford,' ordered King Harold after seeing too many of his men fall in this action. In a flash Alric's mounted troops followed him across the ford, then swinging round, they came up around the other side of the bridge. So that the horse's legs would not be chopped by the powerful swinging of the Berserker's sharp battle-axes.

Alric shouted an order, *'Javelins - loose!'*

Instantly following this order, dozens of these lethal weapons were hurled into the backs of the frenzied Berserkers. Turning too late, they saw their enemy now had both ends of the bridge. They all died under the hail of javelins. The way was now open for the whole of King Harold's army to cross the River Derwent, some by the bridge, and some by the Roman ford.

'Form the Shield-wall!' bellowed Alric. 'Drummers beat out the Shield-wall order.'

Wilfred and his fellow drummers, responded and confidently beat out on their drums, the given order. The Housecarls dismounted quickly, taking up formation in the front ranks of the English army. The Fyrd filled the back rows and the flanks, making a solid formation of angry men. Ricbert hung around the right flank, by its edge, as the Saxon shield-wall was much larger and deeper than that of the Vikings. It swept in a semi-circle around the wedge of the Norse. Chants, taunts and shouts came from both sides as they were forming up.

'Send a herald to me,' King Harold ordered. Then after receiving the message from his king, the herald nervously walked to within shouting distance of Tostig's standard.

Cupping his hands to his mouth the herald proclaimed, as loud as he could, 'Tostig Godwinson, your brother the King of England offers you peace.'

A thousand jeers and swear words came from the densely packed ranks of the Vikings.

'Enough!' ordered Tostig, 'Let us hear what he has to say.'

'Accept your brother as the rightful King of England, join with him now and he will restore your Earldom to you.'

'And what will he give King Hardrada?' was the questioned reply.

The herald turned and walked back to his line to where King Harold stood. After a few expectant minutes, the herald returned. Again cupping his hands to his face, he answered Tostig's question, 'To you, his brother, King Harold will return to you the Earldom. It is not right that brother should fight brother.' Then pausing to get his breath back from this shouting, he continued, 'To King Hardrada,' the herald paused again, then raised his voice even louder, 'he will give six feet of earth – or a little more, because he is taller than most men.'

The reaction from the English was spontaneous laughter. Both sides now screamed and shouted abuse at each other. 'Kill! Kill! Kill!' was the chant from the Vikings, as they banged their weapons on their shields. The English reciprocated with their chant of, 'Go back! Go back! Go back!'

The drumbeat changed and the English advanced, slowly at first, Gyrth took the left flank and Leofwin the right. King Harold and Alric were with the centre.

Javelins - loose!' barked Alric.

There was a deep grunt from the ranks as hundreds of slender shafts now flew through the air clattering into the shields and back ranks of the Norse. The range was short, and scores of Vikings were struck down. A reciprocal reaction for the Vikings to launch their own javelins and spears was not followed. They held on to theirs, to enable them to hold back the English line inflicting greater pain by jabbing their shafts into the English line. The last few yards of the advance turned into a run, the English running straight at the closed ranks of the Vikings. Many English died from the spear thrusts. However, the sheer numbers of the English soon made headway, as both shield-walls met.

Alric concentrated his mind, as he swung his long handled battle-axe crashing it into the nosepiece of a warrior, the impact jamming it into the face of the Norseman, splitting the front of his face, with bone fragments and teeth spilling out. All around him was the thump of shield against shield, and the cry of men in their death throws.

Harold saw a crazed Viking fighting a path toward him; others were quickly following in his wake. Harold darted forward with a sword in his fist, punching it into the throat of the Norseman, so that he fell back with a chocking cry. The others were soon intercepted and struck down by Harold's personal guard.

Bodies began to sprawl on the grass, many struck through more than once. Some who fell, but were not yet dead, used their prone position to stab their knives into the legs and genitals of the enemy above them, resulting in piercing screams, the perpetrators being quickly dispatched by those following on behind the front ranks of fighting men.

Wilfred was left standing with his drum, at the back of the fight, not sure what to do, nor where his father was. He had never seen such horror of men screaming in pain, of un-armoured Vikings disembowelled and of the smell of fear. At Fulford he had seen very little, now though he had a grandstand view.

Ricbert was sending in arrow after arrow, but in the confusion of battle, he had to be careful not to hit his own men. He thought about joining the fracas with his sword and shield, but then thought better of it. A sudden wave of fear came over him, 'Maybe his friends were right,' he thought to himself. 'Those who fought hand-to-hand were better men than an archer, who just picked off men from a long distance.'

Now he could see Hardrada and his size amazed him. He wondered, 'how brave those men were, who got so close to this frenzied giant.'

In spite of it all, Hardrada was still managing to enjoy the thrill of battle. He had seen men face death many times before; he had given them the last darkest rites, sending their souls spinning away. He revelled in his own power to overcome any who tried to better him; they never did better him. He was the most feared among men. This bloody hand-to-hand combat went on for more than an hour, with Hardrada barking order, after order. Yet slowly the English started to force back the Viking wedge, which began to break up, with some Norse groups becoming isolated and fighting in little bands of their own, until they were hopelessly overwhelmed. Hardrada's battle order was beginning to break down.

King Hardrada saw this weakness. Seeing the need to join his two large, but separated groups of his men together, each of whom had become surrounded. He took the only action he knew. Running into the melee, he began to swing his battle-axe, as he had done at Fulford. With both hands on his famed axe, he forced a path for himself, killing many English as he cut his way forward with great power, until he forced a way through for his men to rejoin and reform their defensive wedge. Seldom had men seen such a valiant and brave action.

'*Follow me!*' he yelled above the noise of the battle. '*Follow me...! Follow...! Follow...!*'

Why weren't his words coming out? He again tried to shout his orders, but nothing came out! He felt dizzy. His world was spinning. What was happening? We must fight on. We must fight on. What was happening? Only then, as his knees began to buckle, did he become aware of the arrow shaft sticking out of his throat. For King Harald Sigurdsson of Norway, the feared King Hardrada, Valhalla was beckoning.

Ricbert's skill as an archer of the Fyrd, had paid off. He had found his mark. As a bowman, well versed in his art when hunting food for his family, had brought down the King of Norway, who up until this day, many had considered invincible.

An unexpected lull came over the battlefield at the death of Hardrada. This was partly due to the death of Hardrada and partly the need for both sides to get their breath back. Their exhaustions in the heat of the day had left both sides panting, gasping for air. Slowly each side pulled back. Was it over?

The cries and moans of the wounded and dying were disturbing to both sides.

Taking advantage of the lull, King Harold had a loud proclamation made, 'The King offers a truce to his brother Tostig and to those who will surrender with him.' A short silence ensued.

'Bollocks,' Came the shouted response from the ranks of the Vikings. 'We will never surrender.' Copsig cringed when he heard this.

'To me men,' Tostig cried as he made his way to the black raven banner. 'To me, we will avenge our king.' The Vikings began to encourage one another; they had no wish to surrender. 'Help is on its way. The men from Riccall will be here soon.'

The Viking war horns sounded again and the cry went up, 'For King Hardrada,' as both sides once again clashed in battle. This time Tostig was leading them and the Norsemen were set for revenge, but the superior numbers of the English soon began to tell again. The Vikings were now surrounded and fighting on all fronts. With each minute, the number of Norsemen dwindled. The bodies of their dead comrades became a bloody, slippery obstacle, as others fighting wildly for their lives, stumbled over them, only to be pierced through once their defences were down. Tostig saw that each thrust of the English warriors brought them closer, and closer to him, and the precious Viking standard he now defended.

A sudden scrum of English heaved and pushed forward; heaving toward the hated Tostig, with all their might they pushed, until at last, he too was overwhelmed. Tostig disappeared under a pile of men, all thrusting their weapons into his hated, shattered body.

Almost at the same moment in which Tostig fell, another war horn of the Norsemen was heard. It was now several hours after the battle had started, and the sun was beginning to go down, when Eyestein Orre arrived with the men from Riccall. Since receiving the message from Hardrada to come to his aid, with all haste, they had run the full twelve miles from Riccall to Stamford Bridge, carrying their weapons. Many had become too exhausted to either wear or carry all their chainmail, so they had been force to drop much of it as they ran as fast as they could to the aid of their king. Inevitably, many had been unable to keep up with the front-runners and fell back, even though they still did their best to keep on running: still others had died on the way, from the stress of this forced run.

Alric looked up at the sound of the Viking horn, 'What the hell is this,' he cursed. Then seeing Eyestein's men running he bellowed at his own men, 'Look to your rear, they have reinforcements.'

Wilfred, still in shock but responding to his training had also had seen what was happening. He was quickly ordered, to begin to beat the signal, 'Enemy Behind!'.'

The English, who were being attacked from behind, had been unaware of the men from Riccall arriving, until they heard the drum. Many were cut down before they realised what was happening, as several hundred new men suddenly crashed headlong into the fierce fight. With the element of surprise, the Norse quickly took a heavy toll on the English. Harold looked more intently at these new arrivals, and saw something that came as a surprise to him. He could not believe what he was seeing. Turning to the commanders of his bodyguard, close by, he said, 'They have no armour, they have no armour.'

Alric heard his King, and then turning to those close to him yelled hoarsely, 'Come with me, come with me.'

As many men as he could gather pulled away with him and followed Alric, as he ran around the back of these new arrivals. By the time he arrived, the rear of the English main force had now turned to face their new attackers. With Alric's advance, Eyestein's men were in turn surrounded. Their lack of body armour swiftly began to tell, now Alric was joined by Harold and his bodyguard; together they hit out wildly at the unprotected parts of these Norsemen. Arms were cut clean through, muscles, bone and flesh hung from their bodies. They presented easy targets for the English. Copsig took the opportunity of this distraction; he dropped to the floor by a pile of bodies, pulling them over him, hoping the English would mistake him for dead.

Soon the English in the main forum of the melee began to look around them. Each man was covered in sweat and the blood of both friend and foe, when their immediate contest of death with an enemy had been fought; they instinctively looked around for the next enemy combatant. Gradually they realised that they had run out of opponents. Most of the invader's chiefs were dead, including Hardrada, Tostig and Eyestein. The flower of the Norwegian army lay dead on the English battlefield of Stamford Bridge. Many of these fearsome Viking warriors had suffered the same fate they had meted out five days before to the English troops under Edwin and Morcar. The English had hit the Viking invaders with an armoured fist. Copsig now meekly surrendered, hoping his life would be spared.

As darkness fell across the field, more than five thousand Vikings lay dead, along with two thousand English. It had been a hard fight. Exhausted men dropped to their knees, too tired to move, amazed that they were still alive.

As the twilight gathered, Ricbert ran around the camp eager to find his son. When he finally found him, he saw there were tears in the boy's wide eyes, and in a state of shock. Ricbert put his arm around him and held him in the embrace of a loving relief.

Forty-eight hours later, on the twenty-seventh day of September, the stench of death hung as a thick, all embracing pungent smell over the battlefield of Stamford Bridge. The Viking prisoners, which included Copsig, had been set to the task of burying the dead. There were so many to bury, that pyres were also lit to cremate many of the slain.

The prisoners had been subject to a continuous torrent of verbal abuse from the English warriors, who now taunted them whenever they could. Copsig afraid to let his position be known, pretended to be a sailor of low rank, often having to avoid the accusing glances coming his way from his fellow Viking prisoners, who now considered him a sniviling traitor.

King Harold and his war council were now at Riccall where the many ships of the Norse invasion still lay. Harold's brothers, Gyrth and Leofwin, sat at the centre of a table under a campaign tent, with Alric and Ordgar seated each end. Outside the tent flew the banner of the golden dragon. Spirits were high; they had just beaten one of the greatest armies in Europe.

Ordgar was especially pleased, for, as he put it, 'That one of the lowliest Fyrd archers has brought down one of the highest kings.'

King Hardrada's son Prince Olaf had been summoned to attend this council and now he stood before them. Harold and Gyrth were seated, while Alric and Ordgar got up to stand either side of Olaf. The prince, around nineteen years-old, looked pale and drawn. His sword, a cherished gift from his father, had been removed from him, as had his chainmail. He wore a linen shirt covered by a fur jacket, and laced leggings. The last two days had been hard on him; he still could not believe his father and his strong army had been so clearly defeated. Having been unable to sleep, his eyes were heavy and he felt very nervous, fearful of what was to become of him.

King Harold remained unmoved as Olaf sank to his knees before him. 'We did not want this war,' said Harold accusingly. 'Yet you sought to invade my kingdom. You have paid a high price for this venture,' he paused reflecting on events of the last few days, 'and we also have paid dearly for your evil presumption.' Harold felt sad and sorry for the loss of so many of his men, yet understandably, he felt nothing for the loss of his brother Tostig. 'Tell me,' he went on, 'what would other Kings in my position do with you and what remains of your men?'

Olaf looked up, for this was a loaded question and he needed to be careful with his answer, 'We would be held for ransom sire', was his considered reply.

'True,' replied Harold. 'I would get a great ransom for you, and also for Earls Paul and Erlend of Orkney.' Then Harold looked him straight in the eye, 'And what of your warriors of lowly birth, whose families could not pay me a ransom? What of them?'

'Sire,' Olaf again thought carefully for his words, 'they could be sold as slaves.'

'And?' Harold raised his voice, for he would not let it end there.

Olaf gulped for air, then he stammered, 'They could be put to the sword sire.'

'Exactly.' Harold had made his point. 'There are many kings who would do all this and also torture those they chose to. Is this not so?'

Olaf did not answer; he just cast his eyes down to the floor.

'Is this not so?' his voice raised a pitch.

'Yes sire,' came the whispered reply.

Harold waited for this to sink in, not only to Olaf, but also to his council. 'We could also, of course, keep you and the Earls of Orkney in a dark cold prison.' Fear was now displayed on Olaf's face. 'We could do all these things, could we not?'

'Yes sire,' Olaf was preparing himself mentally for the worst.

'The English,' King Harold continued, 'The English are not like that. We pride ourselves on a higher moral Christian standard than others have shown.' Harold stood up and walked over to the kneeling figure of Olaf. He reached down with one hand, gripped the prince's chin and forcefully lifted his head up. 'Yes, we could hold you for ransom; - but we will not. Yes, we could sell your men as slaves; - but we will not. Yes, we could execute any, or all of your warriors; - but we will not. Yes, we could confine you in a prison; - but we will not.'

A hush fell over all those within the tent. They all realised they were now witnessing something special, something almost unheard of before.

Olaf looked up, scarcely able to believe his ears. 'Then what is to be our fate sire?' he asked, his voice quivering.

Harold let go of the prince's chin, he slowly and deliberately walked back to his seat, and sat down. No one moved, or spoke.

There was high tension in the room. Finally Harold spoke, 'I will show great magnanimity toward you, even though you would not have shown it to me.' The council all turned to look at their King. 'You will swear to me, in the name of God, that you and your chiefs will never again return to England, to neither raid, nor to invade. If you swear this, you and your men will be free to leave these shores; but you must be gone by this time tomorrow.'

Prince Olaf was near speechless. Never had he heard of such a gesture as this. 'Sire, I will swear this now, in front of whom so ever you may wish.'

Harold just nodded, then, turning to his brother, he said, 'Gyrth inform him about the ships.'

Gyrth complied, 'You came onto these shores in three-hundred ships; you may only take back with you twenty-four of these. This will be enough ships to accommodate all that remains of your men.'

This stark statement was enough to show everyone just how complete had been the loss of life to the Norsemen.

From this victory, Harold considered he would reap a rich reward with these expensive ships. He reasoned this would greatly help him cover the expense of this campaign, and would increase the protection of his shores for years to come. Harold was right, there really was not enough Vikings left alive to sail more ships than twenty-four back to Norway, in any case.

When Olaf had been dismissed, Harold turned to his brother, 'We must now return to York and make ready for a great celebration, not only for our victory but also for the freedom we have bought to Northumbria.' Then he paused, waiting to consider his next words, 'The body of our brother Tostig must not be left on the field of battle. See that he is taken to York, for an honoured burial.'

'Gyrth forced a smile, ran his fingers through his hair, and then shaking his head, in an act of almost disbelief, he turned to his brother, 'Never, did a king show more mercy than you my brother. Your actions today are truly merciful gestures of a

Christian king; this will be spoken of for hundreds of years to come. I am proud to be your brother Harold.'

Alric returned to York that same evening, along with Harold and his brother. Alric's spirits were high, even though his Housecarls had suffered heavy casualties at the two battles so recently fought. His men had won a renowned victory over one of the greatest armies of the time. It was time to celebrate. They had survived, life was good.

That night the soldiers of King Harold's army were treated to a feast, a feast of celebration. They deserved it. Every man had all the beer he could drink. The King was paying for it all, out of the royal coffers. No man was sober, and had not been for two days now. Some drank to help ease the pain from their wounds, others just for the joy of being alive, and for the part they had played in helping to protect their country from the invader. It was a good feeling. Alric and the King were happy, as they drank each other's health, along with the health of Earl Edwin and Earl Morcar. Earl Morcar was still suffering considerable discomfort and pain, but he would live. He was luckier than some men, whose wounds had become infected, and were subsequently now delirious with high fever.

After the hard won fight at Stamford Bridge, the amount of weapons the Viking army had left behind was enormous. A huge stockpile of weapons had become available to Harold's army: valuable weapons. Not just weapons, but armour, clothing, food and beer; all left by the campaigning Viking army.

Typical of the man, King Harold had been generous to his people, 'See to it that all men who fought with us, and any who have since joined us, have the weapons and armour they need.' Then smiling said, 'It may be they will use it in the spring, if Bastard William comes to these shores. Although, when he hears of our victory here, he may soon have second thoughts.' They all laughed.

Ordgar, who had been overseeing the stockpiling of the seized weapons, was particularly keen to see the Fyrd had all the weapons they needed. There were so many weapons; more than enough to go around. 'Your success and fame is spreading sire,' Ordgar told the King. 'Men are still coming to join us from the farthest corner of your kingdom.'

King Harold left the men to their rejoicing; he needed time to think. His thoughts, like many of his men, were of those he loved. He regretted how he had hurt his first love, Edith Swan-Neck. His time with her had been his happiest. He had lived with her in the 'Danish manner', as they called it, but the Danish manner was not accepted by the church as a legal marriage, and so the church did not recognise Edith as his true wife, even though he had six children by her. The people themselves accepted Edith, but to the clergy she was considered only Harold's mistress. Still, he loved her deeply and no church ruling could change that. As things had turned out he felt it was perhaps a good thing he had not been legally married in the eyes of the church to her, for this gave him the freedom he needed to form this valuable alliance with Earls Edwin and Morcar, when he married their sister, Ealdgyth, in the Christian manner.

Would they have won the North if he had not formed such an alliance? Would the Earls have stood against the Norse army, or would they have joined with them? He dismissed this latter thought, after all they could not have sided with Tostig. He certainly needed their support to protect his kingdom; after all, they controlled the second largest part of his kingdom. Now, their sister, Queen Ealdgyth, was pregnant with his child, or was it children? For they told him, they thought she was pregnant with twins, who would be born in November. How he longed for that day.

The flickering light, encased in a lantern slung from the masthead of the Mora, could clearly be seen. The sun had gone down below the horizon some time ago, but in the long twilight of the north, there was still enough light for all to see the Norman invasion fleet, which had finally left the confines of Saint-Valery-sur-Somme, in Normandy. This was the evening of the twenty-seventh day of September, just two days after the battle at Stamford Bridge. The waters of the sea were calm as the Mora headed a large flotilla of six-hundred ships, bound for England.

The golden gilt figure of a child on the stern of the Mora, was pointing across the crew and beyond to England, with the flag it held in one hand and holding an ivory horn to its mouth with the other. Atop the masthead was a golden cross, from which hung the framed banner from Pope Alexander II: a red cross on a white background; the holy sign from God and the Pope. The single billowing sail displayed upon it the two rampant lions of Normandy. At the prow of the ship was an ornately carved head of a lion.

The invasion fleet was carrying more than fifteen-thousand infantry, archers and cavalry, along with two-thousand horses. It was the largest army in living memory, and the largest to attack England since Roman times. Duke William knew he was taking a risk by being the first invader, of English shores, to bring so many horses with him; he had been warned by scholars that even the Romans had not done this. The horses took up a lot of room on the already heavily laden ships. Each horse was tethered and packed into the tight confines of his longship. In this way, William sought to surprise the English with mounted cavalry. He well knew it was the English tradition to fight on foot, and so by bringing large numbers of mounted cavalry it would, he hoped, have a greater impact upon the balance of power, in any assault.

This fleet not only carried with it the nobility of Normandy, but also many soldiers recruited from all over northern France, the Low Countries and the German States. Many soldiers in his army were men who had little or no inheritance due to them, so William promised them, if they brought their own horse, armour, and weapons to join him, they would be rewarded with lands and titles in the new realm. Now they crowded on board the ships, heedless of everything, save that they were not left behind, and had their armour and weapons ready for use.

Duke William travelled with his brother Odo, Bishop of Bayeux, in the Mora, while Richard Fitz-Gilbert and Robert Count of Mortain were each in separate ships. Bishop Odo had blessed the fleet and all the soldiers, before they sailed. He reassured them that their invasion was God's will and all would be fine with them, after all, they did have the Pope's blessing. Beneath his chainmail and padded tunic William carried a small silver box, in which was the finger bone of Saint Nicaise of Rouen, one of the most precious things he owned. Saint Nicaise had been instrumental in turning pagan Gaul into a Christian land; he believed this would surely bring him success, for he now risked everything in trying to bring it about.

Now though William was tense, as the gathering gloom of the night started to fall over his fleet. He did not know where the army of King Harold was. He had planned to sail overnight so that no early warning of his presence could be delivered to the English army.

'The first hours will be the most crucial,' he had informed his generals, before they left. 'We must quickly establish a strong base which will afford us protection before we strike out against Harold's army.'

No one dared to sleep, as the night plunged them all into total blackness, the heavy clouds blotted out any light from the moon and stars. William kept glancing up at the dim lantern light on the masthead. In his mind, he kept thinking to himself, 'Prey God they can all see this light and follow us safely across this sea.' He could not even see the ships that had been closest to the

Mora. It was a long night, so dark, so very dark. William looked intently at Stephen Fitz-Erard, the Captain of the Mora, 'When will we make landfall captain?'

'By day-break, my lord,' was his reply as he stared into the blackness before him.

Hours passed, long hours. Then gradually, there was a slight change in the colour of the night. A lighter colour on the dim horizon, slowly giving way to the first hints of a new day. The twenty-eighth day of September was dawning.

William looked about him in panic, ahead was the dim outline of the English coast, but where was his fleet? William shouted out, 'What in God's name has happened captain? Where are they?' The captain looked just as startled as William, both straining their eyes to look around them. There were no other ships, the Mora was alone on the sea, no ships of the fleet could be seen anywhere!

'My Lord,' the captain sought to reassure the duke, 'your ship is the finest ever built, she is much faster than the others. We must have out-sailed them. They will soon catch us up.'

Odo pulled William to one side and whispered in his ear, 'William, do not panic your men. Let us hove-to here and await the arrival of the fleet. And to show all is well, let us make a great show of taking breakfast.'

William knew his brother was right. Therefore, breakfast was served, to William and Odo, with bread, fish and warm spiced wine. This had the desired effect of keeping his men in good heart. Within an hour, the loitering forest of masts rose into view. For this short time, William knew very well, he had been at his most vulnerable. If the English navy had known his current situation he could have quickly been over powered. Now however, the fleet was reassembling, to continue its progress on to England.

The Mora was the first ship to make landfall, with the rest quickly following. They landed near to Pevensey, in the county Sussex, a county named after the South Saxons. William had chosen this landing area deliberately, for this was close to

Wessex, King Harold's heartland. There was excitement and high tension all round when William jumped from his ship to the shore: in doing so, he stumbled and fell. A hush suddenly came over the noise and bustle from those who observed this. Was this a bad omen? William instinctively knew of their fear and superstitions. He thought quickly; grabbing two handfuls of sand, he stood up and bellowed for all to hear, 'See, look; I have already seized the land of England.'

A great cheer went up, and the stunned silence was suddenly transformed into uproarious laughter.

With the ships either beached, or anchored close offshore, the archers were the men who stepped ashore first, just in case the enemy came upon them. There were hundreds of them, so unlike the English army, who only used archers as snipers. Each archer had his bow strung, and a quiver full of arrows at his side. They were clean-shaven and had short haircuts, so different was their facial appearance to that of the Anglo-Saxon English. They wore light clothes to give them freedom of movement and were all at the ready should they be attacked. Quickly these archers formed a protective semi-circle around the bay, the knights, sailors, soldiers and their officers jubilantly made their way onto the beach. With some rudimentary defence in place, the squires carefully unloaded their ships; carrying out shields, saddles, and spare weapons.

Landing the war-horses proved to be tricky, for the horses were nervous and there was no quay or jetty to make this easier. Many men stumbled into the water trying to get the horses safely to the shore. The war-horses were naturally nervous anyway, but especially so after their voyage. Each man who was responsible for a horse was doing his best to calm the spirited animals, holding onto the reins and talking soft words into the ear of his charge. They remembered Duke William's words, 'Your horse is a fighting machine, look after it well.'

It took time for the main force of the army to disembark; many men were fully armed, wearing their long tunics of chainmail, with their shields slung across their backs.

Robert, who was himself in charge of a company of knights from Mortain, began to form them up on the shore, each one mounted.

Soon the support cargo ships began to arrive. They carried the supplies of food, tools, weapons and craftsmen; these had been much slower with the sea crossing than the warships. The carpenters landed, with great axes in their hands, and adzes hanging at their sides, these men were vital to William's battle plans. The beach was soon abuzz of activity, with more people now on the beach, than there were in some English towns.

After making sure all the key stages of the landing were going well, William and his brothers Odo and Robert along with Richard, gathered on the beach away from the main force.

'I had expected some resistance to our landing,' William declared, 'but look, no one is here.' William shrugged his shoulders in disbelief.

Richard, looked concerned, 'I don't like it. I have sent scouts out to see what they can find. It could be some kind of trap. What do you think brothers?'

William shook his head, 'I think not Richard. If it were a trap, it would have been sprung by now. I am overjoyed we met no resistance to our landing.' William was now striding along the beach as they spoke; he did this so he could be seen by his men, to be in a confident mood. 'However, I am not happy that this is the best place to defend if we are attacked.'

William turned to Robert, 'Robert, start the temporary defences as we planned.' Then looking toward a rise in the land above the beach, he pointed to it, 'Over there will do for now.' They had brought with them some prefabricated heavy wooden fencing for just such a need. 'We must find a better place for a stronger structure. Send out scouts to find such a place.'

The whole scene was one of frenzied activity. They each knew that if the English army was close by, they had no time to waste.

The nobility of Normandy sat around a hastily constructed table, on the beach of an alien shore. This temporary table had been made up from the shields they carried. With Duke William sitting to his right, Bishop Odo in full chainmail armour blessed the food of fish placed before them. As was the law of the church, fish and not meat, had to be eaten on a Friday, and today was Friday, the twenty-ninth day of September. Just a day and a half since their landing near Pevensey, the invasion force had now moved along the coast, eastward, to the coastal town of Hastings. This meal was a public show, both of piety and of being in control, as well as a symbolic serving of the Duke's first meal on English soil. He made sure that many knights and commanders were on hand to observe this spectacle.

Using the materials they had brought with them, William's army were in the process of constructing a defensive holding, should it be needed. It was made of wood, some of which had come from dismantling one or two cargo ships, and some from the prefabricated fencing they had carried with them across the sea. The timbers from many ships provided a readily accessible timber source, with which to build these defensive fortifications. In his planning, Duke William had tried to think of everything that would be needed.

In front of the Duke's table stood a frightened English woman and her young son. Her manor house, on the hill beside the beach was ablaze, for Norman's had torched it; having been the finest house in the district. The woman held her son tightly to her, as they stood in front of these invading lords of war. The troops had pulled her out of her house, shouting words she did not understand, then, they set fire to it. Now she was both frightened and puzzled, why it is, she thought, they seem to be putting so much effort into eating a meal on the beach. William was getting annoyed. He had asked her where the English army was, but she did not speak French and could not understand him. He found this irritating. Most of the Norman army spoke two languages, French and Latin, but few, if any, spoke English.

'Are all these peasants the same?' said the Duke, frustrated. He had expected even the common people to speak Latin, but this woman did not. 'Latin is a language all speak, why doesn't she understand it?'

Odo was equally disparaging, 'Looks like we will have to educate them, as well as conquer them.'

A Norman who spoke some English was soon found and ordered to translate for them. After some time, he addressed the Duke, 'My lord, the English army are in the north, where they have gone to fight the King of Norway, King Hardrada. She does not know the outcome my lord, nor if there's been a battle as yet.'

William did not know what his reaction should be. 'This is mixed news indeed,' said William.

'Why mixed news?' asked Robert.

'Because it is good we were not opposed in landing. This gives us time to prepare ourselves.' Looking pensive, he continued, 'Now though, we have a major problem. To start with we do not now know who we will fight.' William picked up one of the fish bones to use as a toothpick, while he continued, 'Will it be Harold's army or that of King Hardrada?' William was becoming really worried now. 'Whichever army it is, if it stays in the north, we are buggered. We will have to march through a very hostile country in order to meet them; and during winter at that. This is something I do not want to do. If we move north, we will be away from our ships and stretch our supply lines too thinly.' William stood up and shook his head. 'If we move north, Harold's army could cut us off from our base here in the south. We are too few to risk that.' His eyes blazed, as he hit his fist into his hand, 'Damn them! Damn them, this is not what I wanted.'

One of the lieutenants, by the name of de-Vitot, had been watching all this. He was a man who wanted to be seen as an active participant, so he rashly spoke up, without being asked to do so, 'Should we now march on London, my lord?'

William was offended by this upstarts question, he did not invite comments on his war from lesser men, his quick temper flared up, 'You would not understand the implications of your question, let alone the answers,' was his demeaning retort. Then pointing with one finger into an unknown distance, he ordered de-Vitot, 'Go with one of your men to London. Say we wish to speak with their Earl Harold.' William would not use Harold's title of King. 'See what you can find, and hurry. Now go!' The lieutenant's mouth dropped open.

Later that evening, when the night had fallen, the man who had accompanied Lieutenant de-Vitto on his mission to London, rode at full haste into the Norman camp. William hearing the commotion came out of his campaign tent to meet him.

'Back so soon!' queried William. 'Have you reached London already? Where is Lieutenant de-Vitto?'

'Dead my lord!' was the spluttering answer.

In the dim light of a flickering candle, William then took a more careful look at the man in front of him. He saw the man's eyes were black and swollen, his face and lips badly bruised and bleeding.

With difficulty, the man told his story, 'We got as far as a village called Crowhurst; and then we were set upon. We told them we came in the name of Duke William of Normandy and were seeking Earl Harold to talk with him. They were old men, my lord, who were too old to follow their king.'

Duke William's head jerked up instantly at this, eyes glaring. 'Sorry my lord, I mean Earl Harold,' he quickly corrected himself, hoping he would not be on the receiving end of the duke's temper.

'Go on, go on,' snapped William.

'They killed Lieutenant de-Vitto, there and then. I feared for my life. They beat me,' he stammered. 'Then they told me to take a message back to you, my lord.' The man stopped, unsure if he dare go on.

'Well? What did they say?' William's irritation was getting stronger now.

'They said King Harold had beaten the vast army of King Hardrada of Norway. They had destroyed them in a great battle near the city of York. And...'

'Get on with it man,' demanded William.

'And that if you wanted to take on their king, this vast host would overwhelm you and send you back into the sea.'

'Crowhurst, you say?' William's fury flashed, he now sought only revenge. 'Then we will have to teach them a lesson.' He strode back into his tent, where Odo had been standing observing and listening. He looked thoughtful, 'If the English army is in the north, we must tempt them to come back to the south. We cannot risk moving north,' then on reflection added, 'Not yet anyway.'

That night William began to wonder if he had brought enough men with him, and he began to feel just a little insecure.

The tranquil and peaceful setting of the village of Crowhurst, felt the storm of panic blow through its streets. Hundreds of mounted knights and cavalry surrounded the village. Every man, woman and child the Norman troops caught in Crowhurst, were slaughtered and every building burnt to the ground.

Shortly after the massacre of Crowhurst, all the towns and villages for miles around were similarly systematically destroyed. Foraging parties went out on a daily basis, each man eager to see what he could find. Soon the whole of the south of England was being devastated. Their hapless victims tortured and killed. The Normans had tasted English blood and wanted more, much more. Duke William needed to tempt King Harold to return to the south, so he set about sending him a message, in the most effective manner he knew how. Giving his men complete freedom to do as they pleased, he sent them off on a terror campaign around the whole area of south England. The Normans pillaged and burnt everything they came across. William needed to provoke Harold into an early conflict, before the English were ready and before the winter set in. He could not go north without stretching his supply lines and risking encirclement.

Deep within the dense woodlands of south England, dishevelled groups of English villagers, refugees from the onslaught that had hit them, hid from the sudden violent onslaught of the Norman rape of their homeland. They were wet and cold, not knowing what to do, where they should go, or what they could do. The whole area was swarming with Norman invaders. All these survivors could do was to hide and hope they would not be found.

'So these are the Orcs,' lamented a scrawny old man, bent double with age and shaking with cold. 'I have long heard of them, but this is the first time I have seen them. They are truly terrible. How can they be so cruel?'

'They look like monks with swords,' said one matronly sized woman. 'Their hair is shaved like that of a monk. Who would shave their hair like that, except for a monk?'

'You do not know what you are saying,' said a young mother clutching a bundle of damp wood she had gathered, with the hopeless task of trying to make a fire, in order to keep her child warm. 'They are not monks, but Orcs, demons, sent from hell to take our land.'

'Yes, that is true,' said a newly widowed woman with a sad, dazed look about her. Her large buxom frame denoted the good life she had enjoyed before this invasion. She had been the landlady of a local tavern; now destroyed. 'They must be Orcs, look what they did to those poor girls, no wonder they were screaming to be killed. It was horrible, so horrible. Why did they mutilate them like that?' The woman started to weep at the thought of what she had seen.

'We cannot understand them,' said an old woman, still shaking with shock. 'The language they speak is like none I have ever heard before.'

'Our blessed land is destroyed,' lamented her aged husband, clutching his aching back. 'They kill everyone.'

The rape of England had begun.

Ricbert had a tear of pride in his eye, as he gave his son Wilfred his family sword, 'You did well my son, that was your first battle and now this is yours. It has been in our family for longer than I can tell, but you have earned it. Well done.' With that, he embraced him in a fatherly hug. Ricbert had a new sword, issued from the haul taken from the Viking army, along with a throwing axe and a chainmail jacket. There had been so many weapons handed out, they were now better equipped than they were before the battle at Stamford Bridge.

'We will be able to go home now; your mother and brothers will certainly need our help, it must have been hard for them while we have been away.' Ricbert was still smiling when he was distracted by a commotion taking place, some distance away. A lot of shouting was going on and men were throwing their arms about. 'Something must have happened,' he said to his son.

They walked over to where the crowd had gathered to find out what it was happening. Some men were crying; others just looked blank and dazed.

'The Normans have landed and attacked the south. They are pillaging and burning the whole of the south near King Harold's home.' This was the shock news on everyone's lips. Their joy of victory over the Vikings was suddenly whipped away from them, on that second day of October.

Ricbert for a moment was speechless. As the full enormity of this news crystallised in his mind, he sank slowly to his knees in dismay. He simply said, 'God no!'

'How can this be?' asked Wilfred, unable to think of anything else to say.

'Those bastards,' said Ricbert through gritted teeth. 'We will teach them.' Then standing he thrust his fist in the air, 'We will teach them,' he shouted. Others now began to say the same thing, just as Leofwin came up to them.

Leofwin raised his arm up to command silence, 'Men we have to return to London. Our homeland is still in danger, this time from the Norman bastard.'

'We can beat them sir,' responded Ricbert, 'like we did to the Norse.'

'I, that we can,' acknowledged Leofwin 'Now all men must get ready to move. We march south this day.' Then climbing up onto the back of a wagon, he addressed those there, 'You have proved what a great fighting force you are men. We will drive this second invader back into the sea, as we did Hardrada. We have many new weapons to try out.' With that, he held up a Viking helmet and a great cheer went up.

The damp grey sky reflected the mood of the long sombre procession, as it trudged and rumbled south along Ermine Street. Whereas shortly before they had been full of good cheer, and were elated with their victory, now the English army were grim faced, yet still determined. They were enraged to hear of towns and villages in the south being despoiled by the Normans. Infuriated, they now moved to confront this second adversary. The banner of the golden dragon hung wet and limp from its pole at the head of this long march. The same wagons they had come up in, now carried massive amounts of weapons gathered from the Viking army, along with numerous men nursing wounds.

Earl's Gyrth and Leofwin had done all they could to persuade their brother Harold to wait until their damaged and weary army was stronger. Alric repeatedly pointed out how many men they had lost and how the northern army had been badly mauled by fighting two battles in just a few days.

Alric begged Harold to wait until the army was stronger, rested and fully recovered. 'Many are in no state to travel south yet,' he implored Harold. 'We must rest and strengthen ourselves, before we march south.'

Nevertheless, all Harold could think of was Duke William hitting his own heartland, and it hurt. Alric had trouble in getting Harold to be still, in one place, long enough to talk with him; it was difficult, for Harold was dashing around, from group to group, and leader to leader.

'I cannot ignore the cry of my people,' Harold snapped back at Alric as he persisted in trying to get his King to listen.

'Sire, if we wait we can get stronger. After Fulford and Stamford Bridge, many are in no state to travel. Give just a little time and they will recover.' Alric just did not know how he could get Harold to see reason.

However, Harold did not want to listen to Alric's reasons, all he could think of was the people of his Earldom being hurt and killed. 'The longer we wait the more time that bastard William will have to establish his foothold on our kingdom. He will build fortifications and make our task so much more difficult.' Harold would not be dissuaded. 'If our Housecarls can beat Hardrada, they can beat anyone,' he boasted, slapping his arm across his chest.

And so it was a depleted army, which now marched back along the Roman road to London. Earl Morcar's northern army had fought so well at Fulford, but were now depleted. Because of this, and the wounds he still bore, the brother Earls and many of their northern army did not join them on this long journey south.

Although depleted King Harold's army still consisted of the men from Wessex and Mercia, and the call would go out for still others to join them along the way.

Ricbert and his son started out with the rest of the army on that long, hard march south. Like many in that sombre procession Ricbert was troubled. He had been in deep thought for some time when he pulled his son to one side and spoke quietly to him, 'Wilfred listen to me carefully.' Wilfred observed the tenseness in his father's eyes. 'You must go home, to help our family with the farm. They will be struggling to manage; they will need your help.' Wilfred saw the faraway look in his father's eyes and he could tell he meant what he was saying, so he did not object; but still he wondered why his father would say this. Ricbert continued, 'When we reach the city of Lincoln, you are to branch off on the Fosse Way, then head for Nottingham. Take great care once you are on this road, you must not make any short cut through the Forest of Sherwood, it is not safe for one so young. You must keep to the road and go around it.'

'What about the war father? Should I not stay?' Wilfred was concerned and could see no reason for his father's order to him:

but he said no more. His father's face looked pained. Was that a tear he saw in his father's eyes? Wilfred could not be sure.

'You have been in two battles already my son, that is more than enough for one so young, and I am proud of you.' Ricbert knew a few others were also leaving, slipping away into the night, and yet paradoxically many were still joining having travelled vast distances to be with their king who had won such a great battle.

'No one will blame you, for you will have time enough for more battles, if God decrees it so.' Ricbert held his son tight, it was a difficult thing for him to part from him, but having seen the ferocity of a full battle he did not want him to face another, he wanted to protect his eldest son and the rest of his beloved family; he knew it had to be done.

The days were getting much shorter now, as winter was hastening on, and along with this turn in the seasons came more rain. The rain added to the depressive mood which hung over this army, but it did not detract from the determination of the Housecarls to meet the Normans in battle. The Fyrd, however, were not so minded. Some, who had fought at both battles, had already slipped away, as had Wilfred, to return to their homes, much to the disgust of Harold's fulltime soldiers.

Ordgar pointed out to the King that some of the Fyrd had deserted, but Harold's reply had simply been, 'We will get more recruits in London.'

'Maybe sire', Ordgar agreed, 'but will we have the time to train them properly?' The King had not answered.

Harold then moved among his army, from commanders, to the part-time Fyrd. All the time he was encouraging them, putting fire back into their bellies, showing them all clearly, the stark choice they now had. As he moved around his army, he constantly spoke with every group he could, dispelling their fears, and raising their strength, uplifting them. For when Harold spoke, men listened; he had an art of building men up, to the point where they would willingly follow him and, if need be, lay down their lives for him. It was not long before he made their morale high again, distracting them away from their concerns. With food in their bellies and a flagon or two of beer and cider, the men where now happily exchanging banter between themselves. Harold made weary men smile again. Gone was their fear, returned was their heart, to defend their country.

Even as the days grew dark, the long stream of men continued on their southward journey. Some tried to continue through the night, but without any light from the moon, it became impossible to ensure their horses footing. They had to be ordered to rest up, rather than risk laming their horses.

The one-hundred and eighty miles from York to London was again marched and ridden down for the second time; this time taking just an incredible five days to complete.

The day before they reached London, King Harold stopped off briefly at Waltham Abbey, where he prayed before the altar, confessed his sins and vowed his fealty to God. He gave gifts and money to the monks there, for them to pray for him and the victory they all wanted. He hoped for the sake of his country, that his prayers would be heard.

The first of the King's forces arrived in London on the sixth day of October. It had been just sixteen days since these valiant men had first left London and marched north to York. Never had such an amazing feat been thought possible; but several impossible things had already been achieved. Now everyone could see King Harold's men followed him with their hearts, as well as with their feet. It was not alone out of loyalty to Harold, that they followed him, but for love of England. All now felt and believed that these Norman men of different speech and instincts must be driven off the soil to which they had no lawful claim. Harold's energy and grim determination had clearly won the hearts of his men again.

The fame of the northern victory brought crowds of recruits to the banner of the golden dragon. They were saying, 'If Harold could conquer the great Hardrada, it was surely not impossible to defeat the Normans also.'

New members of the Fyrd rallied to their King, while Harold waited in London. Men flocked together from the west and south, responding to yet another rallying call. Harold was too good a general and knew too much of the Norman soldiery, to underrate the Norman prowess in battle; he shook his head gloomily when his officers spoke with scorn of their foes. He well knew he would have a fight on his hands.

'Just look at them,' said Harold to his brothers Gyrth and Leofwin, as he stood on the steps of his manor house in London, to watch yet another column of men arriving from the countryside to join him there. Ansgar, the Royal Standard Bearer, in the main square was the rallying point for these new arrivals. Harold looked on with pleasure. 'They are wonderful men,' he said with genuine pride.

'That they are,' agreed Gyrth, 'but we need more time to train them.'

Harold's impulsive nature had never been as evident as it was now, 'Alric knows his orders, he has five days to train them.' Harold's curt reply, sought to silence Gyrth, as they continued to watch the new men arrive, but it did not.

'Five days is not enough time,' retorted Gyrth angrily, 'Let Leofwin and I, harry the Normans with our personal Housecarls. We can do this and keep them pinned back for weeks while you build a stronger force here in London.' Harold did not reply, but just shook his head. Gyrth raised his voice for he knew Harold was not listening. 'This will give us time to get strong again.' Gyrth's frustration with his brother was getting the better of him. It was sound advice Gyrth tried to get across to Harold, but he had taken a blinkered view of events, ever since the news of the Norman invasion had reached him.

Leofwin also now tried to persuade Harold, 'Harold, there are many due to arrive from the west country, who will not be here for a few days,' Leofwin was now equally as concerned as his brother Gyrth. Harold did not answer.

Exasperated with his brother, Gyrth argued strongly, 'Look Harold, our army can only get stronger as others come to joins us. The Normans will only get weaker as they lose men and we close their supply route with our ships. Surely we should harry the Normans, while our army gets stronger?'

'No!' barked Harold. 'We cannot let the bridgehead they have established already, become any stronger.' Then thumping his thigh with his fist, he asserted, 'Look Gyrth, it is *my* homeland the Normans are destroying: as I am their king and lord, it is therefore *my* duty to protect them as quickly as I can.' Harold's mind was in turmoil, 'We cannot wait,' he insisted. He stormed out of the presence of his brothers, then turned as he entered the door, 'And we will not wait.' Harold would not be moved.

On the eleventh day of October, Alric set out with King Harold at the head of the army to march the last sixty miles to Hastings. They would then have covered a total distance of two-hundred and forty miles from York by the time they reached Hastings.

For several days, William's army was filled with uncertainty, nervousness mingled with excited expectancy. Clearly, there was no army in the immediate area of Hastings. It was evident to the Normans at the moment they had that part of England to themselves. As the days went by, they had remained undisturbed by any English force whatsoever. Voices now began to be raised, urging that they march further into the country, but William would not have it.

From captured English during the Norman rampage, came more information for the Normans, regarding events in the north. Graphic details began to reach William's men, while they continued to burn and destroy, unhindered in the south. The captives told of news they received; of the great battle in the north, of Harold's relief of York and the terrible disaster that had befallen the multitude of the Norse army. Some were saying, 'Twenty-thousand men have been slain in the north, and that the English were mad with pride and rejoicing.' This confusion of information began to tell on some of William's men, who asked in whispers among themselves, 'Were they strong enough to risk a battle with that victorious English army?'

That evening, on Friday the thirteenth day of October, King Harold's army camped on Caldbec Hill, just six miles north of Hastings. Harold had hoped to repeat the same surprise tactic, which had served him so well at Stamford Bridge. After all, he reasoned, William would not be expecting him to complete this long march already. From this hill, and the south facing ridge sweeping away from it, his army could completely block the road to London, blocking any advance that way for William's invaders. If William wanted to break out from his bridgehead at Hastings, to try a march on London, it would have to be via the ridge blocked by Harold's army.

Harold knew moral was high with his men, from the defeat of King Hardrada and the almost impossible march they had now achieved. Now they had the proof of just how strong they were; surely, this was the finest infantry in Europe. Who could stand against this infantry with their terrible two-handed battle-axes?

Gyrth's failure to prevail on King Harold to wait a little longer for reinforcements to arrive had irritated Alric. At heart, Alric knew Gyrth had been right, but he persuaded himself, their army was strong enough. Even so, this nagging thought would not leave his head, 'Should we not wait another day or two and make the army stronger still?' He wondered why Harold would not listen, for the English wanted to see an end to these invaders from overseas, they all wanted the suffering of the people to be finally over. Alric could only obey his King.

Ricbert's body was aching and his feet hurt and bled. He had ridden most of the way by horse, sometimes riding in a cart, but he had also walked in places for miles, and now he had blisters, which troubled him. Still, as he sat down to eat some dried meat and fresh bread; handed to him by well-wishers along the way, he looked to his arrows. He constantly checked them whenever he could. A number of fletchers, the makers of arrows, had handed him many more while the long column was moving south. Would he be able to kill a second leader of these invaders? He hoped God would give him the chance.

Late that afternoon, two of Duke William's scouts came galloping into his camp shouting the news, 'King Harold is approaching with a great army.'

The watch fires flickered and faded, as the gray morning of the fourteenth day of October dawned. The sweet smell of fallen leaves filled the air; the ash trees had already lost all their leaves, the oak, hawthorn and beech, were now dark golden brown and ready to fall. As dawn broke, Alric woke with a start. Surprised he had been able to sleep at all on the damp ground. The exertion of the last few days had made sleep essential.

Choking down some dried meat and old bread with a little wine from his flask, he strode over toward the King, while many others were also hastily gulping down what food they had. Alric shouted orders, to get the King's army ready to move. King

Harold, as a born general, was choosing his ground well, so directed them to move from Caldbec Hill to the ridge of 'Santlache' – which means, 'The Sandy Stream'. Here he was able to place his army on a ridge of high ground, thereby forcing the enemy to attack uphill, if they were to move toward him. Behind him was a steep upward slope and then woodland, the flanks of his position dropped sharply away and were covered with thick undergrowth. The woody nature of the terrain and the steepness of the sides would make it difficult for his army to be outflanked. Harold was forcing William to take a full frontal assault uphill, with little, or no chance of the invader being able to get around his sides. At the bottom of the ridge, the ground was marshy. Only a narrow strip in the centre was firm enough for the invaders to negotiate. Any army can be defeated Harold reasoned to himself, given the right conditions.

The Housecarls all were in their full armour of chain mail, loose fitting and knee length, split at the front and rear for ease of movement, with elbow length sleeves. Many, but not all, of the Fyrd were likewise so clad, now that they had been able to take so much from the defeated Norse army; others of the Fyrd wore leather hauberks. All the men wore conical helmets and carried a shield, the Housecarls were using shields of the long leaf shape, but the Fyrd favoured the more traditional round shape, gaily painted. Harold's position was strong, but due to the limited space available, his men were becoming crowded together.

It was difficult for Harold to know exactly how many men he had, for men had been joining him throughout the night, and were still coming, but he estimated he had around twelve thousand men.

At the sixth hour that morning Duke William rode on a black stallion at the head of his army, together with his brother Odo, as they set off from their camp in Hastings. Robert rode separately at the head of his knights from Mortain and Richard brought up the rear. They all headed to where their scouts had informed them of the English position. The duke was dressed in full chainmail armour, with long sleeves, covering his whole body, even the calves of his legs: as was his brother Odo. Because he was a Bishop of the church Odo was forbidden to shed blood, so he was riding to battle carrying a three-foot long mace, the end of which was a heavy flanged head of wrought iron. 'I can't shed blood, but I can bash in a few sculls,' was his illogical and typically arrogant reasoning.

William's heart raced with excitement, 'I have waited a long time for this', he thought to himself. All the months of preparation and the vast amounts of money he had spent, would now hang on the outcome of this day.

William rode at the head of an elite mounted military cavalry force, which now led the way for their infantry and archers to follow. Both cavalry and infantry were equipped with long sleeved chain-mail hauberks, long leaf-shaped shields and conical helmets, which had a strong nosepiece in the centre. There were many more Norman archers than the English had. William relied a great deal on his archers, who were lightly clothed to allow rapid movement on the battlefield and easy use of the bow. Their bows were short, about four feet in length. Against chain mail, its effective range was no more than about fifty yards.

As the Normans marched the six miles from Hastings, to meet the English, they were singing. The song they sang was 'The Song of Roland', a warrior hero of Normandy. Roland's warlike example was being used in song to raise the fighter's valour. This song had a rousing chorus, which all joined in with gusto.

Duke William had promised all those who fought with him would be well rewarded, with booty and land. 'Their houses will be yours,' he declared, 'I will give you their farms, and those who gave money, ships and weapons to this crusade, I will return with interest. You will have titles, earldoms, shires, cities and towns. All this I will give to those who have given to me, and I will give in proportion to that donated.' This was a very popular motivation for most of William's followers, but the loudest cheer had been heard when he decreed, 'And I will give you their women.' Their spirits were high as they marched these six miles, to war, singing.

When the Norman force drew close to that of the English, they stopped singing, their hearts sank; when looking up to the top of the ridge all they could see was a forest of glittering spears and shields. King Harold's army was clearly arrayed in great strength; he had deployed his army well with all his military skill, along a ridge of rising ground. The heavily armed Housecarls were placed to the front, while the Fyrd were placed to their rear. In the thickest of the ranks, Harold's royal banner, the golden dragon of Wessex and England, flew proudly above all. Harold himself stood close beside this large banner, together with his brothers, Gyrth and Leofwin and also Alric. Alric's heart raced with uncontrolled excitement as he looked along the lines of men. Their awful battle-axes, which had shed the blood of those who died at Stamford Bridge, were clearly displayed, being waved threateningly in their thousands. All knew this weapon could deliver a devastating blow which no shield or chainmail armour could withstand. Every Housecarl was sheltered by the solid, interlocked shield-wall. Alric was satisfied that these Englishmen looked a formidable force indeed.

Taking his eyes away from the site of his men, his heart full of pride, Alric looked down the slope of the hill and saw the Normans forming up at the bottom. Then, turning to the King with a look of puzzlement on his face, he said, 'Sire they are mounted!' In disbelief he added, 'They are going to use horse against us.'

'Indeed they are,' Harold acknowledged. Then tuning to all who could hear him, he shouted, 'A horse and rider will fall if you hack the horse's legs. They will not stand against our great two-handed battle-axes. Use shields well to protect the axe men. Even on horse they will still fall', then turning his men he laughed aloud, 'only they will fall harder from a horse.' There was gruff laughter from the ranks.

An unnatural silence descended over both armies as the English watched the Normans manoeuvre into position. For a brief moment, each man was alone with his thoughts, contemplating what was to come. Harold seeing this, suddenly raised his voice, 'Let us make sure these Norman dogs know where they belong, together with their bastard leader.' Then he started to chant, 'Out, out, out, out,' he bellowed for all to hear. Immediately his army took up the chant, 'Out, out, out,' they sounded, as each in unison slapped his shield with his weapon. The chant then added a cutting word, as it rose to become a crescendo, 'Bastard out, bastard out, bastard out,' it went on, and on, for some minutes. Then, the English erupted into a thunderous clattering of weapons upon their shields. Their anger made clear to every Norman.

There were not so many war drums, as there had been at Stamford Bridge, but there were still enough to start up a rhythmic beating, following the initial chanting, which soon became the preamble for the chorus of further chants from the English warriors.

If the Normans were intimidated, they did not show it. Yet, as they looked up, the English battle-axes looked gray and cold and they knew they might feel those bitter edges of cleaving steel, before the day was spent.

William formed up his army on lower ground, about one-hundred and fifty yards away from the English, just out of range of Ricbert and the few archers in Harold's army. William's army was set in three divisions, the right-hand division was made up of French and Flemish troops under the command of Eustace of Boulogne, who was more eager than most to wreak his revenge against the English. This was the same Eustace who had caused the people of Dover to riot during the reign of King Edward-the-Confessor and one of the key instigators of the hatred between the Anglo-Saxons and the Normans.

The Normans straddled the London-Hastings road, facing Harold's left wing. Their left division, on flat and boggy ground, was made up of Bretons, from Maire and Anjou, and commanded by Alan Fergent, the Count of Brittany. The centre, which had many more men, than either the left, or the right flanks, was made up of the Normans under the command of William's half brothers Bishop Odo and Robert, Count of Mortain. It was here that William raised the standard of Normandy, two rampant golden lions on a red background, along with the papal banner of the red cross on a white background.

Richard was bringing up the rear, with the reserves.

Each division of William's army consisted of ranks of three rows. In the front were archers and spearmen, the second ranks were rows of infantry, and the third ranks were rows of cavalry.

Leofwin, looking down at the Normans forming up, said in a wistful, casual fashion to his brother, 'They would be easy prey for us now Harold.' Leofwin was impatient for action, as he saw the rows of Flemish and French moving in front of the English line, 'We should attack. We could scatter them with ease.'

'Never,' cried Harold, 'We must not lose our protection or break our shield-wall.' Then turning to his men, he baulked out an order, 'Hold the line men. No one must leave this line without my permission. Our shield-wall must not be broken. If we hold the wall the day will be ours.' A loud cheer went up from Harold's massed ranks. They were now so tightly packed together; it was difficult for some in the centre to move.

Turning to his brother, Harold rebuked him for his young foolhardiness, 'If we were to go down the hill, away from our protection, the Norman cavalry would swing round and be upon us, before we knew what had happened. We must hold this line at all costs.' He then turned again and spoke loud, so that all could hear him, 'The longer we hold this position, the more reinforcements will get through to us from the Fyrd who are still on their way here. Bastard William, on the other hand, is on a foreign shore, he can expect no one to reinforce his men. If we hold this line victory will be ours.' More cheers ensued from the English army.

The Anglo-Saxon war drums now began a profound and menacing beat. Deep and heavy, boom, boom, boom didi boom, rang out which could be heard for miles around. Ricbert felt a pang of guilt as he heard them.

By now it was the ninth hour of the day and William's three divisions began their slow advance up the ridge toward the English lines. In front of Duke William rode a minstrel by the name of Taillefer. He was in full chainmail armour and singing, inspiring the Normans with his 'Songs of Roland and of Charlemagne', at the same time he was throwing his sword up in the air, in a clever juggling action. Prompted by the thrill of battle, he sheathed his sword, grabbed his spear, and charged single handed toward the enemy line, unswerving up the hill toward the English Housecarls. As he drew close to the English ranks, he launched his spear, which was easily deflected by a Housecarl's shield. He then took hold of his sword and rode straight into the heart of the Housecarls. Within seconds, he was engulfed by them and cut down. The English cheered loudly and the Normans cursed back, enraged by the death of their favoured minstrel. First blood had been shed.

'It is as he wished it to be,' declared William to his stunned men.

William's archers now came within range of the English lines.

'*Archers stand to!*' ordered William and the ranks of archers stopped in their tracks.

He cupped his hands to his mouth and roared out an order, '*Front ranks ready!*'

The front ranks of archers rippled forward. Each man reached back to retrieve an arrow from his quiver. They tensed waiting for the order.

'*Release!*'

There was a deep twanging as the archers all released their arrows simultaneously.

Their disappointment was soon evident as most of the arrows bounced off or stuck into the shield-wall.

'*Rapid fire!*' William yelled. There was a hail of arrows, for some time. Volley after volley was released.

The English started laughing and taunting them, as the arrows did little damage.

'Is that the best you can do?' they jeered. Then they started their chant again, 'Bastard out, bastard out, bastard out,' they went on and on, banging their shields as they did so, with the drums joining in.

It soon became clear this attack was ineffectual. A captain approached Robert, 'We must watch our arrow numbers; they will soon get low if we use them at this rate. They are not returning any of our fire, so there are none we can retrieve.' Then he added, 'By firing uphill we are only hitting their shield-wall.'

William watched; he had seen that the arrow attack had been ineffectual. He was now getting annoyed. *'Archers to the rear!'* he barked.

'Keep your shields up men,' ordered Alric. 'They are doing nothing to worry us as yet.' He knew this was a fine start to the battle; but it was far from being over.

William rode out a little, to where he could be seen by his men. His anger blazed as he rebuked these men, 'You are fighting here for survival. If you fail this day, the English will not treat you kindly. Here, this day, we will fight a great victory or we will die. Today you will either have gold or earth; which is it to be?' Then drawing his sword he yelled, 'Are you ready?' A great cheer went up.

'Infantry forward!' roared the duke.

Lines of heavily armoured foot soldiers now began their, tromp, tromp, tromp, up the hill toward the English ranks, with William and Odo to their rear.

'Javelins ready!' came the duke's following order.

'Javelins ... loose!'

Several thousand javelins flew over and into the English shield-wall. The affect was immediate. Many found their mark, killing or wounding effectively. The ranks of the English were so densely packed together the Norman javelins could not fail, either to hit a man, or to become stuck into the shields of the defenders; thereby rendering the shield too difficult to hold up, with the extra weight of the shaft sticking out of it. Gaps in the shield-wall appeared as the defender either died or tried to break off the javelin stuck in his shield. The Norman infantry charged the English line with full force and fury. Some, who were more powerfully built than their comrades, burst through making a gap between the shields, but they fell straight onto the points of swords and spears.

Alric braced himself, clenched his teeth and tightened the grip on his battle-axe. For the first time in this battle, he came to blows with the enemy, but he had to give ground, as a group of crazed Normans threw themselves into the centre of the English around Alric. As Alric backed away, he saw these hot-headed Normans cut down by the frenzied thrusts of Housecarls to his right. While Alric gathered his senses, another Norman was on him. Alric summoned all his considerable power and struck; his axe found its mark and the Norman's head snapped back, his blood spraying into the air, splattering all those around. The men around Alric steadily closed up the gap in the shield-wall, making an unbroken line, once again.

Ricbert frustrations grew; he tried in vain to find a target to shoot at. There were so many men in front of him, it was impossible for him to see the enemy. All he could do was to shoot up into the air with the hope it would find its mark.

The English fighting style and aggression now broke forth in its full fury and in all its gory glory. Their deadly battle-axes crashed into the Norman infantry, pounding through chainmail and helmet alike. Men fell, with sculls split and limbs cut through. The Norman sword was no match for the traditional Anglo-Saxon axe. Ordgar and the Fyrd moved in close behind the Housecarls. The Fyrd were holding on to their spears, using them effectively to jab at the enemy through any gaps in the ranks of the Housecarls. These jabbing spears were bringing men down in large numbers, others from the Fyrd simply hurled rocks and other missiles onto their foe. Ordgar was a bundle of energy, directing his men and using his spear well whenever he could.

The impetus of the charge had been broken, and the Normans backed away amidst the tangle of dead and writhing wounded.

'See the shield-wall works to perfection,' cried Alric to his King, above the noise of battle. 'There is no break in the line.' Harold felt his heartbeat pounding in his chest as he acknowledged this with a clenched fist salute to Alric.

The fallen of the Norman infantry now lay on the ground, with shattered faces, broken legs and pierced stomachs. While others endeavoured to hold in their intestines, as battle-axes had disembowelled them. Bodies now piled up on top of each other.

Odo now rode his horse into the English ranks, swinging his deadly mace and shouting and cursing as he did. His great mace he swung in all directions, onto the sculls and shoulders of all he could reach. He was a fearsome sight, but even his intervention was not able to break the English shield-wall. Odo pulled away, for fear of his horse getting hurt, but he had already caused great damaged, which inspired his brother to carry out his next move.

'Infantry pull back!' bellowed William through cupped hands to his mouth. Men now ran back down the hill as fast as they could, tripping and stumbling over; so badly did they want to escape the rocks and spears.

After seeing the relative success of his brother, William barked out an order, *'Send in the cavalry!'*

Pulling his horse to come alongside William, Odo expressed his gathering frustration, 'It is too soon, we should wait until there is a break in the wall.'

'We must try,' insisted William.

Odo nodded his reluctant agreement. Robert and William formed the cavalry up into line, facing the hill's incline. At the sight of so many fine horses, snorting and pawing at the ground in excitement, William had every reason to be proud of his cavalry. The infantry stood resolutely still, their grim faces helped to steady the others, as the cavalry readied themselves.

William gritted his teeth, said nothing, then pulling his horse to the front, drew his spear and at the top of his voice yelled, *'Follow me!'*

William, Odo and Robert led the charge together, up the hill toward the massed ranks of the English behind the still intact shield-wall. In unison the cavalry lowered their spears, to use them as lances. With these long wooden spears couched under their arms, the cavalry charged. The thunderous throng of mounted men soon reached the shield-wall. As they did so, many became awestruck by the English array of sharp spears, bristling out of the wall, impaling many horses. The momentum of the charge was turned at the wall, forcing them to gallop parallel with the wall, instead of straight at it. As they rode along side of the shield-wall, many Normans hurled their spears at a sighted target, finding their mark, killing or maiming the Housecarls. Gaps in the shield-wall now began to appear, as row after row of Norman cavalry threw their spears into these tightly packed ranks of Harold's army. Some of the riders reversed their grip on the spear holding it above their heads, striking down at the English in a jabbing motion. It was a costly charge to both sides, but still the English wall was not broken.

The mounted Normans sped back down the hill in a sweeping semi-circle, to return to their men at the base of the hill, disappointed at the failure of this charge to break the wall.

'The wall has held,' declared King Harold. 'If they come again release your javelins,' he ordered, above the cries and screams of the wounded.

With fresh spears gathered, the second Norman charge now came up the hill, but this time they were met by a hail from thousands of javelins and other missiles, directed by the agile Ordgar. When a horse fell, a Fyrd man ran out from the ranks, to dispatch the prone warrior with his axe or sword, then quickly retreated behind the shield-wall: unless that is, a Norman rider got to him first. William again lost many of his men from this attack, as did the English.

'Ride again into the shield-wall,' ordered William.

For a third time the Norman cavalry rode up the hill, to attack the shield-wall on a full frontal assault. As they approached, each Norman rider was again forced to turn his mount side-on, this time to be able to use his sword more effectively. By this action the horse was more open to attack. Often a long battle-axe would cut through both a horse and its rider in one mighty swing. When a horse had been cut from under a rider, the Norman in his heavy hauberk was suddenly defenceless, unless he could quickly regain his footing, but even then, he was targeted by the infuriated English. Swirls of blood shot up into the air, as the legs of horses and riders were cut through. Odo fought wildly with his mace, killing many men. Still the exhausted shield-wall held its ground.

With the failure of yet another attack, there was a lull in the fighting as the Normans re-grouped. For a moment, the battleground went strangely quiet.

'One more attack and we will have them,' William sought to rally his army's flagging morale. 'We will combine the infantry and cavalry in the next attack. This time we will break them.'

The English took this opportunity in the lull to move their dead and wounded to the rear, these once brave, bright-eyed men had now become just a bloody mess. The dead horses were also creating an obstacle to easy movement, but a dead horse was too heavy to move. Men were panting heavily for breath. They searched for some jars of water to quench their dry mouths, as their breath laboured through open mouths. It was now near mid-day, and both sides were exhausted.

'The shield-wall is strong again sire,' Alric informed Harold as he saw to the removal of the dead away from the wall. Harold looked grim and just nodded to Alric.

'*Archers stand to!*' William again wanted to try an aerial barrage. A more nervous look now appeared on their faces as they took up line formation.

'*Release!*'

This time more arrows found their marks, but they still had little effect on the shield-wall.

'*Cavalry, with me!*' William dug his heels into his horse.

Archers fell back to the rear of the ranks to let the cavalry through.

'Infantry forward!' Robert called out.

The massed ranks of foot soldiers once again set off up the hill behind the cavalry. The bulk of William's army now began to march once more toward the English defences, cavalry at the front, accompanied by infantry close behind.

The encounter was as fierce as ever. As soon as the Normans came within range, they were again met by a murderous assault of spears and axes, causing numerous casualties. Horses lay dying and kicking wildly, a danger to anyone who came too close to them. One writhing animal, caught a soldier in the shield-wall, with a large cracking sound, the man's leg doubled back on itself; broken at the shinbone, sending him tumbling over in great pain. The man pleaded for someone to help him, but to reach out and pull him back behind the wall would have meant certain death for whoever tried to do so. Instead, he disappeared under the bodies of Normans cut down in their attempts to break through the wall.

Alric carried on swinging his deadly axe. He hacked at anything that moved in front of him, with a style honed from years of training and warfare; he could keep this up for hours.

Suddenly a cry went up from the Norman ranks, 'The Duke is dead!' The Norman advance stopped in their tracks and panic began to set in among them. A look of absolute horror quickly spread across the faces of the attacking Normans as the word flashed across their massed ranks. 'The Duke is dead,' they all repeated, in wide-eyed fear, almost stopping them in their tracks. Immediately, some began to fall back, not willing to be in a leaderless fight.

An English battle-axe had killed Duke William's horse from under him. He struggled to his feet as his bodyguards quickly surrounded him, fighting off a concentrated assault around him. The duke then lifted off his helmet, turned to look at his men coming up the hill, so all could see his face.

'I am not dead,' he shouted. 'Your Duke lives.'

He instinctively grabbed another's horse, mounted it and rode out along the ranks, still with no helmet on, showing his face and shouting, 'Your Duke lives, your Duke lives.'

'Advance, advance!' William screeched at the top of his voice.

The infantry recovered and continued their attack, but the incident had unnerved some. William was beginning to get desperate, with up to one quarter of his force now either killed or wounded. Such high losses and yet the English line was still intact. The Norman position was looking precarious. William knew if the next attacks failed, it was likely he would face defeat in a foreign land. Defeat he knew would mean almost certain death for all the invaders.

King Harold wanted to change tactics and so pushed his way over, through the densely packed ranks of his men, over to where Alric was fighting, swinging his mighty battle axe around him. 'Alric!' King Harold shouted, distracting Alric. As Alric turned to see his King, a Norman foot soldier broke through the wall, and came rushing toward him with his spear held low and out stretched. 'Alric!' Harold shouted a warning, then instantly added, 'Look out, a Norman is on you.'

Alric quickly turned, and with the skill of a trained specialist, in the blink of an eye, he cut through the assailants' spear shaft with his axe. Swinging his axe hard in an upward sweeping action, knocking off the Norman's helmet while separating his upper and lower jaws as his battle-axe cut deep into the face of the Norman. This act brought a smile of satisfaction to both Alric and Harold.

'Alric, you must order the right flank to *"About Arms,"* Instructed Harold. 'We will win this fight, but we must hang on until night fall. Bastard William cannot stay here all night and must then retreat to a safer area. If he does this, we have him, our forces will be stronger as more join us and he will be much weaker. So give the order.'

Alric immediately moved back away from the front line, calling upon the trained left-handed Housecarls to ready themselves and get in position. There was a great deal of bustling behind the right flank of the shield-wall, signifying the compliance with this order. A new row of Housecarls now stood behind those fighting on the front line.

'*About Arms!*' bellowed Alric, at the top of his voice.

Suddenly the front row of Housecarls on the right flank stepped back, to be replaced by those behind. Using a right-handed grip on their shields, they could now swing their swords toward their opponent's unguarded right-hand side, requiring the right-handed attackers to shift their shield over toward the defending Housecarls. This unexpected action exposed the Norman foot soldier to sword thrusts from their unguarded side. This tactic quickly diminished the attacking speed and ability of the Normans and they visibly began to slow. The Bretons on this left flank of the Norman infantry were now faltering.

The English seeing the weakness of the Bretons threw themselves forward and broke their attack, routing them. As they fled back down the hill in disorder, the Fyrd on the English right flank moved forward away from their shield wall and ran after the fleeing Bretons. The Fyrd attacked the centre division on the Norman's now open flank, forcing a disorderly retreat of the Normans. It was a rout. The confusion quickly spread to the centre right; the Norman line gave way as a whole.

Excited by their success, many of the Fyrd broke ranks and ran even further down the hill after their fleeing foes

Ricbert joined with the pursuing Fyrd. At last, he thought I have a chance now to do something. He stopped, while he gathered his remaining few arrows taking aim to shoot. This was easy, he reasoned, as several of his arrows found their mark. His disappointment with his earlier perceived failure now turned to elation. He shot arrow after arrow down the hill at the fleeing Normans. His emotions were running wild, but then his elation suddenly turned to fear when he realised he had shot his last arrow.

'Come back, come back!' yelled Harold. 'Do not follow them.'

'*Stop them! Come back!*' barked Alric also, horrified at the action of the Fyrd. In the noise of battle, most of the energized Fyrd could not hear this order; but Ricbert did, and somewhat sheepishly returned to his line.

'What are they doing?' Harold looked on in despair, knowing what was soon to happen.

Duke William seeing the Fyrd break out from their shield-wall, could not believe his luck, 'We have them,' he shouted. 'We have them. *Cavalry - with me – now!*' Then at the top of his voice he yelled, '*Charge!*'

The Norman cavalry thundered along with their duke, swinging round and up the hill; surrounding the hapless Fyrd, who had broken away from the protection of their ranks. Clearly in the open, they were no match for mounted cavalry in full armour. Hundreds of English were cut down; few who had left the shield-wall survived this onslaught. King Harold and Alric looked on in horror as in front of them, valiant men, who had followed their King were now being cut down and slaughtered.

Following this episode another lull came in the battle. The English shield-wall had become noticeably smaller. Duke William called the captains of his archers together, 'You are to change the trajectory of arrows,' he ordered. 'Instead of aiming at the shield-wall, shoot high above it so that the arrows fall on those behind.'

One of the captains responded to this order, 'My lord, we are running low on arrows, we have barely enough for another few volleys.'

'Then they must all count,' said the Duke with a determination none dare argue with.

The order was given throughout the ranks of the archers. '*Archers - forward!*' A bustle of movement rippled through the ranks, as the archers again took their stance to the front of the Norman troops.

'Make your arrows count. Aim high men, above the shield-wall.' William waited while all bowmen pulled back their bows. '*Release!*'

The sky was suddenly full of arrows aimed high above the front ranks of the English. The effect was immediate as the hail of arrows dropped on the men behind the shield-wall. Ordgar's men were hit the hardest, as his men fell dead by their dozens. Ricbert had not at first seen the hail of arrows coming. Only when he felt a sudden pain in his leg did he realise arrows were now falling down on them from the sky, instead of as before, being shot at the shield-wall. The pain was intense, but with his sword drawn and his bow discarded, he continued to stand.

The duke, pleased at the effect of the arrows, ordered, *'Again captains!'* he hollered. *'Again! Again!'*

Simultaneously all rows of archers dew back their bows, and rapidly shot them above the English ranks. Volley after volley of arrows rose against the afternoon sky, falling into the back rows of Harold's army.

Satisfied at the affect from the repeated hail of arrows, William voiced another order, *'Archers withdraw!'*

Changes had also been made in the English position. The shield-wall was now too thin to adequately defend the entire ridgeline, due to their heavy casualties. As a result, the wall now shifted to concentrate on the slightly higher positions in the centre. While this allowed the Normans to attack from level ground from the west, it would still be no easy task though for them.

'Infantry forward!'

The Norman foot soldiers moved forward, their ranks close together. This wave of assault was the fiercest of the day. The two sides crunched together, shield-to-shield, close enough to hear the panted breath of the enemy straining in their throats. By mid afternoon weaknesses now began to appear in the English defences. William, seeing this, kicked into the sides of his horse and the cavalry again followed up the hill. The weakened right flank of Harold's army was now exploited by William as he poured his force into it. A gap had been created and the Normans now wheeled around into it, constricting even more the limited movement of the English. Gyrth and Leofwin immediately saw the danger to the King. Flinging themselves, with their bodyguard into the encroaching Normans, they began to drive them back. Steadily the gap in the line was closed. As the line was closing a mounted Norman threw himself and his horse sideways onto those defending Gyrth and Leofwin, crushing them beneath. Thus exposed, the attackers reached and then pierced through Gyrth, killing him instantly, before the horrified eyes of his brothers Harold and Leofwin; the bile rising in their throats.

It was with herculean effort from the English, that the wave of this Norman attack was beaten back, but Harold felt frozen with shock. Harold's line of defence still held, but it was much weakened and the men were stunned at the death of Earl Gyrth.

William sensed the flow of battle was turning his way. Harold's defensive core had been greatly reduced in size. Dazed and rooted to the spot, Harold was in a state of shock. Harold, Alric, a few Thanes, blood soaked Housecarls and the remaining Fyrd, stood around the banner of the golden dragon. The day was now drawing to a close, as the afternoon gathered on a pace toward evening. It had been a very long day for all, but now William smelt victory.

Simultaneously, William's forces struck hard at both ends of the wall and the centre. The defenders were already thinly stretched and now Harold was forced to concentrate his forces into even smaller groups to meet this attack. It was desperate fighting. When at last they had again thrown back the Normans, Harold's men were in a desperate shape, they were exhausted. Many could barely stand.

Alric was panting heavily, leaning on his shield, waiting for the next onslaught. Turning to Ordgar, Alric gasped, breathless with exertion and finding words difficult to form, 'We must ... protect ... the ... King.' Ordgar looked toward Harold and nodded, when he saw the state of disarray that now surrounded their King. They both started to move across, through the exhausted warriors, men with staring eyes, their clothes blood soaked, some crouching down to rest their tired legs. Everyman was covered in blood.

'They can be held,' shouted Alric to reassure them, as he and Ordgar moved through the throng.

Tragically they failed to see six mounted Norman knights, chosen for this deed, led by Duke William himself and accompanied by Count Eustace. William had formulated this next move when he realised he now had an opportunity to strike. This specially chosen band now charged the weakened English line, immediately breaking through. They spurred their horses forward, hacking their way amidst the defenders, straight toward the banner of the golden dragon, where King Harold stood; the blood of others dripping from him. These knights, with one purpose of mind, were soon upon the King, slashing and hacking as they went. The remains of Harold's guard were quickly felled as Duke William found himself close to the banner of England. He saw his men with swords raised high, thrusting them down repeatedly. In the blind fury of war, they repeatedly hacked at the now lifeless body of King Harold, as he lay prone on the earth; the earth he had fought so hard to defend. The Normans did not stop and continued to decapitate and dismember their hated opponent.

'The King is dead!' this appalled cry went out from the distraught English army. The English war machine had now been reduced to a series of isolated groups, with each man fighting for survival and each fighting to the death. The Norman's gave no quarter as they cut down and slaughtered every English defender they could. The Normans cut them down as if they were firewood. More than two thirds of King Harold's army now lay dead, or wounded.

Ricbert found himself using his sword in hand-to-hand combat. He felt so tired. Throughout all his training he had concentrated on his bow, now his bow was gone. Sword fighting was never his best skill, but he gave it all he could. So concentrated were his actions, he did not even notice the pain in his leg from the arrow, all he could think was, 'I must fight on.'

Swinging wildly he stumbled over the body of another. An intense pain racked his hand, as a Norman foot stamped down hard upon it, breaking the bones. He turned only to see, when looking up, a spear thrust into his chest. The noise of battle quickly receded from him, as he looked up to the cloudy sky; his last thoughts were for his family. Had Wilfred made it home all right...?

Leofwin and Alric were the lone surviving leaders. Leofwin sought to gather some remaining ranks around him, but with the crush of dead bodies and the many wounded thrashing horses around him, he could not move. He held his sword high, pointing it toward the enemy; he was lost in a desire to kill. Leofwin was in a combined state of grief and frenzy, knowing his brothers were dead. Though he bawled frantic orders, no one heard him. Ahead of him came the Normans, with battered shields and blood covered faces. Truly looking like Orcs.

'Dismount!' William ordered. 'Finish the work.'

The Norman troops moved through the field, stabbing any Englishman who showed any sign of life, Leofwin being no exception. Hands gained purchase on some part Leofwin's armour and to his horror, he felt himself begin to slip. He swung out and killed another man, only to see the sword torn from his arm. The pain was intense as he met a hard death, beneath a myriad of stomping armoured feet, holding him down while he was impaled, again and again.

These Norman troops looked like butchers from the shambles, as they destroyed all who were before them, the dead now lying in heavy heaps of human flesh. A youthful generation of English manhood, slaughtered.

In absolute horror, Alric and Ordgar had both seen their King, and his brothers' fall. It was plainly clear to them, and to those who could still understand anything, that their situation was now hopeless. There was only one thing left for them to do; they beckoned to those remaining to flee this field of death.

'Retreat if you wish to live,' Alric said to those still standing around him. 'We have seen enough of our people die here today.'

The golden leaves of a nearby beech tree, fluttered down to the ground, as the sun set.

Stumbling through the trees with daylight almost gone, Alric, Ordgar and a few dozen other survivors, fled wildly away from the carnage: to where, they knew not. Furtive glances were constantly being cast behind them, no one daring to speak, save to whisper under their breath as they ran, 'Oh my God! Oh my God!' Were they being followed? They did not know. Their singular thought was to, 'Just keep running, while we can.'

The dense woodland helped conceal them in making this mad dash to some form of safety. Breathless, some began to ask, 'Where are we heading?'

'As far away as we can get,' confessed others.

'We will head along the north road and try and make for London as quick as we can,' panted Ordgar, his eyes beginning to sting with the blood running into them. He was not sure if it was his own blood or that from someone else.

'Quiet!' Alric said in a loud whisper. 'Someone is ahead of us.' The group abruptly stopped running and peered into the gloom. A large body of men were approaching, he could not tell how many, but they were on foot. Then they all froze, the reason was not so much as to whom might be ahead of them, but because of the sound of mounted cavalry behind them. They were surrounded.

All crouched down in the last tall bracken of summer, now brown and dying, but still standing and providing a good hiding place. Ordgar suddenly stood up, 'They are speaking English,' he declared. 'Who goes there?' he shouted.

'Fyrdmen, come to join our King,' was the unexpected, but welcome reply.

Alric, Ordgar and the others now stood up and walked to the new arrivals.

'Good God in heaven,' a startled Fyrdman declared in shock, looking at the ghastly shapes now emerging from the undergrowth. About thirty newly arrived Fyrd gathered around them. The look of horror on the faces of these new men, said it all. Alric realised how dishevelled they must look, so he spoke up, 'You come too late brothers, the battle is lost and good King Harold is dead.'

'What! How? When? Where?' Were all the words these startled new arrivals could utter. Then looking at the survivors and seeing the obvious truth in the matter, these new men were stunned with such news, they simply said, 'Dear God! What will become of us?'

The noise of the mounted men grew closer. Alric saw an open area of grassland a short distance away. 'Prepare for battle men,' he shouted and started to run forward. Turning to the new arrivals he said, 'You may get you chance to kill Normans yet. Now move yourselves, quickly,' he ordered. Finding the new arrivals gave a renewed strength to the veterans of the battle, they all ran to where the land opened up, forming a clearing. At the far end was a large drainage ditch, built to carry water away and drain the land. As they reached it, Alric, and all of the men who had survived the battle, threw themselves down at the water's edge, desperate to gulp their first drink that day; they were so thirsty that it was several minutes before anyone spoke.

'Form a shield-wall on the far side of this ditch,' ordered Alric.

'It is getting too dark to see,' said a new arrival.

'Exactly,' was Alric's retort, 'now shout.'

'What?'

'Shout! Bring them over here,' Alric glared at them through the blood, sweat and mud on his face. He had found his old authority coming back to him. The others were unsure, but could see Alric meant what he said and that maybe he knew what he was doing.

'Bastards! Devils! Go home!' Their voices were shaking as they shouted into the gloom.

At first, there was no response. 'Bastards! Devils! Go home!' they all repeated, this time more loudly. Then the mounted Normans came crashing through the woodland and undergrowth. It had been difficult for them to find a track and the trees made it tricky to spread out, so they came out of the woods and into the open ground in single file. The Norman cavalry dimly saw about one-hundred of their English foe, lined up against the far tree line, across from an open clearing of pasture land. After a short time around fifty Normans lined their horses up in a single line, facing the English. These men had their blood lust up; after fighting all that long day, they were keen to see that none escaped them now.

The English could plainly see now what Alric had in mind and waited in excited anticipation. The English line was on the far side of the ditch, which because night was now falling, was difficult to see from a distance.

The Normans reigned in their horses, and then slowly manoeuvred into one long line. Kicking their spurs, they charged forth toward the English at full pelt. All they could see, with their fixed vision, were the English awaiting them; too late did they also see the ditch into which they now charged, headlong. Both horses and riders crashed into heaps at the feet of the vengeful English. Vengeance was taken. Pent up anger, frustration, fear and hurt, a jumble of emotions, were now unleashed in full fury against the fallen foe, who were writhing in the water of the ditch. A Norman raised his arm across his face in protection, as he looked up and saw Alric, his face full of hate, with his battle-axe raised. An instant later, the axe swept down towards the Norman, it barely shuddered as it cut clean through the

Norman's forearm, shattered his helmet and buried itself deep into his skull.

Within half an hour, all Normans lay dead. 'That was a bad ditch for them,' declared a member of the Fyrd, as he plunged his knife into the throat of a prone Norman, just to make sure he was dead.

'Bad ditch it maybe,' said Alric, picking up an extra sword from a Norman, 'but no doubt they will use the Latin word and call it "Malfosse"'.

Alric's band of men now turned and walked off into the dark night, their emotions a mixture of fear, anger and trepidation.

It had been a restless night. Some of the Norman warriors had slept exhausted where they could, on the cold, damp grass, but the cries of the wounded and dying, pierced the air all night long. The smell of blood enraged the nostrils. It had not been easy for the men to sleep and William was no exception. As he lay there throughout the night, his mind kept reeling with the same thought, 'William the bastard, the dishonoured and insulted grandson of a tanner, was now Conqueror of England.'

When William rose in the morning, he looked out at the battlefield. The stench of death was everywhere, 'What is the name of this place?' he asked his commanders. A captain replied, 'We are told it is called "Santlache", which means "Sandy Stream."' William looked up at the ridge above where he stood, piled with bodies, 'From now it will be called "Senlac", which means "Blood Lake."'

William remained standing outside his campaign tent for some time. A group of men saw William and brought the banner of the golden dragon over and laid it at his feet. William looked down at it as it was placed before him. 'Send this Saxon banner to the Pope in Rome. Tell him God has heard his blessing of our crusade and our prayers, for God has granted us a great victory.'

Like many men William still felt weak from the exertions of the battle. He looked up at the pile of bodies on the ridge of Senlac Hill. Many of the bodies were now naked, for throughout the night and early morning, anything and everything of value had been stripped from the prone English warriors. Weapons and chainmail were especially sought after.

William walked slowly up to the top of the hill. There he saw the red cross on the white background, the standard blessed by the Pope. It had been planted where the banner of the golden dragon had flown so proudly, just a short while before. By the side of this standard was the banner of the two rampant lions of Normandy, gently waving in the cool wind. William had never felt so satisfied.

Odo, Robert and Richard now joined William. They were still feeling in a dazed state after their exertions of yesterday. William eyed Richard, but said nothing; he could not remember what action, if any, Richard had seen yesterday. Robert had been the first of the brothers to go up to the ridge that morning, to view the carnage. 'We must bury the dead quickly,' Robert had been visibly moved by what he had seen. 'I will get burial parties ready.'

William looked grim, 'Yes we must bury our dead with all military honours, as you say.' Robert nodded and was about to move off, when unexpectedly William added, 'But no English are to be buried.'

Robert could not believe what he had heard. 'Brother we must bury them all,' he indignantly declared.

'Robert, we *must* do nothing,' William insisted, slowly. 'We are now the masters of this land and I will say what *must*, and *must not* be done.' Then turning to Richard, he said curtly to him, with a hidden anger, 'Call the captains together.'

Within a short time, commanders, captains and knights stood before William. With his face taught, he then made a pronouncement, 'Our noble dead, who fought with us on this field, will all receive a warrior's Christian burial. This you must do immediately.' Then kicking the limp arm of a dead Englishman, he added, 'These English dogs, who tried to refuse me as their rightful king, will not be buried; neither today, tomorrow, nor ten years from now. Let them rot where they lie, as a lesson to all.' There was a murmuring among those listening; even the most hardened Norman soldier was shocked by these words.

'What about Earl Harold?' asked Odo. 'Should he not receive some honour, a Christian burial?'

William did not answer and thought it over for a moment, then, reluctantly agreed, 'For him I will make an exception. After all, he was a true warrior and he did give us a hard fight.' William realised this order was not popular, but it did not concern him what others felt. 'Once our dead have been buried, we will make for Hastings and rest there for a few days, where we will await submission from the English nobles.' With that, William returned to his campaign tent.

Several hours later, Robert came back into William's tent. With his arms wide open, he gesticulated, 'It is impossible brother. The bodies are already stripped of the armour and their fine clothes, they are so badly mutilated we will never identify the body of Earl Harold. We just cannot find him.'

'So be it,' William snorted. 'It is God's will.'

Robert was still very uneasy about all this, and sought to make some kind of amends, 'I will send for one of his kin to see if the body of Earl Harold can be identified.' So saying, Robert walked out, disgusted with his brother, and leaving William to brood by himself.

WINTER

To hear about the terrors on the field of Senlac Hill was one thing, but to actually see its appalling aftermath was another. A sad group of weeping men and women stood mesmerised at the sight before them. Edith Swan-Neck had been called to identify the body of King Harold, she wanted so much to do this, but the process was too difficult to comprehend. So many dead men still lay strewn across this ridge. Alric, who was now in London, had told her, as best he could, the whereabouts their king had stood at his last; but it was so difficult. The bodies were far too heavy for one woman to move by herself and so Duke William had allowed her to take a small number to help. So two women and four men now set to this awful task.

Most, if not all of the bodies had been stripped of much of their clothing and anything of value they had once possessed. Not only were many bodies piled on the top of each other, wild animals, rooks, crows and seagulls had removed the eyes from many of the corpses, rats and foxes disfiguring them further.

Duke William had forbidden the burial of any of these English warriors, except the remains of Earl Harold. To disobey this order was to risk death. However, the Normans had yet to understand the tenacity of the English spirit and their ability to do what they thought was right, regardless of the consequences. Men had been coming in the night, to take a few bodies for a Christian burial, whenever they could, and at great risk to themselves should they be caught.

Edith Swan-Neck now walked through the carnage of the battlefield with great fortitude. She was determined to do what was right in her eyes, for the man she had loved for twenty years and whose children she happily mothered. Looking at the mounds of corpses all around her, she uttered, 'If the monsters that have done this are to rule our country, what will become of us?'

An oft-repeated expression from the men who were secretly transporting away a few of the slain warrior's remains was, 'Prey God, the Witan can help us from this misery.'

Edith and the other woman with her, clutched their veils tightly across their nose and mouth, in a vain effort to try to reduce the vile stench, which pervaded everywhere. It did not work and they vomited, as they went about their duty.

For several hours, they methodically moved and lifted corpse after corpse. Edith had told them to look for a certain mark. The task seemed endless. After a long time, Edith gave a sudden cry, her whole body trembled and she sobbed uncontrollably. At her feet was the decapitated body of a man, but high on the bicep was the tattoo of the golden dragon of Wessex and England.

'This is the father of my children,' she said as she collapsed into willing arms enclosing her, to hold her from falling. 'This is he, the one I loved the most on this earth.'

After a short search, the head of Harold was found. 'Now we can lay him to rest, with a Christian burial,' Edith said wiping her tears. 'He shall be laid at Waltham Abbey, which he had rebuilt in happier times and where he prayed on his way to Hastings.' Then looking around in disgust, added, 'Away from this vile field.'

As she watched the body of her beloved Harold being loaded onto a cart, her mind flew back to when they had been lovers and how witty and hansom he had been. These invaders could never take these precious memories away from her. Then on reflection, she drew some contentment from the thought that she still had his children, and his noble blood lived on in them.

The news of the defeat of King Harold travelled fast throughout the land of England. The English felt a sense of numbness and a cloud of despair and gloom hung over them all, they were unable or unwilling to comprehend what had happened to their nation. Norman heralds of victory set sail across the sea, exultantly proclaiming their great victory.

After the battle William returned to his base at Hastings. Many men had wounds needing treatment; some being beyond treatment just lay on blood soaked blankets, waiting for their inevitable death to arrive and put a stop to their torment. William set about reorganising his camp. The wounded he moved into the houses of the local people, demanding that they look after them. He ruefully acknowledged his army had suffered more than thirty percent losses, so replacements from Normandy were needed immediately, as were fresh supplies of food, wine, horses and weapons.

Not long after returning to Hastings, William called a council of war. He knew Earls Edwin and Morcar could still raise an army against him, if they so wished; at this stage he did not know how badly mauled the Northumbrian's had been at the battle of Fulford. He well knew these earls could possibly bring an army to attack him and he had to be ready.

William and his brothers moved into a local manor house, after ejecting the family. He sat with the generals and the captains of his army to discuss what they should do next, 'We will rest in Hastings for a while, while we await submission from the nobility of all England.' William fully expected the official surrender of England to take place within a few days.

'Replacements for the valiant men we have lost must be sent for. I have therefore ordered today many more armed men from Normandy to come and join us.' William then sought to counteract those who were over anxious to move on to London immediately. 'The English are beaten, but not yet broken,' he warned. 'Our supply lines across the sea could still be attacked by the English navy, which is largely intact. London and other cities may yet still raise another army against us and we do not know if the north of England will submit to our rule. Earls Edwin and Morcar, could between them, raise the north against us and even call on their people's blood ties with Denmark, for that country to come to their aid.'

All in the room went very quiet at these wise words coming from their Duke. Most had not thought of these matters before. For in truth, if the English could find a good leader, then they were still more than capable of forcing another battle. 'It is Earls Edwin and Morcar which now worry me the most. They were not here with Harold. We do not know why they were not here. Are they ready to submit to us, or are they getting ready to attack us? Until we know the answer to these questions we must keep up our guard.'

Richard shuffled in his chair, 'This is true William and well said. We must certainly keep our guard up, for we are in a foreign country and until we get fresh men from Normandy and France to join us, we are vulnerable.' Richard smiled, 'However, while we are here, can we not send out bands of men to subdue the surrounding countryside and towns?' Those listening grinned, as they comprehended what he was saying. 'A time of sport for our men; I am sure they will find much to amuse themselves.'

William remembered his promise to his men for loot and plunder. 'Yes Richard, why not?' he agreed. Realising the need to keep his men motivated and well rewarded for their efforts, William concurred, 'While we wait here for the submission of England, you may go hunting, seek out what you may find.' Those attending the Duke now laughed, for they had been told to take whatever they wished, whether it is plunder or women, or both. Their shouts of praise compared William to all the paladins of Charlemagne. William had now unleashed his savage soldiery, without check, upon southern England.

Throughout the next week a great deal of coming and going made the Norman camp a hive of activity. New ships arrived with men and supplies. Everyone seemed to be busy. The nights became drunken orgies as William indulged his men in the fruits of victory. William was pleased to see those who had won him a kingdom, get pleasure from their efforts. The cries and screams of women could be heard coming from many houses and field tents throughout each night. It was a time of debauchery, while the Normans raped and tormented any girl and woman they could take hold of, and whom they found pleasing to their eyes, often passing them from one group to another.

Yet as the week wore on, no envoy came from the English lords, no noble to give him homage; not even a herald. William's period of rest and contentment, quickly gave way to his usual rage. Again he was seen with his face wearing a brooding expression and a deep frown.

'Where are those dogs? Why have they not come to give me homage and accept me as their King?' William's irritation was plain for all to see.

On the sixth day, William decided to wait no more. He called all his generals and captains together. Robert and Odo stood either side of their brother, when William spoke it was again in his old fury. 'We have waited these last days for homage to be paid us, and none has come. Tomorrow we march out of

Hastings to let these English dogs see their true King. They will feel our wroth.' William paused and they wondered what he was going to say. 'When our fleet sailed from Normandy, two ships went astray and landed in a town called Romney,' William glared above their heads, and then went on. 'They slaughtered every man on board those two unfortunate ships. We will begin our march to London by first paying a visit to the town of Romney. Others will hear of our vengeance and consider what it means to them. We will set Romney as an example for others to fear.' Then turning to Count Eustace of Boulogne, 'Count Eustace, you have served us well, and you were one of those brave knights who stood with me in that noble band which slew Earl Harold, for that reason I give you the honour of leading this expedition against Romney.'

Eustace smiled, bowed and said, 'I thank you my Lord.'

William went on to make his point clear, 'We will not accept tribute, nor will we accept surrender. We will make a lesson of them. Let this be a warning to all, that we will not be resisted.'

'It will be done, my lord.' Eustace knew this would give him and his men great pleasure.

The Witan were assembling at Westminster Palace, Alric, Ordgar and many other Thanes had hurried to get to this important meeting. The faces of those in attendance were glum and displayed signs of strain. Seated on a central chair was a thin, slightly built, and very nervous fourteen-year-old boy. The boy's eyes and mouth were wide open. His trembling appearance blighted the fact he was Prince Edgar Atheling, the grandson of

King Edmund-Ironside and great-nephew of Edward-the-Confessor. Edgar was the last surviving male relative of King Alfred-the-Great. In spite of his pedigree, he was no leader of men and far too young to be considered as such. Edgar had a sister, Margaret, but she could not be considered for the crown, because it was a war leader that the Witan now wanted. To Edgar's right sat Ealdred, the Archbishop of York and on his left sat Stigand the Archbishop of Canterbury. In attendance was also Earl Edwin of Mercia, his brother Earl Morcar of Northumbria and Alric, General of what remained of the Housecarls.

Ealdred, like Stigand, was dressed in the ceremonial robes of the church; he now rose to address the Witan, 'My Lords, Royal Thanes and Noble Housecarls, this is a sad meeting for us all. A great disaster has befallen our country, one without equal. The sadness in our hearts knows no bounds; our hearts are breaking with grief.' Ealdred paused, searching for words and finding the whole thing very emotional. 'We meet this day to elect a new king, for our good and noble King Harold fell on the battlefield near Hastings.' He sighed deeply, 'Before we proceed further, I now ask that General Alric read out a list of our noble English who fell on that accursed October day.'

Alric stood up, with a parchment scroll in his hand. As he unrolled it he said, 'This is a grievous list we have to record.' Then he proceeded to read, 'Our most noble and brave Harold II, King of England fell that day, as did his two brothers, Gyrth Earl of East Anglia and Leofwin Earl of Kent. Also fallen that day were, Hakon, the nephew of King Harold, the man who had been held hostage by William the Bastard in Normandy, whose release was obtained by Harold when he was Earl of Wessex.' This list was so sad; it was difficult to comprehend what they were now hearing. Alric continued, 'Also to fall were, Aelfwig, King Harold's uncle and Abbot of Winchester; Leofric, Abbot of Peterborough; Godric, Sheriff of Berkshire; Esegar, Sheriff of Middlesex, and the Royal Thanes Aelfric, Breme and Thurkill.' Alric lowered the list, looked at the audience and concluded, 'These are only the most senior of the nobles; the fact is that half the nobility of England died that day.' Then shaking his head, he sat down.

For a long while no one spoke, nor moved, trying to absorb this grim information. Then Ealdred rose again, 'Men of the Witan, we may have suffered defeat in a battle, but we are not a defeated nation.' A few nods came from those seated, their eyes unblinking, staring in shock and amazement. 'I therefore say we should declare Prince Edgar, King of England.'

Earl Edwin immediately jumped to his feet, 'No! Never! It cannot be so,' he shouted. 'The boy is too young to lead us at this time. We need someone strong who can take control and deliver us from this invader. I submit my brother Earl Morcar to you all, he is the one we should elect as king. Has he not proved himself a great warrior at the battle of Fulford?' Some nodded in approval, including Alric.

'This is true, we need a warrior, a war leader at this time to lead us,' asserted Alric in agreement.

'No, our king must have royal blood,' was Archbishop Stigand's shouted reply.

Then the assembly erupted into a full-blooded argument, shouting across at each other, all at the same time.

'Earl Morcar has no royal blood,' one grim faced Thane declared.

'Neither did Harold,' retorted another.

'Do not slander King Harold's great name,' sharply responded an offended Thane, at this. 'Harold did have royal blood, he was brother-in-law to King Edward, therefore of the royal family, he was also from the family of Harold Bluetooth, King of Denmark.'

'Harold was a great king,' shouted an unrecognised voice from the back of the hall.

'We elect kings, whether they have royal blood or not.'

'Edgar has the blood of King Alfred in his veins; surely he is our natural king.'

The shouted words crossed the hall, with no one taking proper control. This chaotic scene continued for some time.

Violent arguments erupted, as each shouting man was trying to put his point of view across to the assembly. Weeks of tension and frustration now exploded into one of recrimination and of accusations. No one took control.

Earl Edwin grabbed hold of Morcar's arm and raised it up. 'What say you? Declare Morcar as king now.' A few agreed, but not many. Edwin glared at those who had not raised their hand in support of his brother. Edwin was incensed, angered by this perceived insult. He now shouted across the assembly, 'If Morcar is not to be King, we will have no part in this meeting. If we have to, we can defend the north from this invasion by ourselves. We will have no part in this weak and insipid assembly.' So saying, the two brothers strode out of the assembled Witan, along with their supporters.

There was now a silence. After a prolonged wait, one of the Thanes stood up and said, 'I declare for Prince Edgar to be King.' Then another did the same, and another; but it was not a tumultuous response.

'Let us hear from Prince Edgar himself,' stated Alric.

All eyes looked intently at the boy, who did not move, but just shook with nerves. After much persuading, he finally stood up, but continued to look down at his feet.

'T-t-th-thank you,' he stammered, and sat back down again. The boy's nervousness made his weak voice to seem even weaker.

If the Witan expected to see and hear the natural spark of authority, which many of Edgar's ancestors possessed, they were instantly disappointed. After further questioning of the nervous boy, it became evident the boy's character would no doubt be unequal to the tremendous burden suddenly being thrust upon him.

Undeterred by the boy's lack of apparent ability, and the chaotic nature of this assembly, Archbishop Ealdred continued, 'It is the wish of this Witan, that Prince Edgar Atheling is proclaimed the next and rightful King of England. How say you, Archbishop Stigand,' Ealdred looked intently at Stigand.

'I am not so sure,' replied Stigand quietly, so as not to be heard by all.

Infuriated Ealdred stood up looking at the silent, downcast faces, and then he raised his voice above all, 'God save King Edgar!'

'God save the King,' was the less than enthusiastic, muted response from the Witan. 'God save the King.'

'Let it be known and proclaimed, the Witan declares Prince Edgar to be our next lawful King of all England.' Ealdred laboured the point, but no one dared to mention anything about a coronation for this boy-king, least of all to set a day for it.

Alric looked despondent; he was acutely aware of his country's military nakedness at this time of crisis. Not only did they now have a nervous, inexperience boy-king to lead them, they also had a split kingdom, with the north going a separate way to the south. Rising to his feet, he looked for silence from these chattering Witan members, who were all still talking across each other, completely ignoring their newly chosen king. The Witan members continued to carry on chattering in excited tones. Alric clenched his fist then slammed it onto the table. The new king nearly jumped out of his skin. Everyone suddenly stopped talking and looked expectantly at Alric.

'We have plans to make and an enemy to fight,' Alric stated the obvious. 'William the Bastard is already on the move from Hastings and we must be prepared. Many of the Fyrd were late in getting to Hastings in time. I will gather these men together and call out to any man who can fight, to take up arms. All warriors now in London must report to Ordgar here at Westminster, by tomorrow mid-day.' Then giving a cursory bow to the new king, he walked out with Ordgar following him. 'We have much to do,' were his depressed, departing words to the Witan.

Just as dawn was breaking, a boy struggled to carry the slop-bucket, full of stinking night soil from his family's house. He was taking it to the slop-pit, in a field at the end of the street, in the town of Romney. It was a job he hated, the foul substance of the bucket splashed onto his clothes. He was being punished for being rude to his father's friend; the two men had become drunk on the cider, which everyone was busy brewing, now the autumn apple harvest was in. The boy had been too outspoken regarding their drunkenness, which angered his father, and this was his punishment.

As the boy struggled down the dirt road, something moved just beyond the main street. This movement made him look up, but in the dim light of dawn, it was difficult to see clearly. Startled, at first he just stared. It was not easy for him to register what he was looking at. He could vaguely make out dim shapes that looked like mounted ghosts, standing on the brow of the small hill near his town. Grey faced men, dressed in grey steel, against the backdrop of a grey sky; so sinister that they frightened him. Then, as their dark horses raised their heads and the riders rode down toward the town, horrific realisation slowly dawned on him.

'Orcs!' he yelled. Orcs! Orcs! The slop-bucket dropped from his hands, the foul substance spilling over his feet and legs; but he did not notice.

With a bone-chilling yell, these alien invaders started to gallop down the main street. The boy stood open mouth in panic; then his fear jolted him back to his senses as he ran screaming for his father, toward his house.

Count Eustace of Boulogne watched, as his men charged into and around the buildings, rampaging through the town of Romney. He took great delight in seeing the local people, running in frantic wild panic. His men kicked open the doors, then on entering the houses, broke open the iron stoves and scattered the burning contents on anything that would burn.

Most of the men of fighting age, were away, either gone to London, or were already dead on Hastings field. The few men who were left were the elderly, or infirmed.

The inhabitants of the first house, where these Norman assailants had entered, ran screaming outside onto the road. A soldier drew his knife across the throat of one, a struggling woman, while others clubbed the heads of her children. The soldiers took up pieces of the burning material, taken from the iron stove, then riding their horses through the town, set fire to the thatched roofs wherever they could. They spread terror everywhere.

It was not long before every house was ablaze; even the church. Startled citizens ran about wildly, in confusion, as Normans clubbed and hacked at anyone they could reach, children were no exception.

Eustace coughed as he breathed in the thick grey smoke. A group of five children ran in panic out of their house, weaving around the back of the small houses, darting, twisting and turning about quickly. They were bare-chested boys who had had no time to dress, their long hair flying behind them. Some boys carried knives, which they lacked the strength to use effectively, although a few did manage to cut the faces of their attackers before being cut down themselves. Small groups of men and boys held their ground as the Normans thundered towards them, not one was left standing as they rode by. One Saxon youth managed to shoot an arrow, which hit the horse of Count Eustace, wounding it badly. Eustace raged at being unhorsed, ran over, drew his sword and killed him before he could loose another arrow. Two old men shouted at a Norman charging toward them, 'We surrender. Spare us.' Only to be ridden over by the horses and trampled underfoot.

A group of men dismounted to rape a girl on the ground in the street. One was tearing at her clothes while two others held her down. Amid the panic they had created, they had not seen the girl's mother. With speed and tenacity of a mother protecting her young, she plunged a knife into the throat of the rapist, and lashing out at another she thrust the knife into his naked loin, from which gushed a river of blood. Turning to look at her daughter, it was the last thing she ever saw, as a Norman sword split her skull in half. Her daughter was also subsequently dispatched.

Romney paid the price for resistance against the rule of Duke William. Every man woman and child was slaughtered and every house destroyed. Thick black smoke rose from what had once been a peaceful and quiet town.

William shrugged as he turned to look back at the desolation he had left behind, 'Now this country will know the price they will pay, for any who resist my rule.'

'Brother shall we now march on London?' asked Robert.

'No!' was the concise answer. 'If we move on London and attack the capital it might push the English into further resistance to us. Let them tremble first. Let them shake in their beds. Let them scurry around and sweat with fear. Let them see and hear what happens to those who dare resist us.' William's eyes glared with hate, then he added, 'Let them see how merciful we can be to those who side with us.' Pointing toward the smouldering town of Romney, William gritted his teeth, 'Brother, we shall put on a morale-sapping display of frightfulness.' Then laughing, kicked his horse into a canter and bellowed, 'We move to Dover.'

The invading army moved on. When they approached Dover, William sent heralds ahead to announce his coming. 'Tell them either to accept me as their King, or suffer the fate of Romney.' This was William's stark message to the people of that town.

In the days of King Edward, the people of Dover had shown their contempt for Norman over-lords, when the Anglo-Saxons reacted against the arrogance of Count Eustace of Boulogne, by causing a riot and sending that vengeful man packing. It was he, who had told lies about this incident, instigating a rift between

King Edward and King Harold's father. This caused Harold's father, Earl Godwin, to be exiled. Now this same man had been one of the knights who had finally killed King Harold at Hastings. Eustace looked down on Dover with satisfaction. Now would be his chance to seek full and terrible revenge on them.

William saw the look in the eyes of Eustace and knew his thoughts. 'Remember, we are setting examples, let us see what they have to say, before you act further.' William was not sure Eustace had heard him, so he suddenly yelled at him, 'Understand?'

'Yes my lord,' was the reluctant acknowledgment from Eustace.

Both could see the elders of Dover coming to meet them. Eustace felt his heart sink with disappointment as they prostrated themselves to the floor, before the mounted duke. 'We surrender Dover to you, noble lord,' they said meekly, complying with the demand of Duke William.

William felt satisfied. 'This town will provide all the supplies which my army needs, it will not be sacked and its people will be spared.' Thus William informed the elders of the town; then added, 'We will be staying here for a while.'

During the next several days, Duke William inspected the white cliffs of Dover and decided this would be a good place to start the building of a new castle. He informed his generals, 'If we are to subdue this land we must have safe places to station our troops. Such castles will become the focal points of our Norman strength and the English will then understand who their masters are.' William's military brain knew that if he intended to control a restless country, he would need safe places of refuge for his garrisons. From the start of this conquest he let it be known the building of a castle stronghold was a prerequisite to control a population that did not want the invader to be there.

Eight days later William moved his troops out of Dover; this time along the old Roman road to Canterbury, where again the inhabitants submitted to him. He knew though that London was the key and that London was a law unto itself, which could still pose a serious problem for him.

While William was in Canterbury he became gravely ill with dysentery. Many men of his army were also succumbing to this same disease. His already reduced army was being weakened even more. The urgent need for reinforcements of fresh troops to cross the English Channel to join him was now becoming critical. November was a cold, wet and dark month, which did little to improve the mood of his men.

After two weeks in Canterbury, a messenger came to see him. William was still weak and looked ill; the stresses and strains of his great venture were beginning to take their toll on him. Still he was determined to proceed on to London and take by force *his* capital city; if need be.

The messenger bowed low before Duke William, 'Queen Edith, the Dowager Queen of England sends you her greetings.'

William looked puzzled for a moment; here was the wife of King Edward-the-Confessor, and the sister of the late King Harold, sending him a messenger. 'What could she want?' he was keen to know, but would not let his feelings show. He still had a fever, but struggled to disguise his illness; he did not want this to become common knowledge. Even so, his voice was hoarse, 'What is your message?' He said almost in a whisper. He was clearly uneasy, wondering what was to come.

'Queen Edith has lost four of her brothers and her husband this last year. She says enough men have died. While her brother, King Harold, has been away for much of this year, she has been holding the city of Winchester in Wessex for her late brother, in the capacity of Dowager. She bids you to listen well to her words.' The messenger could feel the hostility of those standing around the duke and did not want to say anything that would cause them to react violently toward him. He paused for breath and continued, 'Queen Edith, the Dowager Queen of England has now reflected on the relationship her late husband, good King Edward, had with yourself and your Norman people. This was a good relationship and was one her husband cherished most dear to his heart. The Queen says,' and he paused for effect, 'she says we have had enough of war.'

William's ears pricked up at this last sentence, 'Go on,' he said weakly.

'Queen Edith, the Dowager Queen of England, hereby formerly submits the city of Winchester to you, and thereby the county of Wessex.'

It took a few moments for the full meaning of this message to sink in. Then William's frown turned to a smile, he was delighted. This was the news he had been waiting for, it meant that much of southern England was actually submitting to his rule. All he had to do now was take London; and then the north.

The river Thames looked cold and dark-grey, as the fierce, threatening water flowed fast along its length. The sky was heavy, thick with brooding black clouds, from which a dank mist of continuous fine drizzle fell. These were the last days of November and they chilled the very bones of Londoners, both noble and common. An unpleasant time of the year even in normal times, but this November was far from normal. Depression hung over the city, a city unsure of what the future would bring. The days were now very short and the nights long and dark. People no longer smiled and greeted one another as they passed in the streets; they just pulled their cloaks or shawls around their heads for protection against the damp, the cold, and went about their business, with heads lowered. The city of London was a city belted by a sturdy wall, raised corner turrets for archers, pierced with loops, whence the bowmen may discharge their arrows. Stone-capped places of shelter were the guard's platforms, where the sentinels sheltered themselves during these cold days. Outside the city to the west, raised above all around it, was the magnificent structure of Westminster Abbey, King Edward's proud and final monument.

From the centre of the city wall, crossing this wide river, was the rickety wooden structure of London Bridge. The bridge was raised on piles of rough-hewn timbers; it accommodated two drawbridges along its length, which could be lifted to allow vessels to pass through. This bridge had replaced earlier structures, more robustly made, constructed during the Roman times and then one raised early during the Saxon settlement of England. However, this present one was inferior to those preceding it.

On the south side of this lone bridge, stood the small town of Southwark, guarding the southern entrance to the city. All around the south entrance to London Bridge was a bustle of frantic and fearsome activity. Throughout this dark and dismal morning, English troops had formed a shield-wall, in a convex semi-circle around this strategic point.

Alric and Ordgar had spent the last six weeks training hundreds of Fyrd to the highest standard they could in such a short time. A few dozen Housecarls, most of whom had been too late in arriving at Hastings to take part in that battle, took up the training of others. Both Alric and Ordgar were looked on as national heroes, by all those who now willingly spent their days training hard under the command of these two men. They were held in awe and reverence by the population and their deeds spoken of far and wide. Ordgar's agility and fiery nature had not deserted him; indeed, it had come well to the fore during his training of these men. Alric had become hardened by the things he had seen and his hatred of the Normans knew no bounds. He would do anything to get revenge on these invaders of his fine country.

It was a fact that Alric and Ordgar now led the English army, which took its stance, around the entrance to London Bridge, as the vanguard of Duke William's army approached London from the south. The hatred held for these Norman invaders was so great the new English recruits had needed little motivation to train hard in the arts of warfare during these last few weeks. The stories of the Norman treatment of the English dead at Hastings were on everyone's lips, as was the slaughter of the populations at Crowhurst and Romney and many similar towns and villages in the south.

Having been forewarned of the Norman advance on London, Alric had made everything ready to repel them. They waited in pent-up anger and anticipation, eager to deliver some retribution to these alien invaders.

Four-hundred mounted Norman cavalry emerged through the dank wet gloom of the day, from Southwark toward London Bridge. They reigned in their horses when they saw in front of them this unexpected English resistance, massed around the entrance to the bridge. Once again, the English were keen to ready themselves for a Norman attack, with their battle-axes held high, keen to draw Norman blood.

The newly elected King of England, King Edgar, stood on the city walls of London, his sister Margaret standing by his side, looking out across the river, to see what events would follow. Neither of them were versed in the arts of war, for they had had much to learn in a very short time.

Hugh de Grandsmesnil was the captain of this Norman vanguard. He was a politician of some note in Normandy and had taken part in the battle at Hastings. On seeing the shield-wall already in place around the entrance to London Bridge, he was initially unsure what to do. Should he attack or should he send reports back to the Duke William and wait for his orders? Arrogant and impulsive as ever, expecting little resistance, he saw a chance for personal glory, so gave the order, *'Advance!'* On seeing their approach the English tensed, gripping their shields and weapons tightly, eager for some revenge.

Ordgar shouted for all to hear, 'Now come on, you son's of the devil, we are ready for you.' Ordgar's need for retribution was high. He had seen so much slaughter, brought on by this hated Norman invasion. He needed a chance to get revenge over them, and now felt he was about to get it. Alric and Ordgar readied themselves as the Normans got their horses to prance along, parallel with and in front of, the English ranks. The Normans began to taunt them and demanded they submit to Duke William, the victor at Hastings.

Hugh rode to the front, just out of arrow range and shouted to the defenders, 'Who do you think you are to try and resist us?'

Most of the English did not understand what Hugh had said, however, shouts and barracking followed his attempt to speak to them. Alric held his hands up high and suddenly and unexpectedly, the English fell quiet.

Raising his voice in answer, Alric replied, in fluent French, 'We are the people of this land, the land of England. We will fight those who seek to take it from us. You will not prevail over us. We will drive you back into the sea. Our King is Edgar, we know no other.' No cheering followed this, just an unerring silence, for most English had not understood what was being said.

Alric repeated what he had said, only this time in English. Cheers now abounded from the English ranks. Then they started to beat a slow, purposeful rhythm on their shields, but this time without the Saxon war drums to accompany them. 'Death, death, death,' they chanted. With intense hatred glaring from their eyes at the Normans, they threateningly lowered their spears to a height level with that of a horse's breast, ready for any charge.

Hugh was incensed, how dare they still resist, he would have to teach them a lesson. When the charge came Alric raised his two handed battle-axe above his head, as the mass of spears bristled out from the shield-wall. The Norman riders, which managed to get close enough, had their horses spiked from under them. The thrown Normans were now at the mercy of the English battle-axes. Ordgar swung his axe at one of the unhorsed Normans; the nosepiece of his helmet was jammed in with the impact, smashing all his teeth. The Norman was desperate to find his sword, which had fallen from his hand with the impact. His legs buckled from under him, as he flailed around, knowing the death blow would come, but not where from.

Many fallen Normans were culled by Alric himself as he quickly, by the lightening sweep of his deadly axe, cut into the bodies of the unhorsed riders, swinging it down, in a large arc, cutting into and crunching their shoulders. Alric could smell their fear as Normans fell around him. These fallen riders were then quickly finished off by the Fyrd soldiers, who came running out from behind the wall, with long daggers fit for this purpose. Several times the Normans tried a fresh charge and each time they were cut down, greatly reducing their numbers. Hugh had no infantry with him and no archers; too late he realised he had made an elementary mistake of engaging his cavalry, without such needed support. Subsequently he suffered many losses.

Shocked and embarrassed by his unexpected failure, Hugh pulled what remained of his men away and retreated to a safe distance. Hugh was in a state of bewilderment, nervously wondering how he could explain this to the duke; when shortly after Duke William arrived with his main force of men.

William cast his eye around the scene; it was immediately obvious to him what had happened here. He was furious, 'Hugh de Grandsmesnil, why have you have been so foolhardy, as to take on an English shield-wall without infantry and archer support?' William knew he could ill afford to lose so many men, before any replacements could get to him from across the Channel. In addition, here was a captain of his army who had shown little understanding in the art of warfare.

'Why did you not wait? Why did you not inform me?' William ranted on.

Hugh was mortified for his foolishness, casting his eyes down to the floor. William then saw more reason to add to his fury,

263

'These Londoners,' the words stuck in his throat. 'These Londoners are still trying to resist us? How dare they, don't they know when they are beaten?'

William dug his heals into his horse, riding up to within earshot of the shield-wall. Infuriated he yelled in French across to them, 'Submit to me Duke William of Normandy as your rightful ruler. Submit, or pay the price.'

Ordgar's anger sparked, he replied in Latin, so most would understand, 'You are not our ruler, bugger-off back to Normandy. You the bastard, who would seek to rule what is not yours to have.' The English started to slap their weapons on their shields to emphasis their defiance.

William was well aware of an unspoken nervousness among the Normans as they approached London. Would there be another great battle to fight there? Yet he had not expected such insolence as this. Irate at these words, William turned in his saddle, then shouted an order, 'Archers!' he screamed, 'Take up your positions.'

Several hundred bowmen ran at the trot forming up in three lines in front of the English. Many more shields in the English ranks were instantly placed over the heads of the defenders. The arrows mostly hit the shields and failed to have any great affect, as they had done at the start of the last battle.

Infantry now clattered forward to engage the English in battle. *Forward!* ordered William. The infantry had learnt from Hastings, in hard hand-to-hand combat, of the need to remove as many shields as they could from the wall by spearing them with javelins, making them too heavy to hold. Even so, little headway was made; the shield-wall was solid. William saw he would need to mount a full frontal attack, if he was to make any progress. He was about to order such when Odo approached him.

'Brother, wait a moment; we cannot afford to lose too many men until replacements arrive. The English have a backdoor of escape across that bridge, if they retreat along it, a few men will be able to hold off many hundreds before we can cross. We cannot take this bridge by storm.'

William reluctantly could see Odo was right. 'Then we will set fire to the bridge,' he replied.

'In this weather?' Odo looked up wiping the rain from his eyes, 'I doubt the structure would catch fire and burn, it is far too wet. We could send for our ships, but that will take some time.'

'God send them to hell,' shouted William for all to hear. 'Send in our full force, at least we will drive them off this side of the river.'

The Norman troops moved forward en-mass; then just as Odo had predicted, the English fell back in an orderly retreat across the bridge, shouting insults as they did. Repositioned, they were again ready to hold off any advance along the narrow bridge. William could see plainly that to try to cross the River Thames by this bridge would cause many hundreds of causalities for him. He could not risk that. He had sent for more troops from Normandy to join him, but they had not arrived yet on these English shores. Reluctantly William realised London would have to wait, but Southwark would now feel the full force of William's rage.

His soldiers were soon kicking down doors, killing the few inhabitants who had not crossed the bridge earlier when they could have done so. After killing all they could find, they systematically set fire to anything and everything they could. Southwark burned.

In the days following this rebuff, William had settled into his old fury, which his brothers knew he could maintain for days or weeks, if he so wished. He set himself on the path of a movement on a large scale, intending to isolate the city of London, by the destruction of a broad belt of the country all around it. Firstly, he headed west along the south bank of the Thames. The dark mass of this Norman army moved methodically westward; when it passed by villages and hamlets, farmers and inhabitants, either ran away, or just stared in dull, gut wrenching fear.

William's army was now very wet, bitterly cold, bedraggled and frustrated. They bemoaned openly at their apparent lack of advancement.

The mournful bell of the abbey rang out its slow, repetitive death knell, for Leofric the Abbot of Peterborough had died. He had been badly wounded at the battle of Hastings yet he had managed, with many willing helpers, to make his way back to his abbey. Sadly, after a few days of arriving he had died from his wounds. Alric had read his name out at the last meeting of the Witan, and listed him as one of the key men to fall that day. The abbot was a greatly loved man for the many kind works he had done for the people, helping the poor and setting up medical help for many communities there. Through his good guidance, he had brought prosperity to the land through profitable trade, so Peterborough prospered. Yet the consternation among the monks was not simply because they had lost their beloved and respected abbot. True he would be greatly missed, but their concern now was because the king had to approve the appointment of a new abbot.

The monks met to discuss what they should do. Amid fear for their future, a new abbot had been elected from one of their own to replace him. The man chosen was called Brand, who before his election had been the Provost of the Abbey. Now they debated to whom they should go to for approval of this appointment. King Harold was dead, Duke William was ravaging the countryside, because he thought he should be king, but the

Witan had elected Edgar Atheling as the new King of England. It was a dilemma for the monks.

After many hours of fearful debate, the monks decided to seek the consent of King Edgar and declared him the true and rightful King of England.

'This may cost us dear,' lamented one monk, as he prepared the written message to be taken to London and King Edgar. 'Duke William could cut off our hands, or blind us, if he is of a mind to. He has done these terrible deeds to many others. Pray to God we are doing the right thing.'

'Would you have a Norman bastard rule us as king, when we have the royal blood of Alfred-the-Great to rule us?' The young messenger was incensed at the negative thoughts of the doddering old monks. 'I will take this message with pride to King Edgar,' shouted the young man as he mounted his horse, to ride to London. 'Let the country know, we declare for King Edgar.'

Thick fog had hung around the Thames Valley for several days, impeding the progress of the Norman army as it moved south west, away from London. They were cold, chilled to the bone. Their noses were red and running, their breath was visible, their hands numb.

'This hateful weather,' cursed Richard, as he, William, Odo and Robert rode together through the chill air of early December. 'Everything is so damp and wet, I can't see for more than a few feet in front of us. I must tell you, the men are complaining William. They don't like this.' Richard was beginning to wonder if they were making a mistake in moving on before reinforcements arrived. He was in fact reflecting the mood of the whole army, who were not used to such damp, dense fog, where visibility was so bad men could hardly see more than a few yards in front of them. Progress had become painfully slow.

William was aware of the grumbling coming from his men, 'Any man who is heard to be complaining will have his pay stopped for a week and put on kitchen duties; I will not have it. If any man instigates trouble, I will make sure he regrets the day he was born.' Then pointing his arm out, decisively toward the line of men following, he added, 'Tell that to your men.'

William squinted through the fog as his army slowly trudged onward. They struggled to find the road, William half turned in the saddle to his brothers, 'We will soon be at Portsmouth where we are to meet up with our new reinforcements from Normandy. That will brighten the buggers up. We will more than double our strength then. Our success has been so popular in Normandy they will be falling over themselves to join us, so sure are they of pots of gold for the picking.'

William went quiet for a moment; he could see the need to raise the spirits of his men. He was heading for Portsmouth, but an idea now amused him. Lifting his head he smiled, 'Robert, inform the men, we will make a small detour to Winchester, we will let that hometown of Earl Harold see who their new masters are. There will be good pickings there.'

This message spread quickly throughout the ranks and a livelier, brighter step in the army could be seen immediately. William's army suddenly did not feel as tired as they had. Winchester would be ravaged.

It was not long before a large camp was set up outside the home city of the late King Harold. Winchester was nervous. They could not close the gates on this new conqueror, as Queen Edith had already seceded the city to William, also the men from the English army were now too spent and scattered to put up any strong resistance. William, Odo, Robert and Richard rode up to the castle of the Earls of Wessex, where nearly a year before, Alric had first brought the news of King Edward's expected death. This was where the dramatic events of this past, sad and eventful year had all started. Now Norman knights rode their horses into the living quarters of the Godwinson family, while their army freely plundered the city. It was what they did best. Riding together into the dwellings of a terrified enemy made them feel strong and powerful. They bloodied their swords at will, without fear of retribution. There would be rewards for their efforts, rewards of weapons, silver and gold. Such was the sadistic pleasure of these invaders; it was the women who suffered the most at their hands.

When Queen Edith tried to protest to William, concerning the actions of his soldiers and the fact she had already submitted the city to him, William simply replied, 'Queen Edith, you and your country have much to learn. My men were getting restless and needed some diversion. Remember the old saying, "To the victor go the spoils."' William was bent on an action of intimidation, a fearful and moral sapping display for all. Submit or die, was the choice now laid before the English. Yet even by submitting this could not guarantee they would still not be killed, as Queen Edith was now finding out.

The water was icy cold, as the Normans trundled their baggage carts across the ford of the river Thames. Those who could crossed the river by the narrow wooden bridge nearby, but it was too narrow and weak to take the heavy baggage train of the Norman invaders. Duke William was at last crossing the Thames at Wallingford, nearly fifty miles west of London, just south of Oxford. The Normans now had a reinforced army, for many new recruits had joined them as planned at Portsmouth. These new elements were keen to profit from a successful invading army and had come readily across the sea to join their duke, as soon as the opportunity arose.

William with all this force, intended to cross the Thames and then turn east to head for London, with this freshly invigorated army. While crossing he was surprised to see waiting for him on the other side Stigand, the Archbishop of Canterbury. Waiting with Stigand was Esegar, the Sheriff of Middlesex, who had been carried wounded from the battlefield of Hastings. They both waited at Wallingford to meet Duke William, for they had been secretly corresponding with the Norman Duke, in the slight hope that they might be allowed to retain their offices by supporting these invaders.

Stigand and Esegar were shown into Duke William's tent where he was camped, on the Oxford side of the river. William sneered, looking down on them prostrating themselves on the floor before him.

Stigand tensed himself, 'My lord, we come to offer our loyalty to you. We offer you our service and the service our office brings with it. From this day we will serve only you.'

William waited, allowing the tension of the moment to mount, 'What office?' he asked, in French, barely able to hide his contempt for Stigand. 'You have no office. Did not King Edward appoint the Norman, Robert of Jumieges, as Archbishop of Canterbury? A position you illegally took from him.' William sat back in his chair, waiting for a response he knew would be difficult to form.

Stigand breathed deeply, 'If we have sinned in your eyes and the eyes of God, then we will repent our ways and subject ourselves only to your will.'

William was pleased with this, but did not let it show, and kept a cold face before them. 'Will you accept me as the rightful King of all England?' he challenged.

'Willingly, my lord, willingly,' Stigand replied.

William pursed his lips, 'I doubt you will keep your position Stigand, for neither Rome, nor the barons of Normandy will accept this: but I will need local people to administer my affairs of state,' then folding his arms he added sinisterly, 'At least, at first.'

Stigand and Esegar remained prostrate at the feet of William, while the Duke made pretence to be deep in thought and then spoke slowly, 'There will be a forfeit to pay in gold and property, from your own estates for usurping the position of Archbishop of Canterbury.'

'As you say my lord,' Stigand had wondered if he would be killed and was glad of any escape route.

William then turned to Esegar, for he was aware through captured English, who had revealed under torture, that Esegar was now called 'Esegar the Staller'. Esegar had sought to stall, or delay, William's advance on London. He was now hoping, rather unwisely, to feign peace with William, while defences at London were prepared.

Addressing Esegar, William's voice took on a more friendly tone, 'I wrote you a promise that if you supported me you will hold your estates. You now come to submit to me as your King, and for that you will remain as Sheriff of Middlesex.'

Esegar could hardly believe his ears.

William continued, 'If you now submit London to me I shall make you the lord of two dozen manors. What say you?'

Esegar was suddenly tempted to forgo his previous arrangement with the people of London and accept the Duke's offer instead. It was a tempting prize; but one that William had no intention of keeping. Esegar, still prostrate before William, went quiet for a moment.

'Well?' asked William, his eyes flaring. 'What say you?'

'My lord, I humbly accept you as the rightful King of England.'

'Then it is agreed. You will march with us on to London,' then William added, 'You will not leave us until I am crowned.'

William had stalled, the Staller.

'Then go, both of you. You must each swear an oath to me in public, and I will accept your service.' With that, William stood up and walked out of the tent, still leaving Stigand and Esegar prostrate on the floor.

Shortly after, William's forces continued their march, but they still did not go straight to London. Instead, they headed in a north-easterly direction, not turning southwards until they had spread destruction across mid-Buckinghamshire and southwest Bedfordshire; spreading further terror among the English population.

The weakened Witan had followed the approach of Duke William to London, with all the courage of sheep being stalked by circling wolves. Riots ensued in the streets of the city, especially from the traders, who wanted to protect their interests and investments. War was no good for their trade and they demanded the remaining authorities now seek peace with the invaders.

The Londoners looked on with dismay while William burnt a path toward them, now without much opposition. King Edgar Atheling was proving himself daily to be weak and indecisive, unfit for the throne of England; the house of Godwinson had fallen, as had many nobles, and now Duke William with the Norman army was heading straight for them. Panic was in the streets; exactly as William had planned.

'Let me smell their fear,' William had said, when asked why he did not go straight to London.

Meanwhile, Alric and Ordgar had argued long and hard with the timid Witan for a new army to be formed, but even they knew the odds were now against them. The humbled earldoms, now willingly or unwillingly, began to talk of receiving their new lord. The defection of Stigand had been a major blow to English resistance, and the submission of Winchester had started the surrender of the southern towns to William, with only the north showing any signs of open resistance. Earls Edwin and Morcar headed north to their strongholds when they had disagreed with the election of Prince Edgar to be King. Their initial thought had been to divide the kingdom, with William in the south, and the brother Earls in the north. Now, after reflecting on the situation, they hurriedly returned to London.

So it was, on the shortest day of the year, the twenty-first day of December, a sad sombre procession headed out of London. Having failed to muster an effective military response, King Edgar's leading supporters had lost their nerve. With barley six hours of daylight available at this time of year, this sullen group had started out from London while it was still dark, to ride the nearly thirty miles to Berkhamstead, northwest of London, where Duke William now had his military camp. This party consisted of the proclaimed King Edgar Atheling, Ealdred Archbishop of York, Earls Edwin and Morcar, Wulfstan Bishop of Worcester, Walter Bishop of Hereford and Alric, General of the Housecarls: along with many of the Thanes of London. They rode out not knowing what the outcome would be. Messengers had preceded them the day before, to inform Duke William of their intention, so that everything was ready for them in William's camp.

It was hard on Alric, Morcar and Edwin, men who had fought so valiantly and so hard to keep their country free from invaders. Many men had died fighting for England's freedom and yet now this freedom looked to be lost.

The sky reflected the mood of this band of Englishmen, above them hung a heavy thick layer of impenetrable grey cloud, increasing the darkness of the day. Not even a glimpse of sun would get through this cloud cover, which hung like a gloomy shroud over the land. Riding through this murkiness each man was deep in thought, lost in his own world of despair and dread. Dread for the future of their country, what would become of it? Dread for their lands and possessions. Dread for their families and possible retributions. Dread for their own lives, or worse; would William disfigure and maim them as he had done to so many others before? They knew that many English would now lose their lands. They would have increased taxes to pay, and be forced to work for new, foreign speaking, and harsh lords of the land. These new lords not only would not understand the English ways, they could not even speak the common English language. Englishmen who had had their own lands would now be reduced to serfdom, a form of life little removed from slavery. The natives of this rich land would now be controlled by a conquering invader, who would show little mercy or understanding toward them.

Alric thought Ordgar had been right, when he had declared he would form a resistance to this Norman invasion in the east of England. Ordgar had departed London in anger and fury at this lack of strong leadership in England, at a time when it was needed the most.

'I will have no part in this betrayal. I will not bow the knee to The Bastard. Did I not say to his face at London Bridge, "You are not our ruler, bugger-off back to Normandy. You The Bastard, who would seek to rule what is not yours to have."' Ordgar's insult to William would not be forgotten, neither by the Normans, nor by those English who vowed to continue their fight for freedom.

Ordgar vehemently let his feelings be known, before finally storming out of the Witan, vowing to carry on the fight. 'I will not become a slave and puppy-dog of the Normans. I am English and a free man. If you bow to these Normans, you will become like a bird in a cage, unable to fly away and follow your heart. Better to die, than become subject to Norman barbarity.'

After leaving London, Ordgar rode away toward the northeast, rather than join this procession of surrender. He was determined he would organise a resistance movement against the Normans, so that the bastard duke would know the English spirit had not died at Hastings. Like many English, Ordgar did not consider the English to be a beaten nation. He would continue the fight. By God, yes he would.

Alric prayed for Ordgar's success as he looked up and saw the camp of Duke William coming into view. He had been sorely tempted to ride away with Ordgar, but this he felt he could do later. He reasoned that now he must support what was left of the English nobility.

The Norman soldiery stood in silence as this subdued English procession passed through their midst, toward Duke William. A platform had been constructed with William seated upon it, either side of him were his brothers, Odo, and Robert along with Richard. All four were in full ceremonial regalia, including the two heralds who stood at the foot of the stage. It was clear William wanted this to be seen, and to be understood for what it was, namely the formal surrender of England.

The damp and bedraggled group, who approach the wooden platform, were in sharp contrast to the appearance of William and his brothers. There was no spirit left in this English delegation, save for that of Alric, who managed to look resplendent in his chainmail armour, conical helmet and leaf-shaped shield. Although he wore a sword, he did not carry his feared battle-axe. Alric had seen Duke William in battle at Hastings, all covered in blood, as he himself had been; but now he viewed him for the first time as a new conquering king.

'So this is the leader of the Orcs, as the common people call him,' he thought to himself, when the party approached the platform.

William was seated on an elaborately carved heavy wooden chair, slightly larger than the chairs of his three brothers, each arm of which terminated in the head of a carved lion. He kept a cold face, expressionless, with his hands outstretched along the arms of the chair. Above the platform was the banner of Normandy, two golden rampant lions on a red background. Ironically, Alric thought, it was the same colours as the golden dragon of Wessex. A herald held the papal banner at one side of the platform, which many Norman soldiers now considered to be a holy relic, which bore some magical power within itself and that somehow this red cross had been responsible for their victory.

The English party dismounted, allowing their horses to be led away. Archbishop Ealdred nudged elected King Edgar to take his place at the front of their group. Edgar though, was rooted to the spot. Ealdred nudged him again, this time with a little more force. Edgar stepped forward, nervously holding in front of him a crown, a band of pure gold. For a moment both groups stood looking at each other, unsure what to do next.

William broke the silence, 'I give you greetings to my camp. What is the purpose of your mission?'

Edgar tried to speak, but nothing would come out. Annoyed at Edgar's lack of movement, and forgetting he was only a boy unsure of himself, Ealdred stepped forward in front of Edgar, bowed low and said, 'We, the nobles England, come to offer you the crown of our country.' Taking the crown from Edgar, he held it aloft.

'Then I take what is rightfully mine.' William, unable to hide his obvious delight, smiled broadly. 'You may do me homage,' and nodded to his brothers either side of him. They knew this was not a request, but an order.

Edgar mounted the platform, kneeled before William, putting his hands flat together in front of his face in the form of a prayer. William then clasped his own hands around those of Edgar, thereby accepting the homage done to him by Edgar, no longer a king; now just a prince. A loud cheer went up from the massed ranks of the Norman army. Their obvious delight would soon become a cause for lavish celebrations for the Normans.

Archbishop Ealdred then in turn mounted the platform and carried out the same symbolic gesture of subjugation. Earls Edwin and Morcar were next, then the Bishops, who were followed by Alric, who hated this very act, but saw no way out of this. This process went on for some time, as Thane after Thane subjected himself to Duke William, the conqueror. It was not just men, who now subjected themselves to Duke William, but also, all the land they owned, their estates and buildings thereon; all now belong to William.

After more than an hour, it was finished. Odo stood to address the assembly, in French, still with a stern look on his face.

'From henceforth', he lifted his voice for all to hear, 'Duke William of Normandy is hereby proclaimed King of England.' He clenched his fist in the air as huge cheers went up from all the Norman military. Cheer after cheer echoed across the valley, shields were slapped with swords and this great rejoicing from the gathered soldiers carried on for some time.

Odo then lifted both hands to quieten the shouting soldiers. When all was quiet, Odo continued, 'King William the first of England is the rightful King of all England. King Edward promised the kingship to him, and Earl Harold of Wessex swore to uphold this,' he lied. Odo continued with his lies, which no one would now dare to challenge. 'Duke William had Earl Harold swear under an oath the kingdom would be his, an oath which Harold broke.' Seeing the intense attention he now had, Odo continued to cement this lie, 'Not only did he swear an oath, but he swore it over the holy relics of the bones of a saint.' A large audible gasp went up from the soldiers. The English just listened, unable to believe the depths of lies Duke William was prepared to go to, in order to justify his invasion of England. 'Yes,' Odo repeated for emphasis, 'Harold swore over the bones of a saint, to give this kingdom to the noble Duke William. This is why God has given us victory over the English. The Pope of

Rome blessed our crusade, and he has delivered England into our hands.' Odo waited for more cheering to subside, 'Tonight there will be a royal celebration, before we march on London to crown our new King.' Odo waved his hand toward the English nobles, 'King William's new subjects will stay with us at his court, from now on as our guests.'

Alric and all the English knew that this was another way of saying; they were now King William's hostages.

'When will this agony cease?' Alric whispered under his breath, to no one in particular.

William left the platform, and went over to the English party and embraced Prince Edgar, the Archbishop and both Earls. He embraced them all like long lost brothers. Alric found it hard to smile, but smile he must, if he was to live.

'Archbishop,' William addressed himself to Ealdred, but did so in a manner that all could hear. 'You and your party of English noblemen will come with me to London, where you shall crown me as King of all England.' William turned to make sure everyone heard, 'I shall not be crowned by Archbishop Stigand, for his position as Archbishop of Canterbury is illegitimate, and as such is not accepted by the Pope of Rome.' William's smile at this statement made Alric feel sick to the heart.

Afterward, William briskly walked away from the English group, beckoning to his brothers to follow him into his tent. His expression suddenly changed from the smiling man, seen outside, to that of a stern commander. 'Until we hold London we will continue to let the English fear our presence. Put no restraints on our men if they wish to amuse themselves with women and line their pockets with plunder. We will make sure they have no heart to resist us further.'

'When will the coronation take place?' inquired Richard

'The time is just right brothers,' William beamed, 'for I will be crowned on Christmas Day. This will be the same day that Charlemagne-the-Great was crowned.' William intended this to make a statement, not just to England, but to Europe as well.

'And where will you be crowned brother?' asked Robert.

William looked up surprised at such a question. 'Why, Westminster Abbey of course. We will then have continuity with King Edward, who promised me this kingdom!' All four laughed.

Christmas Day 1066 was yet another dark and wet winters' day. Rain droplets hung off the eves, off the roofs and from the doorways. Those invaders from the south of France, who had joyfully joined William for this great venture for the promised plunder, had never seen such cold, wet, damp and dark days as this. Today was a traditional time for rejoicing for all Christians, but no English were doing so this year. The native English were in a state of depression and the Normans were very tense, in case something should go wrong with their hastily made plans.

During the two days the Normans had been in London, they felt rather unsure of themselves. They tried to make up for this apprehension by making their presence felt. The Normans held the English cheap and often humiliated them. If a dozen English met a single Norman, it went badly for the English if they did not bow to him. If a group of English met a single Norman upon a bridge across a stream, they had to stand back and wait for him; or there would be some retribution for moving before the Norman had passed. As their paths crossed they were required to make obeisance to the Norman and whoever failed to do this was shamefully beaten if caught. So cheap were the English held and so much did the Normans insult them. Even so, in spite of this, the Normans now suddenly felt insecure. Here in the capital of England, they knew how much they were hated. Would the English rise up? Was there another army ready to take them on? All sorts of whispers were going around the Norman soldiers, stories of imminent uprisings and the subsequent dangers to them. No one was sure what to expect; and neither did King William.

William had ordered that all his force should be fully armed and ready, in case of any uprising at his coronation in Westminster Abbey church. At the same time he banned the carrying of weapons by any English on the day of his coronation. This ban on weapons included the English nobles who had surrendered to William just a few days before. Alric felt naked as he stood in the cold abbey with the same group of English nobles who had surrendered to William. No sword, no armour, and not even a dagger, could they carry. All Londoners of rank had been rounded up by aggressive Normans, and told they had to attend this ceremony today, whilst the general population had been ordered to line the streets to greet their new king. The nobles now stood silent and en-mass toward the back of the nave, many with their wives and adult families. Alric seethed, he was full of pent up tension and hidden rage. Like other English who stood there with him, his inner personal thoughts were, 'To crown such a man who is covered with the blood of our brave Englishmen, on the birthday of Jesus Christ is a sacrilege.'

Outside the abbey the Norman infantry had formed a human chain around the church, ready to thwart any attempt at disrupting the service. Another group of Norman soldiery now slowly filed inside this holy place, until they stood shoulder-to-shoulder around the inside perimeter of the church, looking inward toward the assembled English. A large number of Norman knights and commanders entered the abbey and made their way to the front of the nave, where they stood in silence and waited. The tension grew. The cold of the English winter weather and the unheated cold stone of the abbey began to get through to the Normans. Some were shaking with the cold, unable to hide their involuntary trembles. One or two had drops of nasal fluid dripping from their red noses, which made the English smile to themselves. Still they all waited; both sides were now just as tense as the other.

In front of the high altar stood Ealdred, Archbishop of York, waiting uneasily for something to happen; with him were several priests, all ready to officiate at the ceremony. To the other side of the church's altar stood a Frenchman, Bishop Geoffrey of Coutances. It was his role to act as translator, should one be required.

The great doors of the abbey suddenly opened, allowing a blast of ice-cold air to rush in, further chilling the congregation. All eyes turned to see what was happening. Several Norman knights in full armour walked slowly through the great arch of the doorway, behind them came the single figure of Odo, Bishop of Bayeux. Odo was wearing his full regalia as bishop of the church; a long white under robe, which reached down to his ankles, over which was a purple outer robe, covered in gold embroidered crosses, on his head he wore a gold cloth mitre, symbol of his authority.

Behind Odo came his brother Robert followed by Richard, both in full military armour, over which they wore linen tunics with their family crests embroidered upon them.

A hush fell on the congregation as William himself followed his brothers into the abbey and up along the long nave. William was not in armour, but wore a blue tunic with a gold band around his waist. A red cloak fell about his back, which was held in place by a golden clasp. Behind William came his chosen bodyguard, all looking intently around them as they entered the church.

William and his party walked solemnly up the nave to where the archbishop was waiting. William turned, faced the congregation then sat down on the coronation chair set in front of the church altar.

Ealdred had been told what to say, but he also intended to say a few things for himself; namely, to get William to swear a protection of his new people. After a prayer, Ealdred, speaking in

English, raised his voice to start the ceremony, 'Like the mighty Charlemagne before him,' Ealdred began, 'William Duke of Normandy and henceforth King of England has chosen this holy day, Christmas Day, for his coronation. We, who are assembled here in the sight of God, do come to crown William as our true and rightful king.' Ealdred could feel the tension mounting as he continued, with voice raised, 'Will you have this man to be your king, in the sight of God?' Bishop Geoffrey now repeated this last sentence in French, so the Normans could understand the words.

The Normans shouted out immediately and loudly, to affirm their acceptance of William as the new King of England. The English realised they must also be seen to be accepting their new King and joined in a chorus of, 'God save the King, God save the King.' This erupting cacophony of noise was heard by the guards outside. To them it sounded like a riot. The differing languages made no sensible sound to the soldiers outside; yet they concluded it was an unusual noise

'There's an uprising against us,' one sergeant shouted. 'The Duke must be in trouble, to arms men, to arms.' Whereupon the guards drew their swords, fearing this uprising would now overwhelm them and get out of control. Without justification, the Normans rushed forward to attack and kill some of the English bystanders; people who had been ordered to attend and were there most reluctantly. The chaos outside could now be heard by those inside. Normans inside now drew their swords. Alric's hand instinctively dropped to draw his own sword, when exasperated, he realised it was not there. Women in the congregation began to scream. The Norman guards inside now panicked and started to strike down the unarmed English. A mass of terrified English stampeded for the door to escape this mayhem.

When the English ran out of the abbey and into the street, the Normans outside thought they were being attacked from the rear.

Seeking some refuge in nearby houses some of the Normans ran in, and then began kicking over the cooking braziers inside these houses. A full-scale assault was suddenly in progress, with the fallen braziers setting fire to the local buildings. The whole area outside the abbey was soon ablaze. People were running and screaming everywhere. The Normans did not know or care, which, if any of the English were attackers. They struck out at them all, hacking men and women aside, until bodies soon lay everywhere.

Inside the church Ealdred's jaw simply dropped open, when he saw the throngs of men and women of every rank and condition fleeing out of the church in frantic haste. He turned to look at William who was visibly trembling, fearing this was an armed revolt and he would be struck down.

William did not know what to do, then glaring at Ealdred said, 'Get on with it man – quickly.'

'Yes sire,' Ealdred picked up the golden crown off a cushion, held by a terrified altar boy. A few priests had remained and the ceremony continued, but with very few onlookers left. Holding the crown high above the head of William, Ealdred tried to remember the words he had planned to say, 'Will you swear, to maintain the Church of God and all Christian people in true peace?' Ealdred began to race through his words as fast as he could, 'To prohibit all orders of men from committing injustice and oppression and to direct the observance of impartiality and mercy in all your judgments?' The words were said at such a speed William was not sure what he was saying.

'Yes!' William replied, but he was no longer looking at Ealdred, he was looking beyond the archbishop, for he saw smoke beginning to pour into the church from outside.

Ealdred plopped the crown on William's head, reached for the orb and sceptre, placed the orb in his left hand and the sceptre in the other. Then bowed his head and said, in nothing more than a loud whisper, 'Hail King William: God save the King.' Ealdred had now crowned two kings of England in one year, but this thought was not uppermost in his mind right now.

King William, his brothers and close bodyguard, turned and together headed quickly for the abbey doors. As William appeared outside at the door of the abbey, he, Odo and the other brothers, started to yell and bawl at their troops to come to order.

'You stupid fools,' Odo shouted at the soldiers transfixed in their indecisions. 'Come to order. Greet the new King of England.'

A half-hearted, embarrassed cheer went up from those caught in the act of unjustified reprisals, 'Hail King William, God save the King,' they all but mumbled.

William stood on the steps of the abbey, whilst his soldiers assembled into some kind of order from the confusion; he was still holding the orb and sceptre, and wearing his golden crown. William looked out at the chaos of this, the first day of his reign as king. Dead bodies lay in the street, others clutched at bleeding wounds, houses were burning and the streets deserted of all English, for all who could still move, had done so and fled from this unrequited carnage; including Alric, who saw it was usless to try and fight.

Looking around him at the chaos of his coronation, William felt cheated. He had wanted adoring crowds of well-wishers to greet his triumph; instead, all he saw were the glazed and embarrassed eyes of his assembling army. His brothers had often seen, and been on the receiving end of, his feared temper; but now William looked fit to burst. The fear he had instilled in any who dared to opposed him, made it so no one dared to approach him at moments like this.

Smoke poured from the burning houses and drifted toward William, making his eyes sting. Without speaking, he thrust the orb and sceptre into Odo's hands and stormed out, away from the abbey and its surrounding carnage. True, he had made it. In spite of everything, he had made it. He mused to himself, 'I am now King of England, now let them call me bastard, if they dare. I will demand respect from all, as this office commands.' This was the innermost thoughts of a man in fury, who had killed and maimed hundreds and was determined to continue to do so, on an even grander scale if need be. 'As long as I succeed', was all he could think about, 'I care not for the manner to bring this about.'

Amid all this confusion, Alric had slipped away and was now hurrying from the abbey, running through the dark streets, with the night already falling by mid afternoon. His fists were clenched tightly; he saw nothing and no one, as he fled. He had seen enough. His anger raged, he was determined to make his way to the northeast and join with Ordgar, where he would do all he could to resist and repel these alien invaders, who were now exultant on his beloved English soil.

'By God, yes I will show them. I'll make them pay,' he kept repeating to himself as he went to get his horse, Welland, out from his stable. He knew now there was only one option left open to him, he would join those who wanted to fight, to resist this Norman invasion. Soon he was away, riding through the night northeast to join Ordgar, in his stated resistance campaign. He would do all he could to defy these hated invaders.

HISTROICAL NOTES

Alric, Ordgar and Ricbert and are the only fictional characters in this book, all the rest were real people living through real events.

The name of the Norwegian King was really Harald Sigurdsson, but this could lead to confusion having two leading characters with the same name, although the English King is often spelt as Harold and the Norwegian as Harald, so for the sake of clarity I have mostly kept to his nickname, that of Hardrada.

All main events referred to in this book are real events; I have only fictionalised three sub events; one where Duke William first received the news of Edward-the-Confessor's death and the other two were the murders of Ulf and Einar Jonsson by Hardrada.

It is a cliché, but nevertheless a true one, to say; 'It is the victor who writes the history'. This has certainly been the case with the Norman Conquest of Anglo-Saxon England, where right up until recently, the lies the Normans had told to justify their invasion were accepted as 'facts'. We now know that the Witan had the power to elect their kings and they certainly would not have elected William. Abbot Ælfric of Eynsham, the leading homilist of the late 10th century, who wrote:

> "No man can make himself king, but the Witan has the choice to choose as king whom they please; but after he is consecrated as king, he then has dominion over the people, and they cannot shake his yoke off their necks."

Neither did Edward-the-Confessor have the right to bequeath his kingdom to William, without recourse to the Witan. The Witan was the beginning, or the embryo of a parliament: sadly it would be another six hundred years, before any such body could again exert significant control over a king.

The story that Harold was shipwrecked off the coast of Normandy and was given hospitality by William; is suspect to say the least. Harold did go to Normandy, but his motive in going there clearly points to him hoping to secure the release of his younger brother Wulfnoth, then aged twenty-six and his nephew Hakon; both being held in Normandy as hostages. Hakon was released, but Wulfnoth was not. There can be no other reasonable argument for Harold putting his head in the lion's mouth, by going to Normandy. Again, the subsequent 'promise' Harold is supposed to have made to William, to give the Kingdom of England to William, must be spurious.

This is plainly Norman propaganda, for Harold did not have the authority to make such a promise without the Witan endorsing it and neither would he have glibly handed over the Kingdom of England to the Normans, at a time when the Normans were clearly so hated by the English: as events in Dover proved. The Norman, Count Eustace of Boulogne, who was married to Duke William's sister, was humiliated in Dover, after visiting his fellow Norman, Robert of Jumieges, Archbishop of Canterbury. This event and the subsequent replacing of the Norman Robert with the Anglo-Saxon Stigand, shows the contempt there was in England for all things Norman. Harold would hardly, in such an atmosphere, even attempt to hand the Kingdom of England over to the Normans: and why should he? The so-called shipwreck, and promise made to William by Harold, while under oath, is clearly Norman propaganda.

The Bayeux Tapestry was a tool of this propaganda. For example, in this tapestry Stigand, Archbishop of Canterbury is depicted as crowning King Harold Godwinson in Westminster Abbey. Stigand was not appointed by the Pope and so was not recognised by Rome, as such, therefore it suited the Normans to depict a questionable person crowning King Harold. We now know it was Ealdred, Archbishop of York, a man accepted by Rome, who crowned King Harold.

This same tapestry depicts some Housecarls fighting with a sword in their left hand, as I covered in the text.

William, who was originally little more than a 'War Lord', after these events ruled as King of England for twenty-one years; and his descendants have done so ever since. All the Kings and Queens of England and later of Great Britain are descended from the Normans. One third of England is still owned by families of Norman descendent to this day. However, even though the Norman families controlled much of England's land and titles, the two nations eventually merged, and some genealogists tell us the current ruler of England, Queen Elizabeth II, is the 29th great-granddaughter of King Harold II and Edith Swan-Neck.

It took King William most of his reign to consolidate his conquest and very brutally so, but consolidate it he did. It is estimated that one-fifth of the population of England was killed during William's rule, by war, massacre and starvation. Historians now say that the one-hundred years following 1066 were the worst in English history for the suffering of its people. After spending the Christmas of 1069 in York, William's soldiers destroyed every town, village and house between York and Durham, slaughtering anyone they could find, whether old or young, men or women and children. They destroyed all food stocks and farm animals. We now know that, after this cruel treatment of the north, the land did not fully recover for more than one-hundred years.

William administered the same punishment so effectively to Stafford, Derby and Chester, that Gerbod, the new Earl of Chester, soon became so tired of this desolate Earldom, that he went back home disappointed to Flanders. William's devastation was so fierce and his ethnic cleansing so complete; the north was de-populated. Norman soldiers destroyed anything that might have been of use to those who lived in the north. It is estimated that as many as 100,000 people of the north died because of this iron grip. This northern region ended up deprived of, and losing forever, what had been up until the conquest, its traditional autonomy: a period the Normans euphemistically referred to as, 'Harrying of the North': today we would call it 'genocide'.

Eventually, the Pope himself protested against this excessive mistreatment, which had been exerted by the Normans against the English people. It was said that, 'William created a wilderness in the north and called it peace.'

Although the south of England had submitted quickly to Norman rule, resistance continued as long as it could in the north and east, until at least 1072. The strongest resistance to this Norman occupation come from Northumbria in 1068 and 1069, when the forces of Earls Edwin and Morcar allied themselves with Prince (or King) Edgar Atheling. Prince Edgar Atheling had fled to Scotland with his mother and sisters, where they were well received by King Malcolm. One of Edgar's sisters, Margaret, then married King Malcolm. From Edgar's point of view, this meant he was now allied with the powerful King of Scots, a warrior who provided him with armed support against the Norman usurpers.

Incidentally Margaret became such an important influence in Scotland that later she became 'Saint Margaret', where her ancient chapel still has pride of place in the centre of Edinburgh castle.

Almost immediately after the conquest, William set about an intense castle building programme, the like of which had never been seen before, nor has been seen since. In order to keep an iron grip over the English and keep them suppressed, over one-thousand castles were built, many of which can still be seen to this day. Originally most castles were of the Mott and Bailey type, but through a massive building period, most castles soon became the monoliths of stone we know of today. Each Norman nobleman who received land was expected to build a castle there.

These Norman lords and knights were invaders and building a castle was essential to act as a refuge for them and their soldiers. This was basic commonsense, for they were understandably highly unpopular with the English.

William carried out his promise to reward those who fought for him with land and estates. He is said to have eliminated the Anglo-Saxon aristocracy in as little as four years, handing their land over to his Normans. William's brothers were given large chunks of England. His half brother, Robert of Mortain, became the second most significant landholder in England, being given the whole of Cornwall and five hundred and forty-nine manors scattered across the country. Odo of Bayeux was made Earl of Kent and given control of Dover and was effectively 'Ruler of England' whenever William was in Normandy. Richard Fitz-Gilbert was granted land all over the south of England, being rewarded with one hundred and seventy-six lordships and a large estate at Clare in Suffolk. He subsequently became Richard de Clare and as Earl of Clare, one of the most significant Norman families in England and Wales.

Ironically, Copsig, Tostig's associate in those dark days of 1066, did homage to William and was consequently made the new Earl of Northumbria, replacing Morcar. How the Northumbrians must have hated this.

All lands of the English who had fought at Hastings were confiscated and given to Norman supporters of William. The seizure of lands and property was brutal. Only two Englishmen were left as the remaining Anglo-Saxon landowners in England, both of whom had turned traitor and supported William against the English. Thorkill of Arden was one of these Anglo-Saxons, yet even he was to have his land taken from him during the reign of William Rufus. The wily Wulfstan, who had become Bishop of Worcester in 1062, was the only Anglo-Saxon Bishop allowed to keep his post by William.

The language would change drastically, as would the government of England; French became the official language of the royal court for nearly three-hundred years. William and the

Norman kings who followed, considered themselves French, with England as a colony, or province. It was many years later before English became the first language of the court, during the reign of Henry IV, who ascended to the throne in 1367; the first king since 1066 whose mother tongue was English.

The ramifications of that momentous year of 1066 are still with us, up until this day. The year 1066 was truly a turning point in English history. Eventually these two warring nations did become one powerful English nation, whose English language would eventually replace Latin as the world's international language.

Had there been no Norman invasion, the history of Britain could have been entirely different. The instinctive aggression of the Norman race would not have become indigenous within the future English people and England may well have settled to a more 'quieter' development; as did Denmark and Norway.

There is no doubt that William's reign was one of unbridled cruelty. On his deathbed in 1087, he is supposed to have confessed: 'I persecuted the native inhabitants of England beyond all reason. Whether nobles or commons, I cruelly oppressed them; many I unjustly disinherited; innumerable multitudes, especially in the county of York, perished through me by famine and sword ... I am stained with the rivers of blood that I have shed.'

Thanks mainly to the legacy of King Alfred-the-Great, before the Normans arrived, England was the wealthiest, most stable nation in Europe and it had the strongest currency, based on the silver penny. These coins were strictly regulated at a national level to ensure their purity. England also had the most efficient tax gathering system and sufficient local input to ensure that it was assessed fairly. It had a strong law code, which was enforced at local and national level. England was also highly cultured. It was renowned for its arts and crafts, which were known and valued all over Western Europe, especially the illumination of manuscripts, embroidery and gold and silver work. The gold hoard found in 2009 in the county of Staffordshire well illustrates this.

I have not depicted King Harold being killed by an arrow in the eye. Accounts of that time tell of him being cut down and mutilated, as depicted in this book. The arrow in the eye comes only from the Bayeux Tapestry and that 'arrow' is now thought by many historians to be really a faded spear held by the man next to Harold as he was cut down. It is understood that some well meaning restorers, two centuries ago, 'repaired' this part of the tapestry and added arrow flights onto this spear in error. Also the earliest accounts of the battle from, *"Carmen de Hastingae Proelio" (the Song of the Battle of Hastings)*, written shortly after the battle by Bishop of Amiens, says that Harold was killed by four knights, one of whom was Duke William,

It is interesting for the modern person to note, that a number of senior churchmen took a fighting role in the Battle of Hastings: Odo, Bishop of Bayeux, Aelfwig, Abbot of Winchester and Leofric, Abbot of Peterborough.

That William could not read and write is displayed in the document entitled the *'Accord of Winchester'* dated 1072. This document is signed by both William and Matilda; their signatures being no more than rough rudimentary crosses.

I have 'modernised' the hatred between William and his oldest son Robert. His father gave him the nickname, Curthose, and he has gone down in history as Robert Curthose. Curthose comes from the Norman French *Courtheuse*, meaning Short Stockings (or in English - curt & hose), as it is sometimes translated. William of Malmesbury and Orderic Vitalis, early writers of these events, report that William called his son *brevis-ocrea* (short-boot) in derision. It would appear Robert had inherited his mother's shortness, for Matilda was only 4' 8" tall. Therefore, I use the modern vernacular 'Short-arse', which imparts the same meaning to the modern reader.

What happened to the Housecarls? After the conquest, the Housecarls seem to have completely disappeared. The vast majority died on Senlac Hill, fighting around their king, but not all. Most of those who did survive, along with many of King Harold's Thanes, either fled to Scotland, or crossed to the continent as mercenary troops. Many of these made it as far as Byzantium and became members of the Varangian Guard, so much so that, by the twelfth century, they were sometimes referred to as 'The English Guard'.

There were many other revolts against the harsh rule of the Normans, particularly in Dover, Mercia, and Exeter. King Harold's sons from Edith Swan-Neck headed an army into Devon and Cornwall, but they were defeated by William. It was in the north and in Suffolk, where resistance was the strongest, in particular around the Isle of Ely. In June 1070 Hereward-the-Wake seized the Isle of Ely. It was here William met the strongest resistance in any armed uprising against Norman rule. Earl Morcar and King Sweyn of Denmark joined Hereward the following year.

It is unfortunate that Hereward-the-Wake's heroic stand against this invading tyrant is not more widely known. In modern times, television, books and movies have all too often clouded the real historical events of Hereward-the-Wake, with the fictional events of Robin Hood, although 'a' Robing Hood could well have been part of a traditional folk story involving the numerous English resistance movements. Many have correctly interpreted these legends as generic tales of resistance to Norman oppression. The fact remains, rebellion was endemic and William was forced to spend all his reign trying to contain this resistance; but this is a story for a following book, in which the deeds of Alric and Hereward can be told, along with that of the continued rape of England and the violent divisions within King William's dysfunctional family.

Do you want to know the sequel to this story?

If enough people write to

mgkelley@hotmail.com

I will write it

****

Now read Mike Kelley's book,

'The Origins of Faith'.

Order from Lulu - http://www.lulu.com/

When Jacques Gendron experiences the brutal force of Radical Islam, he sets out to find the answer to the question, 'Why?' Why has there been so much violence in the name of the world's leading religions? The answers he uncovers are startling, disturbing and dangerous. Jacques takes a roller-coaster ride through many countries, from Canada to Pakistan, with a high price to pay. Find out why Jacques' search also reveals that *"Israel does not have, and never did have, a divine right to the land of Palestine"*

Why not write to Mike Kelley at - mgkelley@hotmail.com

The Origins of Faith

Israel Does Not Have, And Never Did Have, a Divine Right to the Land of Palestine

Mike Kelley